Savings and Bequests

Savings and Bequests

Edited by
Toshiaki Tachibanaki

Ann Arbor

THE UNIVERSITY OF MICHIGAN PRESS

1997   1996   1995   1994   4   3   2   1

A CIP catalogue record for this book is available from the British Library.

Library of Congress Cataloging-in-Publication Data

Savings and bequests / edited by Toshiaki Tachibanaki.
        p.   cm.
    "Papers . . . presented at the International Conference on Savings
and Bequests held in Tokyo, Japan, March 17–18, 1992"—Preface.
    Includes bibliographical references.
    ISBN 0-472-10498-5 (alk. paper)
    1. Saving and investment—European Economic Community countries—
Congresses.   2. Saving and investment—Japan—Congresses.
3. Saving and investment—United States—Congresses.   4. Inheritance
and succession—European Economic Community countries—Congresses.
5. Inheritance and succession—Japan—Congresses.   6. Inheritance
and succession—United States—Congresses.   I. Tachibanaki,
Toshiaki, 1943–   .   II. International Conference on Savings and
Bequests (1992 : Tokyo, Japan)
HC240.9.S3S28   1994
339.4'3'094—dc20   94-6418
                                                          CIP

Preface

Preliminary versions of the papers included in this volume were presented at the International Conference on Savings and Bequests held in Tokyo, Japan, March 17 and 18, 1992. The conference was organized and financed by the Institute for Posts and Telecommunications Policy (IPTP) of the Japanese Ministry of Posts and Telecommunications (MPT). We are indebted to the Institute for their support. We also thank Professor Yasuhiko Ohishi, Director of the Institute, Mr. Yutaka Harada, Director of Research Section II, Mr. Patrick Fulner and the staff members of the Institute who gave us useful advice and help at various stages.

Contents

Chapter

1. Introduction: Savings and Bequests   1
   Toshiaki Tachibanaki

2. Intended Bequest Motives, Savings and Life
   Insurance Demand   15
   Hiroyuki Chuma

3. Cost of Care and Bequests   39
   Tadashi Yagi and Hirohisa Maki

4. Storing the Option and Saving for Retirement in Canada   63
   Anil K. Gupta, Steven F. Venti, and David A. Wise

5. Measuring the Bequest Motive: The Effect of Children
   on Saving by the Elderly in the United States   111
   Michael D. Hurd

6. Bequests, Fiscal Policy, and Social Security   137
   Toshihiro Ihori

7. Intergenerational Altruism and the Effectiveness of Fiscal
   Policy—New Tests Based on Cohort Data   167
   Andrew B. Abel and Laurence J. Kotlikoff

8. Bequest and Asset Distribution: Human Capital Investment
   and Intergenerational Wealth Transfers   197
   Toshiaki Tachibanaki and Seiji Takata

9. The Effect of Bequest Motives on the Composition
   and Distribution of Assets in France   229
   Luc Arrondel, Sergio Perelman, and Pierre Pestieau

10. Inheritance and the Distribution of Wealth in Britain
    and Canada   245
    James B. Davies

Contributors   285

CHAPTER 1

Introduction: Savings and Bequests

Toshiaki Tachibanaki

Motivations for This Book

Several of the advanced industrialized countries, particularly France, Italy, and Japan, have high rates of personal saving, while a number of other countries, for example, the United Kingdom and the United States, have low rates. In this regard some representative questions arise that the essays presented in this book seek to address: Is a bequest motive responsible for the difference in the saving rates among these countries? Do different initiating motives surface when we talk about bequest motives such as altruistic or strategic (i.e., gift-exchange)? What is the role of bequest in the distribution of wealth? Do bequests explain the greater portion of wealth holding? Are the typical bequest forms real estate or financial asset, or are they human capital? Is it possible to conclude that bequests affect the formation of fiscal policies, or that bequests are neutral with respect to the effect of fiscal policies? Finally, what is the relationship between bequests and public pensions?

In an effort to answer these questions and to gain a more revealing insight into these issues, the Institute for Posts and Telecommunications Policy (IPTP) of the Japanese Ministry of Posts and Telecommunications (MPT) organized and hosted an international conference on savings and bequests in Tokyo in March 1992. Several distinguished specialists from Europe, Japan, and North America were invited to attend and present their papers on the subject. This book is an outgrowth of the conference. Many countries are covered in this book; specifically, Canada, France, Japan, the United Kingdom, the United States, and some others. During the conference's organization stage, a careful selection of both subjects and participants was made to enable the conference contributions to focus on the relatively narrow subject of savings and bequests, with the additional hope of generating excellent papers in this field. Fortunately, it was possible to collect a range of distinguished papers, as presented herein, that are expected to serve as a useful reading list for the analysis of savings and bequests.

Our intention in producing this book was to have it concentrate on savings and bequests essentially through a single voice, as though its contents were written by one author. This is not to say, however, that the book offers several universal propositions that were accepted by all participants. A multiple authorship provides us with a healthy range of opinions essential to facilitating our understanding of the subject at hand. Although this introduction attempts to summarize several almost universal results that were generated at the conference, it is highly recommended that all contributions in this volume be read to gain a greater comprehension of the authors' different opinions.

In our quest to further our knowledge of the subject, it is necessary to describe initially the reasons why investigations of savings and bequests are so important. Four examples will serve our purpose. First, we can cite the famous dispute in the United States about the significance of the role of intergenerational wealth transfers in wealth accumulation. One proponent of the argument, Modigliani, who is an advocate of the life-cycle saving hypothesis, proposes that the great majority of wealth holding can be explained by life-cycle saving motives in the United States, while his counterparts, Kotlikoff and Summers, suggest that the intergenerational wealth transfers, largely bequests and gifts, account for about 80 percent of the total wealth. Since this dispute is far from being settled, it is worthwhile to investigate it further; indeed it is a focal point of some of the papers in this book.

Second, there is a consensus in Japan that a strong bequest motive is observed; it is one of the most salient reasons for the high rate of personal saving. However, it remains to be ascertained what *kinds* of bequest motives prevail. Are the majority of bequests motivated simply by love or favor (altruism), or is the motivation an expectation of gift-exchange from beneficiaries to donors? Often people save a lot of money after retirement to provide for long life spans; as a result, some of them leave a lot of wealth behind at sudden death. This scenario is regarded as an accidental bequest due to uncertain life span. Obviously it is quite useful to grasp the most important specific motive because it influences the effect of policies on the course of the macroeconomy, saving behaviors, and the working of pension systems. Several papers in this book examine various bequest motives and present a range of empirical evidence for these motives in addition to providing us with the policy implications of the motives.

Third, it has been widely believed that bequest contributed significantly to the transmission of intergenerational wealth inequality. In other words, rich wealth holders transmit their wealth through a form of bequest to their heirs, and poor wealth holders transmit nothing or only a small amount to their heirs. Therefore, intergenerational wealth inequality continues as long as bequests and/or gifts are transmitted from one generation to the next. This theory also suggests that a large part of wealth inequality is explained by intergenerational wealth transfers rather than by wealth accumulation within one generation. Simply speaking, bequests and/or gifts account for the largest part of wealth distribution or inequality. The role of an inheritance tax is crucial with respect to this subject. In this regard, some of the papers in this volume address the issue of the relationship between bequest and wealth distribution and investigate the influence of an inheritance tax on various economic variables as well as on wealth distribution.

Finally, we must recognize that various forms of wealth and/or capital are transmitted from one generation to the next. Typically, real estate such as land and a house is used as a form of bequest and/or gift; the financial asset is also used. Some economists find that human capital investment for children is important and can be a substitute for material wealth transfer. It is interesting to investigate the role of these forms of bequests, and their economic implications.

The continually binding central theme throughout this volume is the life-cycle saving hypothesis, or the life-cycle motive of saving. Since this hypothesis is explained in most macroeconomics textbooks, of course, it is not necessary to explain it here in detail. Nevertheless, it is important to underscore the spirit of the life-cycle motive because the majority of the papers refer to this motive extensively in their investigation of savings and bequests. A person saves during his or her working period and dissaves after retirement, with the amount of savings being zero at death under several stringent assumptions. Naturally, no one believes that this is a valid principle for all people, since there are several unrealistic assumptions that violate the spirit of the life-cycle motives.

First, the death possibility is highly uncertain. A person may continue to save after retirement in case of having an unexpectedly long life span. Or, it is possible for a person to die before retirement. In these cases, savings left at death can be transferred as bequests to someone. Thus, the most salient nature of these bequests is that they are accidental and unintended, although some part of savings may have been accumulated intentionally. In the case of sudden death, however, identifying statistically what percentage is unintended and what percentage is intended is not easy. The preceding description suggests that some part of bequests are unintended and accidental. This case is called precautionary saving in preparation for uncertainty in both life span and income stream. Some economists judge that the precautionary saving should be counted as one of the variants of the life-cycle saving hypothesis, which is contrasted with the bequest motive. Some of the papers in this volume investigate these issues both theoretically and empirically.

Second, several empirical studies in some countries report that the majority of retired people continue to save rather than to dissave. This observation does not seem to support the spirit of the life-cycle saving hypothesis. Although the public pension system, which can substitute for private saving to be used for consumption after retirement, is very common in advanced countries, many retired people do not dissave even in the presence of such a public pension system. The relationship between the social security system and saving is a controversial subject. In particular, the presence of the public pension system produces an enormous impact on the understanding of the life-cycle saving hypothesis. In other words, ignorance of the social security system is unrealistic when we study a life-cycle saving motive or a bequest motive.

Third, there remain several technical questions that affect the working of the life-cycle saving hypothesis. The questions primarily center on (a) the number of family members and/or children, (b) the endogeneity problem of retirement behavior and labor market entrance, (c) marriage and/or divorce, (d) the effect of various taxes, and (e) the extended family. One important conceptual dispute is whether educational expenditure on children is consumption or saving. Since countless technical issues involved in the analysis of savings and bequests make it impossible to cover all of them in one book, only some of the questions and unrealistic assumptions are examined in order to enrich our understanding of the subject.

Finally, one note is added about the significance of bequest motives in relation to the life-cycle saving hypothesis. We observed several different bequest motives—accidental (or unintended), paternalistic, altruistic, and strategic (gift-exchange)—which are explained in several papers. Most bequest motives are likely to violate the condition of the simplified version of the life-cycle saving hypothesis. However, the strategic (gift-exchange) motive is consistent with the spirit of the life-cycle motive because a return (or an exchange) from beneficiaries raises the benefits of donors. In other words, a person and his or her children calculate the lifetime allocation of their resources together, and the children contribute to their parents' utility. This is simply a life-cycle motive of a donor. It is impossible to conclude at this stage, however, that the strategic (gift-exchange) motive is perfectly consistent with the life-cycle saving motive. It is, nevertheless, useful to keep in mind that if the degree of a strategic (gift-exchange) motive was strong among various bequest motives, the plausibility of the life-cycle saving hypothesis would be higher when we compare the importance of a life-cycle motive and that of the various bequest motives that are assumed to violate a naive life-cycle saving hypothesis.

Summaries

The book consists of three sections. The first comprises theoretical and empirical studies of various bequest motives. The second analyzes the role of bequests with respect to the effect of tax and social security policies. The third investigates the relationship between bequests and wealth distribution. Since the classification of the three sections is not particularly rigorous, the content of each is significantly interrelated. Thus, I do not provide a summary of each section but a summary of each paper with some discussion added.

Chuma provides a theoretical and empirical analysis of the impact of bequest motives on the demand for life insurance and annuities, and on saving. Specifically, he intends to distinguish two distinct types of bequest. One type is a desire to insure against the risk of dying (i.e., precautionary saving), and the second is a desire to bequeath real and financial wealth. He is interested in proposing an empirically feasible method that makes it possible to measure individuals' intended bequest motives and their effect on savings and demand for life or annuity insurance. He constructs a Yaarian life-cycle model, and applies fruitful Japanese data to his model. The data include the binary information about whether or not an individual has a plan to bequeath financial and/or real assets to his or her spouse or children, and their specific amounts (i.e., intended bequest motive).

Chuma makes three observations in his analysis. First, individuals have a strong intended bequest motive if they are older and married. Also, men whose spouses do not work show a stronger bequest motive than men whose spouses work. Thus, the degree of intended bequest motives is influenced by age, sex, marital status, the number of children, working status of the spouse, and other pertinent demographic factors. Second, the positive relation between the saving rate and intended bequest motives is largely rejected. Thus, it is likely that the implicit annuity hypothesis and/or the strategic hypothesis are much more relevant in Japan. Third, the elasticity of the life insurance demand with respect to a bequest motive is high, about 1.2 percent, which suggests that the demand for life insurance is closely related to individuals' bequest motives. It is accordingly possible to offer a comment on these findings, namely, a motive for the demand for life insurance may differ by age because younger generations buy it to offset their risk of dying, while older generations buy it to pass on financial wealth to their children or spouse.

Yagi and Maki construct a theoretical model that intends to distinguish between the use of annuities and bequeathable assets when an individual determines the allocation of wealth at or after retirement. The authors believe that an altruistic bequest motive is not so important as has been commonly believed, but that a strategic (gift-exchange) bequest motive must be quite prominent. They show statistical evidence for this, in fact, reporting that 42.9 percent of respondents stipulated a return requirement of taking care of their parents in exchange for accepting a bequest. About 38.1 percent said that such a requirement was not necessary. In particular, Yagi and Maki raise the importance of caring for older parents when they are ill.

When parents become older, they cannot buy care services through the market because the price of such services for the elderly is normally high. Thus, parents ask their children to assume such responsibility on their behalf, and children desire a bequest in exchange for taking on this burden. Yagi and Maki construct a fairly sophisticated model that considers a choice between annuity purchase and bequeathable asset under the uncertainty in death and propose several theoretical propositions based on the Hamiltonian maximization. One of the results proposes that a cheaper cost of care is possible when a gift-exchange motive holds between parents and children. However, a higher earning capacity of children owing to increased human capital is likely to encourage a shift from mutual gift-exchange between parents and children to buying care services in the market. One of the phenomena of the shift is an increasing trend toward private nursing homes for the aged in Japan. The increasing number of female labor force participation rate also encourages this shift because it has become increasingly more difficult for female workers to take care of their older parents in their homes. Yagi and Maki present several empirical data to support their propositions.

Gupta, Venti, and Wise report the examinations of registered retirement saving plans (RRSPs) in Canada for savings and retirement, and give some implications for bequests. RRSP allow for the deduction in the participants' contributions from income for tax purposes, as well as tax-free interest accrued until withdrawal, both of which are now a very prominent form of saving. Contributions grew rapidly, and, since 1977, have exceeded contributions to employer-provided pension plans. Thus, it is possible to conclude that one of the most important reasons for a higher personal saving rate in Canada than in the United States may be attributed to RRSPs.

The chapter by Gupta, Venti, and Wise presents several simulation studies designed to evaluate the effect of the newly introduced carry-forward plan on RRSP contribution. This plan allows a foregone contribution in one year to be made in a subsequent year. The actual method utilized by this carry-forward plan is fairly complicated because the number of carry-forward years varies in the future. The simulation is conducted based on two types of scenarios. The first one considers the effect of the carry-forward plan through the first six years following its introduction in 1982, while the second one looks at the "lifetime" effect of the carry-forward plan for 1987 tax filers. The important explanatory variables in the RRSP contribution probability and the amount of RRSP contribution are the respondent's age and income, in addition to several random effects that incorporate an individual-specific saving motive. The simulation predicts that the carry-forward plan may raise RRSP contributions by 40 to 60 percent and possibly more.

The effect of RRSPs on bequests may be summarized as follows. The simulation for individuals aged sixty-five indicates that the carry-forward plan may have a noticeable influence on the financial well-being of the elderly because it increases financial assets by about 80 percent on average. This suggests that the plan may have a substantial effect on bequests. One brief comment may be added; namely, it is likely that the contribution rate and thus bequests increase under the new plan, though it may reduce the amount of other source savings due to the substitution effect. Thus, the entire effect on saving and also bequest may be uncertain. Future work in this field is essential in view of the fact that tax policies considerably influence savings.

The chapter by Hurd is stimulating because he strongly objects to the importance of intended bequests. According to his argument, the great majority of bequests are accidental due to uncertainty about the date of death and a weak or nonexistent market for annuities. Thus, his study supports the spirit of the life-cycle saving hypothesis, but incidentally uses the terminology of the life-cycle *consumption* hypothesis rather than the life-cycle *saving* hypothesis.

Hurd constructs two life-cycle consumption models à la Yaari. The first one is for singles, and the second one is for couples. The distinction between the two models may be characterized by a model for nonparents and one for parents. Also, it is important to note that assets transferred to the surviving spouse on the death of the other spouse are not bequests, but simply the continuation of the household, that is, a continuing life cycle. The theoretical derivations enable him to obtain empirically testable functions, and he applies the U.S. Retirement History Survey data on retired people to test them. The empirical result suggests that there is no significant difference in the rates of wealth decumulation between nonparents and parents. If the intended bequest motive had been stronger, the speeds of wealth decumulation would have been different between the two groups. Parents would have a slower rate of dissaving. Hurd concludes that the great majority of bequests are accidental rather than intended bequests.

If an intended bequest motive was weak, the household would participate in buying annuities. In other words, the great majority of wealth would have been annuitized. The data, however, do not support this. Hurd raises four reasons for this. First, the transaction cost is high while the rate of return to annuities is low. Second, annuities are vulnerable to inflation. Third, liquidity is low. Fourth, some people find that a substantial part of wealth has already been annuitized because the public pension system is established.

Finally, Hurd finds based on his saving simulation that one of the important reasons for the high amount of bequests is the difficulty associated with financing nonhousing consumption from housing wealth, definitely an important subject to be studied more seriously. As is pointed out by many studies in this book, the majority of wealth is placed in real estate.

Ihori presents the taxonomy of bequest models. According to his classification there are four different motives: (*a*) the altruistic bequest motive, (*b*) the bequest-as-consumption motive, (*c*) the gift-exchange (i.e., strategic) bequest motive, (*d*) the accidental bequest motive. He analyzes the effect of fiscal policy and social security programs on the macroeconomy under the assumption of the various bequest motives. Specifically, his main policy tools are public spending, taxation on intergenerational transfers, and reform in the social security system.

Ihori first investigates the normative effects of government spending under the altruistic bequest motive, and thus debt neutrality. He proposes several analytical findings. One result is that it will be desirable to lower the size of public spending, which is consistent with the opinion of the general public that has tended to favor smaller governmental intervention in more recent years.

Second, Ihori assesses the effect of bequest taxes on capital accumulation under the intended bequest motives that cover (*a*), (*b*), and (*c*) in the above taxonomy. His principal theoretical finding suggests that an increase in the bequest tax will normally reduce capital accumulation. Thus, the bequest tax will be detrimental because it reduces long-run welfare in terms of dynamic efficiency. An increase, however, in bequest taxation may have a favorable effect in terms of intergenerational equity. Therefore, the analysis presents a possible trade-off between efficiency and equity with respect to the bequest taxation. The government and thus the people themselves have to decide which is more important, efficiency or equity, when bequest taxes are levied.

Finally, Ihori analyzes the relationship between social security and economic growth. Under the bequest-as-consumption model he obtains the negative effect of social security on economic growth when the social security system follows the pay-as-you-go scheme. It is noted, however, that the fully funded system does not always produce a negative effect, but rather offers the possibility of an optimum-sized social security. Ihori also points out that a high level of intergenerational transfer is likely to raise the growth rate of an economy, which is, however, affected by the pay-as-you-go social security system versus the fully funded system.

The chapter by Abel and Kotlikoff examines whether an intergenerational altruism or a standard (no risk sharing) life-cycle model is operative in the United States. The authors strictly test whether the Euler errors (disturbances in the Euler equations) of altruistically linked members of extended families (clans) are identical. The above proposition predicts that the average percentage change in household consumption within an age cohort should be the same for all age cohorts. Also, differences across cohorts in their changes in consumption should not be correlated with their income changes. The test is made in a nonparametric manner, and is applied to the U.S. consumer expenditure survey.

Abel and Kotlikoff were not able to reject the first prediction, but were able to reject the second. Based on these two findings, they conclude that their results negate the intergenerational altruism model, and, by extension, favor the standard (no risk sharing) life-cycle hypothesis. Moreover, the risk-sharing arrangement within extended families (or clans) is rejected. This rejection of the risk-sharing arrangement is remarkable because many past studies largely assumed the existence of some degree of altruism. This rejection impacts differently on the macroeconomy and the saving behavior that are separated from the usual understanding prominent in the past.

One example is that the intergenerational income transfer from the younger generation to the older generation through public pension programs discourages private savings and thus wealth accumulation. Abel and Kotlikoff propose, in fact, that the lower saving rate in the United States was not caused by excessive government consumption but rather by this high amount of intergenerational income transfer due to public pension programs. This is an interesting subject that deserves further study because the working of the U.S. macroeconomy is influenced strongly by consumption and saving.

The final implication of this study for bequests is that all of the cross-section studies of U.S. private transfers suggest that, except for the very wealthy, bequests are almost always divided equally among children with no regard to their children's current or past earnings. This can be regarded as indirect support of the Abel and Kotlikoff findings. Incidentally, equal division is not true in several other countries. The observation in the United States suggests strong evidence against altruism models with asymmetric information. Asymmetry here implies that parents do not have clear knowledge of their children's ability or earnings capacity.

The chapter by Tachibanaki and Takata presents several empirical results on the relationship between bequests and wealth distribution, and constructs a theoretical model that investigates the effect of human capital and material wealth on savings and wealth inequality in relation to bequest motives. They use Japanese data for the empirical studies. The results suggest that about 45 percent of total wealth is attributed to the contribution of bequests. Although the life-cycle contribution accounts for the majority of wealth, the contribution of bequest is substantial. It is proposed that about 25 to 40 percent of inequality in wealth distribution is explained by inequality in intergenerational wealth transfers. They also give the estimated results of the bequest functions. These empirical results lead to the conclusion that bequests, in particular physical wealth, considerably determine the degree of intergenerational wealth transfer.

Tachibanaki and Takata construct a theoretical model of the bequest and saving behaviors by taking into account the effect of both human capital investment and the contribution of services to the parent provided by the child. The latter aspect is strictly related to a gift-exchange or strategic motive. Apart from several analytical results, the simulation studies present the following outcomes: first, there is a trade-off between human capital investment for children and services provided by children in exchange for material wealth transfer from parents to children. In particular, the able child has higher opportunity cost due to his or her higher earnings capacity. Thus, he or she is less willing to take care of the parent, because time allocated to taking care of the parent is costly. In sum, the paper suggests that the influence of the child's ability (i.e., earnings capacity) is crucial to the determination of education, saving, and bequests. The contribution of the parents' initial resources also has the interesting effect that is somewhat similar to the contribution of the child's ability. The conclusion of this paper suggests the lesser importance of an altruistic bequest motive even in Japan, and the greater importance of the gift-exchange bequest motive. Human capital, however, plays a particular role with respect to the relationship among bequests, savings, and wealth.

Arrondel, Perelman, and Pestieau show some empirical result on the effect of bequests on the composition of households' portfolios and their wealth distribution by using the French survey data. In particular, they are interested in the impact of intended bequests.

Several empirical findings are summarized as follows. First, households who intend to leave bequests have higher values of real assets than do households who have no bequest motives. It is interesting to add the fact that these households with intended bequest motives tend to concentrate on one category of asset holding rather than diversifying their wealth into various forms. Here, four categories are considered, namely, liquid assets, stock values, primary housing, and other properties. Second, inequality in wealth distribution is higher among households who hold the intended bequest motives than that among those who hold no such motives. Third, the contribution of bequests to inequality in wealth distribution is very minor according to the decomposition analysis. Related to this point it is found that inequality in wealth distribution is higher among households who received some amount of inheritance than that among households who received no inheritance. Finally, inequality in wealth distribution is higher among households who have no children than that among households who have some children. In sum, the deciding factors for bequeathing are whether children are present, and whether the bequest motive is present. At the same time, these factors affect the composition of assets and wealth distribution. Some of the empirical results derived by Arrondel, Perelman, and Pestieau are at odds with the widely held yet unproven belief in France as well as in other countries.

Finally, the chapter by Davies presents an overview of inheritance and the distribution of wealth in Britain and Canada. The data in Britain are considerably reliable and cover a longer period than the data in Canada, which are somewhat weak. The findings reveal that a trend existed toward considerably reduced wealth inequality in Britain for 1923 to 1980, but there has been no change since 1980. The most dramatic decrease in wealth inequality is observed by the top one percent wealth holders, namely from the share of 60 percent in 1923 to that of 18 percent in 1989. This shift appears to have been due to a more equal division of assets between wealthy husbands and wives, the cumulative effect of redistributive estate and income taxes, and the spread of "popular" wealth holding (houses and consumer durables).

Inequality in wealth distribution in Canada is nearly the same as that in Britain because the top one percent of wealth holders have a 17 to 18 percent share, and the top 10 percent share is 50 to 53 percent. Regarding Canada, it is important to note that since 35 percent of capital is held by foreigners, the concentration ratio in wealth might be higher in Canada than in other countries because of the "missing millionaires" effect.

The evidence from both countries shows room for a strong bequest motive for saving because no dissaving after retirement is observed for white-collar Canadians and the upper-tail wealth holders in Britain. The contribution of inheritance to total wealth in Canada is fairly high, namely, 53 percent. Incidentally, the most important source for explaining wealth inequality is inheritance. The next important source is the saving rate. The income differential is not so important. Empirical studies in the United Kingdom also support the idea that the most important source for explaining wealth distribution is inheritance, although its importance has declined over time.

One of the most interesting policy matters is the abolishment of inheritance taxes in Canada, because there are not many countries that have similar policies. Several reasons are suggested in the Davies paper as to why the inheritance tax was abolished. Another interesting finding is the effect of an increase in land prices on wealth distribution in Britain. Since real estate, in particular housing, is distributed nearly evenly, an increase in land prices lowers wealth inequality, unlike the case of other countries.

Conclusions

It is useful to describe the several important findings featured in this book since they represent the main messages on which the participants of the conference have largely agreed and present several crucial policy implications for the determination of savings and thus the macroeconomy in general in relation to bequests and wealth distribution.

First, a substantial part of wealth, say 30 to 60 percent, is found to come from bequests and inheritances when total wealth is decomposed into the bequest part and the life-cycle part. Figures are different by country. This implies that bequests are voluminous in quantity. Thus, it is possible to understand that a large volume of bequests contribute to higher rates of savings, making it unreasonable to ignore the contribution of bequests when arguing savings and wealth.

Second, although bequests play an important role in savings and wealth, this does not necessarily imply that people have strong intended bequest motives. When several bequest motives such as the altruistic, strategic (gift-exchange), accidental, and precautionary are investigated for many countries, we find that an altruistic bequest motive is relatively weak: some authors even reject it empirically. Several authors propose the importance of accidental bequests, due to uncertainty in death probability, and of precautionary motives for various reasons. Several authors raise the importance of the strategic bequest motive in exchange for services or care provided by the offspring. Though the importance of each bequest motive differs from country to country, a consensus has been reached; specifically, the degree of an altruistic bequest motive is very weak.

Third, in some countries a form of the intended bequest motive, the strategic (gift-exchange) bequest motive, is quite operative. It is possible, however, to propose that the strategic bequest motive is consistent with the life-cycle saving hypothesis, as was pointed out previously. Therefore, combining the unimportance of the altruistic motive with the consistency demonstrated between the strategic bequest motive and the life-cycle saving hypothesis, it is feasible that the relevancy of the life-cycle saving hypothesis is guaranteed. The importance of accidental bequests and precautionary motives also supports this position. Nevertheless, until more studies are done in this field, it is still premature to conclude that the life-cycle saving hypothesis without a bequest motive prevails.

Fourth, the nonexistence of intergenerational altruism suggests an important implication. Public pension programs provide strong intergenerational income transfers from the young to the old. This reduces the saving rate and thus produces a slower rate of wealth accumulation, which results in a slower growth economy. Fiscal policies that intend to reduce the amount of intergenerational income transfers are desirable in the absence of intergenerational altruism.

Fifth, an increase in the bequest tax normally reduces capital accumulation, and thus it is detrimental for long-run welfare in terms of efficiency. Social security programs also have a negative effect on the growth of the economy if they operate in pay-as-you-go systems. It is important to keep in mind that both tax policies and social security policies may have a detrimental effect on the growth of the economy under the intended bequest motive. However, it should be pointed out that the deduction in the contributions from income for tax purposes and for tax-free interest accrued (e.g., via RRSPs in Canada) are quite effective for promoting personal saving. Thus, tax policies are sometimes useful in raising the personal saving rate despite the fact that some other tax policies, such as the bequest tax, lower saving rates.

Sixth, bequests are crucial in the determination of inequality in wealth distribution in many countries. Wealth inequality is transmitted from one generation to the next. Wealthy households bequeath a large amount of wealth, and, conversely, we see many households that receive nothing from their parents. One exception is France, which does not support the above propositions.

Seventh, the most important form of intergenerational wealth transfer in all countries is real estate—land and housing—for which several reasons can be cited. One is that the inheritance through real estate is beneficial from the tax burden point of view in some countries. Another is that consumption based on funds generated from real estate is difficult; in other words, the liquidity of real estate is low. Still another is that since the public pension system is fairly adequately established in many countries, it is not necessary to receive funds generated from real estate for consumption.

Finally, special attention must be paid to the role of human capital when the issue of bequest is explored. Human capital is likely to be substitutable for material wealth. In view of the extremely high amount of human capital in many countries, it is important to analyze the effect of human capital on savings and wealth distribution.

I have presented the main findings obtained in this book only very briefly. Each chapter contains a large number of interesting issues, as well as useful theoretical and empirical results that have not been described in this introductory section. Also, some authors presented in this book express ideas, opinions, views, and findings that differ from the above summary of conclusions. As we are quite confident that this book will significantly enrich the understanding of savings and bequests, readers are again encouraged that they will learn a great deal from a careful perusing of each chapter.

CHAPTER 2

Intended Bequest Motives, Savings and Life Insurance Demand

Hiroyuki Chuma

As has been shown in Kotlikoff and Summers 1981 and Hayashi 1986, quite a number of economists have started to believe that individuals' bequest motives considerably influence the determination of various saving rates in each country. As a matter of fact, Kotlikoff and Summers have reported that about 50 to 80 percent of accumulated wealth of the U.S. household sector is bequeathed. Also, observing the high saving rates among older Japanese households, Hayashi has emphasized that strong bequest motives constitute the crucial determinant of Japan's high saving rates. Contrary to these results, however, Modigliani (1988) mentions that these figures are an overestimation. According to him, the corresponding figure is only about 20 percent. Sato (1989) also reports that, according to his calculation, the figure in Japan is about 20 percent.[1]

Despite such an important role imposed upon bequest motives, there have been few empirical analyses performed to directly relate individuals' intended bequest motives to their saving decisions. The exceptions are Hurd 1989, Ohtake 1991, and Bernheim 1991. Using the presence of living children as a proxy of the strength of bequest motives, Hurd considers consumption streams that might be significantly different among persons with or without bequest motives. His results are negative with regard to the importance of bequest motives in the United States. Conversely, Ohtake finds, following Hurd, that the bequest motive in Japan does influence savings.

As Ohtake (1991) correctly admits, however, "using the presence of living children as a proxy of the strength of bequest motives" incorporates the

I am grateful to Yutaka Harada, Charles Horioka, Michael Hurd, Takatoshi Ito, Toshiaki Tachibanaki, Seiji Takata, Yoshiro Tsutsui, and Naoyuki Yoshino for their helpful comments and suggestions. Thanks also go to the participants in the IPTP International Conference on Savings and Bequests held in Tokyo on March 17 and 18, 1992. All errors remain the responsibility of the author. This research was funded by the Japan Securities Scholarship Foundation.
1. For a comprehensive survey of these arguments, see Horioka 1991.

Relative (Question) on NLS
Bry motive Ins purchases on NLS
w/ if life

weakness that it could not identify the relevancy of the various important saving hypotheses that I will discuss in the next section. As is well known, even if the aged have no intended bequest motives, the presence of living children poses the possible positive impact on their saving decisions.

Compared with Hurd and Ohtake, Bernheim pays more straightforward attention to an individual's intended bequest motive per se. His main concern is to empirically clarify whether or not the intended bequest motive matters in determining the aged's demand for life or annuity insurance. His results indicate the strong importance of the intended bequest motive. Bernheim, however, does not consider how much such a motive influences the individual's saving decision. Moreover, his definition of intended bequest motive does not have a concrete form, but is merely revealed indirectly through the individual's life or annuity insurance demand.

The purpose of this study is to propose an empirically feasible method that makes it possible to directly measure an individual's intended bequest motives and their effect on saving decisions and on the demand for life or annuity insurance. For this purpose, special attention is paid to the binary information concerning whether an individual has a plan to bequeath financial and/or real assets to his or her children or spouse. To this end: (1) a specific Yaarian life-cycle model is constructed that determines how an individual judges the demand for saving and life or annuity insurance, and also provides the theoretical basis for empirically measuring his or her intended bequest motives; (2) based on this model, a statistical method is proposed for empirically measuring the intended bequest motives and their importance in determining the demand for saving and life or annuity insurance; and (3) an empirical analysis is conducted based on the cross-section data.

The Model

In this section, a brief outline à la the Yaarian life-cycle model (Yaari 1965) is presented, and several specifications are introduced into this model that make it possible to directly relate theoretical predictions to empirical analyses.

À la Yaarian Life-Cycle Model

Arrival of Death
"Death" is a rare event in a very short interval. Also, when it arrives, it is usually perceived as a "sudden event." In characterizing such a specific event of death, it is convenient to stipulate that arrivals of death follow a Poisson stochastic process with a frequency of $\mu(t)$. According to this specification, the probability of the first arrival of "death" in the interval between the present, time 0, and the future, time t, is given by the exponential distribution

$$e^{-\eta(0,t)}; \quad \eta(0, t) \equiv \int_0^t \mu(u)du. \tag{1}$$

When "death" arrives at time t, the remaining family members receive the bequest, $B(t)$, which is the sum of insurance protection, $I(t)$, and other assets, $W(t)$. Bequest, $B(t)$, must be positive because "the institutional framework makes it virtually impossible for a person in our society to die with a negative net worth" (Yaari 1965, 139).

Positive bequest, however, does not imply the positivity of life insurance demand. To be sure, a person with a strong bequest motive might purchase life insurance, $I(t) > 0$. However, an individual with weak or no intended bequest motives might not purchase life insurance, but rather purchase an annuity, $I(t) < 0$, in exchange for his or her assets, $W(t)$, as collateral. Hence, as long as he or she desires to purchase Yaarian annuities, an individual always keeps a positive amount of wealth despite the fact that he or she has a weak or null bequest motive.[2] In other words, the following relation must be satisfied:

$$W(t) = \begin{cases} \geq \text{ or } \leq 0 & \text{if life insurance is purchased,} \\ > 0 & \text{if annuity is purchased.} \end{cases} \tag{2}$$

We also note here that Yaarian annuity contracts are not necessarily made only between individuals and insurance companies; as is indicated in Kotlikoff and Spivak 1981 and Horioka 1984, these contracts are possibly implicitly introduced between aged parents and their children. Furthermore, when the public annuity system is forcefully introduced so that an individual has to purchase $P_{ub}(t) \geq 0$ amount of (fully funded) public annuities, the level of bequest must be redefined as

$$B(t) = I(t) - P_{ub}(t) + W(t) \geq 0,$$

where $I(t)$ is reinterpreted as the demand for private life insurance or annuity contracts. As Bernheim (1991) argues, when an individual is required to purchase public annuities beyond his or her desired level, he or she might adjust the desired level of bequest itself by purchasing private life insurance contracts even at the very old stage.

Bequest, $B(t)$, is evaluated (in a *ex ante* sense) by a monotonically

---

2. In this sense, the phenomenon that it is difficult for elderly people to decumulate their wealth is still possible to explain without introducing imperfections in capital markets as the standard literature does.

increasing concave utility function $V[B(t),t]$, which satisfies the following conditions:

$$\frac{\partial V[B(t),\, t]}{\partial B(t)} \geq 0 \text{ and } \frac{\partial^2 V[B(t),\, t]}{\partial B(t)^2} \leq 0.$$

Here, for simplicity, the consumer price is normalized to be unity for all time periods. Obviously, if a person has no bequest motives, $V[B(t),\, t]$ must always be zero for any $B(t)$. Moreover, as far as time separable utility functions are concerned, the bequest function $V[B(t),\, t]$ can be interpreted as either one's own utility level directly derived from the amount of bequest or the utility level of one's descendants indirectly derived from the bequest. Consequently the present model makes it impossible to identify a "bequest per se motive" from an "altruistic bequest motive."

Assets held by individuals, $W(t)$, are limited, for simplicity, to a safety asset; and its time path is represented by

$$\frac{dW(t)}{dt} = r_\ell(t)W(t) + Y(t) - c(t) - p(t), \tag{3}$$

$$(W[0] = \text{the initially owned asset})$$

where $r_\ell(t)$ is the rate of return to the asset, $Y(t)$ an exogenously determined (labor) income, $c(t)$ the consumption plan, and $p(t)$ the insurance premium paid or the annuities received at time t.

An individual agrees to pay (or receive) $p(t)$ to (or from) the insurance company,[3] while he or she is alive, on the premise that the insurance company guarantees $I(t)$ for his or her survivors—or he or she forfeits $I(t)$ amount of his or her assets to the insurance company—when he or she dies. In the implicit annuity contract model referred to above, the insurance contract may be set up such that parents' living expenses are financed by their children, $p(t) < 0$, in return for the inheritance, $W(t) > 0$. As far as yearly renewable term insurance contracts are concerned, the corresponding insurance premium $p(t)$ must be equal to

$$p(t) = \mu(t)I(t), \tag{4}$$

when no loading factor exists.

From now on, we impose, just for simplicity, this relation between $p(t)$

---

3. In the case that a fully funded public annuity system is available, the government can also be included here in the word *insurance company*.

and $I(t)$. To be sure, in the real world (especially in Japan), endowment or whole life or annuity insurance (i.e., permanent life) contracts with level premiums are so popular that it is better to deal with them as well as the yearly renewable term contracts. As is shown in Chuma 1990, however, in the present Yaarian model, where insurance contracts are neither surrendered nor lapsed, there could be no positive reason for an individual to purchase either permanent or term insurance contracts.[4] That is, both types of contracts are theoretically unidentifiable here.

Individual's Utility Maximization
An individual maximizes his or her expected lifetime utility with respect to his or her consumption plan, $\{c(t)\}$, and insurance plan, $\{I(t)\}$, subject to the wealth accumulation process in equation 3. The expected lifetime utility itself is defined as follows. Suppose that "death" arrives at time t. Then the individual continuously gets a utility of $U[c(t)]$ until just before "death" arrives at time t and a utility of $V[B(t), t]$, in a lump-sum manner, at the time of death. Here the utility function, $U(\bullet)$, is assumed to be monotonically increasing and concave with respect to its argument. Furthermore, according to equation 1, the probability that he or she will be still alive from the present to time t is $e^{-\eta(0,t)}$ and the probability that he or she will die right after time t is $e^{-\eta(0,t)} \cdot \mu(t)$. Then the consumer's expected lifetime utility at the present time is written as

$$J[W(0), 0] \equiv \int_0^T e^{-\eta(0,t)-\rho t} \{U[c(t)] + \mu(t) \cdot V[B(t), t]\} \, dt$$

$$+ e^{-\eta(0,T)-\rho T} \cdot V[B(T), T], \qquad (5)$$

where ρ is the rate of time preference and T is an exogenously given maximum planning horizon.

Applying the dynamic programming method to the above maximization problem, we have the optimal solution $(\{c^*(t)\}, \{I^*(t)\})$ which necessarily satisfies the Bellman-Jacobi equation:

$$-\frac{\partial J[W(t), t]}{\partial t} = -\rho J[W(t), t] + U(c^*) + [r_\ell(t)W(t) + Y(t)] \qquad (6)$$

---

4. Chuma 1990 has shown that, if the possibility of surrender or lapse is taken into account, individuals who face liquidity constraints are likely to purchase contracts with cash values having a level premium.

$$- c(t) - p(t)] \frac{\partial J[W(t), t]}{\partial W(t)}$$

$$+ \mu(t)\{V[W(t) + I^*(t), t] - J[W(t), t]\},$$

with the end point condition being

$$J[W(T),T] = V[W(T) + I^*(T),T]. \tag{7}$$

In equation 6, $c^*(t)$ or $I^*(t)$ itself must satisfy the first order conditions

$$\frac{dU[c^*(t)]}{dc^*(t)} = \frac{\partial J[W(t), t]}{\partial W(t)} \tag{8}$$

and

$$\frac{\partial J[W(t), t]}{\partial W(t)} \geq \frac{\partial V[W(t) + I^*(t), t]}{\partial [W(t) + I^*(t)]} \tag{9}$$

respectively. In equation 9, if inequality > 0 holds, $I^*(t)$ must be equal to $-W(t) < 0$, or, equivalently, $B(t)$ must be zero, which is implicitly assumed in Yaari 1965 when an individual has no bequest motives.

Equation 8 says that the optimal consumption plan $c^*(t)$ is determined such that the marginal utility of current consumption becomes equal to that of future consumption. Equation 9 implies that the optimal amount of insurance is determined so as to make the marginal loss in utility from lowering the current consumption equal to or greater than the marginal gain from the increase in the amount of insurance at the time of death.

Corresponding to the optimally chosen consumption and insurance plans, savings $S(t)$ is expressed as

$$S(t) = \begin{cases} r_\ell(t)W(t) + Y(t) - c^*(t) - \mu(t)I^*(t), & \text{with bequest motives,} \\ [r_\ell(t) + \mu]W(t) + Y(t) - c^*(t), & \text{without bequest motives,} \end{cases} \tag{10}$$

which will be utilized in the empirical analysis that follows. I note here from equation 10 that (i) if no intended bequest motive exists, the corresponding saving is not influenced by it at all; and (ii) even if such a motive is present, it does not influence the savings when its effect on the desired level of consumption and insurance are cancelling each other out. As a matter of fact, as Hurd (1989) shows, the following empirical analysis confirms that the presence of the intended bequest motive is significantly revealed through the life insurance demand, while its effect on savings is negligible.

Model Specifications

The model in the previous section gives the basic structure of the individual's demand for consumption and life or annuity insurance. In its abstract form, however, we still have difficulty in clarifying the close relationship between these demands and such factors as the individual's bequest motives, lifetime income, level of accumulated assets, family composition, and other socio-economic characteristics. In order to empirically measure the effects of these factors on the demand for savings or insurance, the above model needs a further specification. Subsequently, such a specification is introduced following Richard 1975 and Chuma 1987.

As is easily understood, unless the functional form of $J[W(t), t]$ in equation 7 is given in an explicit form, the first-order conditions (especially the one for demand for insurance, eq. 9) are of little practical use in analyzing our data set. As a way out of this difficulty, utility functions $U[C(t)]$ and $V[W(t) + I(t), t]$ are further assumed to be of the constant relative risk aversion type:

$$U[C(t)] = \frac{C(t)^\gamma}{\gamma} \ (\gamma \le 1), \tag{11}$$

and

$$V[W(t) + I(t), t] = n(t) \frac{[W(t) + I(t)]^\gamma}{\gamma}, \tag{12}$$

where $n(t) \ge 0 \equiv$ the measure of the degree that he or she cares about his or her family when he or she dies at time t, and the measure of relative risk aversion is defined as $\delta \equiv 1 - \gamma (\ge 0)$ and $n(t)$ is assumed to be exogenously given. According to this specification, $n(t) = 0$ means that an individual has no intended bequest motive.

Substitution of equations 11 and 12 into the Bellman-Jacobi equation 6 yields the explicit solution for the value function, $J[W(t), t]$:[5]

$$J[W(t), t] = a(t) \frac{[W(t) + L(t)]^\gamma}{\gamma}. \tag{13}$$

---

5. Assuming the iso-elastic functional forms in eqs. (11) and (12) is tantamount to stipulating that the wealth elasticity of bequest is unity. As is exemplified in Kotlikoff 1989, however, such a restriction may not be relevant. As a matter of fact, Kotlikoff derives the estimation result that such an elasticity is less than unity.

In this equation, coefficient $a(t)$ is determined so as to satisfy equation 7 under the conditions of equations 8, 9 with equality, 10, and 11. More explicitly, it is written as[6]

$$a(t)^{\frac{1}{\delta}} = e^{\int_t^T \Gamma(u)du} n(T)^{\frac{1}{\delta}} + \int_t^T \Lambda(u)e^{-\int_t^u \Gamma(k)dk} \, du \tag{14}$$

$$\Gamma(u) \equiv \mu(u) + \frac{\rho - \gamma_\ell(1 - \delta)}{\delta}; \; \Lambda(u) \equiv 1 + [\mu(u)n(u)]^{\frac{1}{\delta}}.$$

That is, $a(t)$ in equation 14 depends only on such exogenous parameters as $t(= \text{age})$, ρ, γ_ℓ, $\mu(t)$, and $n(t)$. Moreover, for such a time-invariant parameter, $\bar{n}$, as the relation $\partial n(t)/\partial \bar{n} > 0$ holds for all t, we get the relation

$$\frac{\partial a(t)}{\partial \bar{n}} > 0 \; \forall t. \tag{15}$$

Thus, an increase in this parameter directly increases, *ceteris paribus*, the expected lifetime utility. We also note here that $a(t)$ does not always monotonically decrease with age.

$L(t)$ in equation 13 is the discounted present value of the individual's expected lifetime (labor) income at time t and is defined as

$$L(t) = \int_t^T e^{-\int_t^u r_\ell(s)ds - \eta(t, u)} \, Y(u)du;$$

$e^{-\eta(t, u)} \equiv$ the probability that the individual who is still alive at time t will live further until time u.

By the use of the value function in equation 13, the first-order conditions found in equations 8 and 9, are simplified to

$$c^*(t) = a(t)^{-\frac{1}{\delta}}[W(t) + L(t)], \tag{16}$$

$$I^*(t) = [\lambda(t)^{\frac{1}{\delta}} - 1]W(t) + \lambda(t)^{\frac{1}{\delta}}L(t), \tag{17}$$

and

$$\lambda(t) \equiv \frac{n(t)}{a(t)}. \tag{18}$$

---

6. For details, see Richard 1975 or Chuma 1987.

The value function, $J[W(t), t]$, in equation 13 is the expected lifetime utility that is obtained on the condition that an individual is still alive at age t, and that coefficient $a(t)$ can be interpreted as the measure of his or her "tenacity for life." Thus, the term $\lambda(t) \equiv n(t)/a(t)$ is literally called the individual's "relative degree of bequest motive."

In equation 16 the optimal level of consumption, $c^*(t)$, surely increases, *ceteris paribus,* with one's wealth, $W(t)$, and lifetime income, $L(t)$, and decreases with the bequest motive parameter, $\bar{n}$, in equation 15. Moreover, in equation 17, the optimal demand for insurance, $I^*(t)$, surely increases, *ceteris paribus,* with one's lifetime income or "relative degree of bequest motive." The effect of wealth on $I(t)$ is indeterminate. That effect, however, becomes positive if the "relative degree of bequest motive" is so large that it exceeds unity. Thus, in order to make clear the effect, it is necessary to specify the determinants that might influence the magnitude of $\lambda(t)$. These will be explained in an empirical manner in the next section.[7]

Empirical Implementation

The Data Set and Its Characteristics

The data set analyzed in this study is taken from a survey reported in "Nikkei Needs Radar: Survey on Financial Behavior"[8] that was conducted from October to November 1990 by the Data Bank Bureau of Nihon Keizai Shinbun Inc., the leading newspaper company in Japan. In Nikkei Radar about 5,000

---

7. The following lemma derived by Chuma 1987 also gives an important clue in clarifying wealth effect.

LEMMA 1. *As long as (i) eq. (17) holds by equality, and (ii) the individual prefers to die later than sooner, i.e.,*

$J[W(t), t] > V[W(t), t]$ *for all t,*

the following three conditions are equivalent to each other:

(a)$\delta > 1$, *(b)* $\lambda(t) > 1$, *(c)* $W(t) + I^*(t) > W(t) + L(t)$.

Proof. See Chuma 1987, 42.

This lemma indicates that whether or not $\lambda(t)$ exceeds unity is equivalent to whether or not the measure of relative risk aversion, δ, exceeds unity. Hence, as long as Arrow's (1974) well-known axiom that "the measure of relative risk aversion increases with wealth" holds true, it is possible that quite wealthy individuals would have so large a $\lambda(t)$ that the wealth effect on $I(t)$ becomes positive.

8. This data set is publicly available. The data set is referred to as Nikkei Radar in this essay.

individuals (not households) aged 25 to 69 from the Tokyo metropolitan area (i.e., metropolitan Tokyo, Saitama, Chiba, and Kanagawa Prefectures, except for the offshore islands) were interviewed. The number of valid observations is 1,996, of which 1,129 are male and 867 are female respondents. In the subsequent analysis, mostly male samples are utilized mainly because: (a) only household income is available, (b) the name of the insured cannot be clarified sufficiently to separate the face value of insurance contracts, and (c) female samples are far smaller than male samples.

The definitions and details of the variables utilized in our analysis are given in the Appendix. The cohort data concerning a few representative variables are characterized in figures 1, 2, and 3, where "bequest motive" means the ratio of samples who plan to bequeath either financial or real assets, "insurance buying rate" the ratio of samples who retain life insurance contracts, and presence of kids is actually "presence of *dependent* kids."[9] The "face value" is the actual face value of the life insurance policies that each respondent has. The figures well suit the typical characteristics of the Japanese cross-section data (e.g., see Horioka 1991):

> savings does not decrease with age even if permanent income eventually decreases with age,
> both financial and real assets[10] are not decumulated even if the respondent's age increases,
> the bequest motive increases with age,
> the life insurance demand is eventually weakened with age.

Equations to Be Estimated

The main objective of the empirical analysis is to estimate the simultaneous equation model that consists of the savings equation 10, the demand-for-insurance equation 17 and the relative-degree-of-bequest-motive equation 18. In estimating this simultaneous equation model, however, both $a(t)$ and $\lambda(t)$ are unobservable even though the binary information becomes available as will be discussed. Furthermore, the desired amount of insurance, $I^*(t)$, is observed only when it is positive; that is, it is possible to observe the desired amount of life insurance but not that of annuity insurance. Therefore, we have to deal with the "simultaneous equation model with discrete and censored dependent variables" (Lee 1981). In the following subsections, I will discuss how to estimate such a model.

As already mentioned, Nikkei Radar does not ask the "relative degree of

---

9. Regrettably, the data of "presence of kids" is not available in Nikkei Radar.
10. The main part of "real assets" is a housing asset.

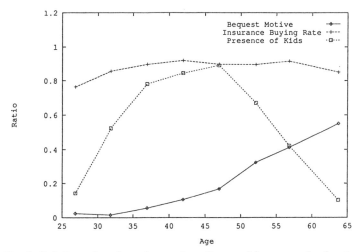

Fig. 1. Relation of savings, bequest motive, and insurance buying to age. (Data source: Nikkei Radar 1990.)

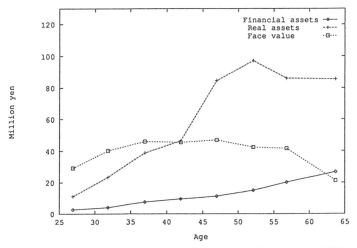

Fig. 2. Relation of wealth and face value to age. (Data source: Nikkei Radar 1990.)

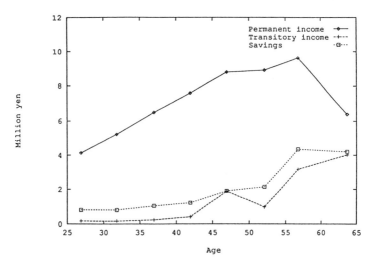

Fig. 3. Relation of income and savings to age. (Data source: Nikkei Radar 1990.)

bequest motive," $\lambda(t)$, in a direct fashion. Thus, I have to somehow estimate it through an indirect channel. To avoid this difficulty, I utilize the binary variable D_BQ,[11] which is defined as

$$D\_BQ = \begin{cases} 1 & \text{if the respondent answers that he or she plans to} \\ & \text{bequeath financial or real assets for children or spouse,} \\ 0 & \text{otherwise.} \end{cases}$$

Moreover, based on equations 13 and 18, the functional form of $\lambda(t)$ is approximated by

$$\lambda(t) = \beta_0 + \beta_1 \cdot Age + \beta_2 \cdot D\_Kids + \beta_3 \cdot D\_Single$$

$$+ \beta_4 \cdot D\_SNJob + \beta_5 \cdot D\_Living + \epsilon_b, \tag{19}$$

where ϵ_b is assumed to follow the normal distribution, $N(0, \sigma_b^2)$. *The variable D_SNJob indicates if the spouse has no job.* The definitions of other explanatory variables are easily understood. See the Appendix for details of the definitions.

Nikkei Radar presents the data on the amount of life insurance but not on the amount of annuities. Thus, the (true) amount of insurance, $I^*(t)$, is censored in such a way that

---

11. The proportion of $D\_BQ = 1$ is 21.5 percent for males.

$$I(t) = \begin{cases} I^*(t) & \text{if } I^*(t) \text{ is positive,} \\ 0 & \text{otherwise,} \end{cases}$$

when $I(t)$ is redefined as an observable dependent variable. The information about both public and private annuities is unavailable in Nikkei Radar except for the binary variable $D\_ARetire$, which means the insufficiency of public or private annuities after retirement.

The demand-for-insurance equation 17 includes both $L(t)$ and $\lambda(t)$ variables. Hence, it is also approximated here as

$$I^*(t) \simeq const + \xi_i \cdot \lambda(t) + \eta_1 Age + \eta_2 \cdot TAsset + \eta_3 \cdot PIncome$$

$$+ \eta_4 \cdot TRIncome + \eta_5 \cdot EduYears + \eta_6 \cdot D\_SelfE$$

$$+ \eta_7 \cdot D\_NJob$$

$$+ \eta_8 \cdot D\_ARetire + \eta_9 \cdot D\_HLoan + \epsilon_i$$

$$\equiv \xi_i \cdot \lambda(t) + X_1 \eta + \epsilon_i, \tag{20}$$

where ϵ_i is a disturbance term that follows normal distribution, $N(0, \sigma_i^2)$, and η is defined as $\eta' \equiv (\eta_1, \eta_2, \ldots, \eta_9)$. The variable X_1 is also defined here as $X_1 \equiv (1, Age, TAsset, PIncome, TRIncome, EduYears, D\_Self E, D\_NJob, D\_ARetire, D\_HLoan)$.

The amount of savings in equation 10 is always observable. However, the explanatory variable $L(t)$ (the lifetime income) cannot be observable nor estimable due to the lack of individual characteristic data in Nikkei Radar. In order to overcome these difficulties, lifetime income is assumed to be a linear function with such observed variables as: $PIncome$ (annual permanent income), $TRIncome$ (annual transitory income), Age (age), $EduYears$ (years of education), D_SelfE (self-employment dummy), D_NJob (non–job holder dummy), $D\_ARetire$ (insufficiency of public and/or private annuities after retirement dummy), and D_HLoan (home loan dummy). Moreover, from equations 14, 15 and 18, $a(t)$ and $\lambda(t)$ are not identifiable with each other. In fact, $a(t)$ is expressed as $a(t) = n(t)/\lambda(t)$ whereas we cannot actually distinguish $n(t)$ from $\lambda(t)$. Hence, $a(t)$ also could not help being approximated by the right-hand side in equation 19. Taking into account these limitations, savings equation 10 is approximated as

$$S(t) \simeq const + \xi_{s1} \cdot \mu(t)I^*(t) + \xi_{s2} \cdot a(t) + \alpha_1 Age + \alpha_2 \cdot TAsset$$

$$+ \alpha_3 \cdot PIncome + \alpha_4 \cdot TRIncome + \alpha_5 \cdot EduYears$$

$$+ \alpha_6 \cdot D\_SelfE$$

$$+ \alpha_7 \cdot D\_NJob + \alpha_8 \cdot D\_ARetire + \alpha_9 \cdot D\_HLoan + \epsilon_s$$

$$= d_s \cdot \lambda(t) + X_1 \alpha + \epsilon_s \text{ (by eq. 20)}, \tag{21}$$

where ϵ_s is a disturbance term that follows normal distribution, $N(0, \sigma_s^2)$, and α is defined as $\alpha' \equiv (\alpha_1, \alpha_2, \ldots, \alpha_9)$.

Estimation Technique

As was confirmed in the previous subsection, the simultaneous equation model presented is very complicated. Let us attempt to mitigate this complexity in the following manner. Our main objective is to clarify how intended bequest motives influence the savings and the life insurance demand. Thus, the equation to be estimated is not the structural savings equation 21 per se but the "reduced form" equation that is acquired by substituting the demand-for-insurance equation 20 into equation 21. Also, as was mentioned above, $a(t)$ in equation 21 is not distinguishable from $\lambda(t)$. What is to be done then is to estimate two simultaneous equation models separately; that is, (i) the relative-degree-of-bequest-motive equation and the reduced form savings equation, and (ii) the relative-degree-of-bequest-motive equation and the demand-for-insurance equation.

The simultaneous equation system in (i) consists of the (almost) ordinary type equation 21 and the Probit equation 19 while the one in (ii) consists of the Tobit equation 20 and Probit equation 19. Furthermore, both of them have a recursive structure, which makes the estimation substantially tractable. The actual estimation technique utilized is Amemiya's two-step Generalized Least Square method (GLS), which is developed in Amemiya 1979 and Lee 1984.[12] In confirming the robustness of our estimation results, we also tried to estimate the systems based on the two-stage estimation method developed by Nelson and Olsen 1978.[13]

Results

Relative Degree of Bequest Motive

Table 1 exhibits the bequest-motive equation estimation results for males of less than or equal to 50 years of age (from now on, the "young age group")

---

12. The actual estimation was done by using the *Limdep* and its matrix language.

13. It is well known that Amemiya's two-step GLS is much more efficient than Nelson and Olsen's two-stage method.

TABLE 1.   Estimation Result of Male's Bequest-Motive Equation (by Probit)

	for ≤ 50 years of age		for > 50 years of age	
Dependent Variable[a]	coefficient	t-value	coefficient	t-value
Constant	−3.5310	(−6.76)*	−2.1296	(−2.43)*
Age	0.0608	(4.93)*	0.0325	(2.20)**
D_Kids	−0.1929	(−0.95)	−0.1087	(−0.68)
D_Living	−0.0203	(−0.09)	−0.0661	(−0.37)
D_Single	−0.6141	(−2.05)**	−0.1764	(−0.52)
D_SNJob	−0.1181	(−0.80)	0.2583	(1.83)***
Log Likelihood	−201.43		−250.39	
Percent correctly predicted	91.46		61.64	
N	773		378	

Level of Significance: (*) = 1%, (**) = 5%, (***) = 10%
[a] Dependent Variable = Presence of Bequest Motives.

and males of greater than 50 years of age (from now on, the "old age group"). For reference, the results for the corresponding female samples are also reported in table 2.

First of all, the results for both male samples show that age (*Age*) itself has a significantly positive effect on bequest motives.[14] This point is also confirmed for the female young age group but not for the female old age group. Although the estimation results are not presented here for the male samples aged over 60, *Age* is no longer significant.[15] It may be natural that bequest motives do not simply increase with age, but rather depend on whether or not an individual has descendants about whom he or she cares. If so, the preceding results stand slightly opposed to such a prediction. However, this positively significant age effect needs to be interpreted with the caveat that due to Nikkei Radar, the variable *D_Kids* is not possible to literally define as the presence of children but only as the presence of *dependent* children. For example, Chuma and Asano (1993) have estimated the similar Probit equation based on the data source from the Seimei-Hoken Bunka Center in which the variable *D_Kids* can be literally defined.[16] According to their results, the variable *Age* is insignificant for both male and female samples even for relatively young age groups.

Even if an individual has children depending upon him or her, bequest motives are not always strengthened. This is partly confirmed by our results that the effect of *D_Kids* is negative in both tables 1 and 2 and significantly

14. The simple correlation coefficient between *Age* and *D_Kids* is relatively low: 0.502 for the young age group and −0.514 for the old age group.

15. *D_SNJob* is only significant for such old age samples.

16. In this data set, regrettably, neither savings nor real asset data are available.

negative for the female old age group. The negative effect is possibly because parents with bequest motives may not retain their income resources for the future bequests but rather spend them on their children for the present human capital investment (Becker and Tomes 1986; Lord and Rangazas 1991) or for some other purposes.

The spouse's job status should be an important factor for the bequest motive because an individual will certainly be concerned about who supports his or her surviving family members. According to the estimation results, the variable representing this factor, $D\_SNJob,$ appears positively significant for the male old age group but insignificant for the male young age group, while it is insignificant for both female groups. The result is quite plausible because as he becomes older, the male (normally as a main income earner) cares much more seriously than before about his spouse's livelihood after his death. The same explanation will apply to the presence of dependent parents living together with the respondents, D_Living. This factor, however, is insignificant for both male and female samples.

The effect of "being single" (the unmarried include those separated by death or divorce) is captured by the coefficient of D_Single. In our estimation, the default group is defined as "married and spouse is not working." Thus, the coefficient represents the contribution of being single to bequest motives relative to this default group. We expect the coefficient to be negative because being single almost always means that an individual has fewer descendents about whom he or she cares. The results show that the effect is significantly negative for the male young age group but not for the male old age group, while it is insignificant for both female groups.

TABLE 2. Estimation Result of Female's Bequest-Motive Equation (by Probit)

Dependent Variable[a]	for ≤ 50 years of age		for > 50 years of age	
	coefficient	t-value	coefficient	t-value
Constant	−4.5418	(−7.65)*	−1.5059	(−1.16)
Age	0.0810	(6.16)*	0.0231	(1.03)
D_Kids	−0.2716	(−1.31)	−0.5537	(−2.20)**
D_Living	0.1535	(0.71)	−0.1409	(−0.41)
D_Single	−0.0758	(−0.28)	0.0271	(0.01)
D_SNJob	0.6597	(0.93)	0.0532	(0.20)
Log Likelihood	−155.97		−126.07	
Percent correctly predicted	92.33		62.96	
N	678		189	

Level of Significance: (*) = 1%, (**) = 5%, (***) = 10%
[a] Dependent Variable = Presence of Bequest Motives.

TABLE 3. Estimation Result of Life Insurance–Demand Equation (for Male Samples of ≤ 50 years of Age)

Dependent Variable[a]	Amemiya's Two-step GLS		Nelson & Olsen's 2SLS		(Simple Tobit) (quasi-*t*-value)
	coefficient	*t*-value	coefficient	*t*-value	
Lambda	29.2643	(2.55)*	32.8343	(2.84)*	(3.54)*
Constant	156.826	(3.18)*	168.657	(3.40)*	(3.65)*
Age	−2.3879	(−2.92)*	−2.6012	(−3.17)*	(−4.00)*
D_SelfE	15.2933	(3.39)*	14.9430	(3.31)*	(3.28)*
D_NJob	−23.2360	(−1.26)	−24.8304	(−1.35)	(−1.33)
EduYears	−0.6064	(−0.85)	−0.5239	(−0.73)	(−0.73)
PIncome	3.1843	(6.14)*	3.2042	(6.18)*	(6.12)*
TRIncome	−0.7886	(−2.32)**	−0.8264	(−2.42)*	(−2.40)*
TAsset	0.0490	(3.91)*	0.0483	(3.85)*	(3.82)*
D_ARetire	−0.8375	(−0.28)	−0.8285	(−0.28)	(−0.28)
D_HLoan	7.6877	(2.26)**	8.4160	(2.46)*	(2.45)*
N			773		
(Simple Tobit:)	$R^2 = 0.1800$		Std. Error of Regr. = 36.63		Likelihood = −3550.0

Level of Significance: (*) = 1%, (**) = 5%, (***) = 10%

[a] Dependent Variable = Face Value of Life Insurance Protection

Demand for Life or Annuity Insurance

In this subsection, the factors affecting the demand for life or annuity insurance are examined. The estimation results are presented in table 3 for the male young age group and table 4 for the male old age group. It should be noted that the explanatory variable $\lambda(t)$ in these tables is an estimated one so that the *t*-value in the last column of the simple Tobit is not the correct one. We include such statistics to indicate the differences in *t*-values among Amemiya's GLS, Nelson and Olsen's 2SLS and the simple Tobit.

First of all, let us look at the "direct" effect of bequest motives, $\lambda(t)$, on the demand for life insurance. Table 3 shows that whether Amemiya's GLS or Nelson and Olsen's 2SLS is utilized, the variable $\lambda(t)$ has a significantly positive effect. This point indicates that the individual's intended bequest motive does in fact exist for the young age group.[17] Conversely, the intended bequest motives for the old age group do not influence the demand for life

---

17. The elasticity of $I^*(t)$ with respect to $\lambda(t)$ at the sample mean values is 1.07 in table 3. This number is substantially larger than those corresponding to the total asset (*TAsset*) and annual permanent income (*PIncome*), where the elasticity of *TAsset* = 0.06 and elasticity of *PIncome* = 0.50. Hence, it is confirmed that the bequest motives represented in the estimates of $\lambda(t)$ strongly influence the demand for life insurance.

insurance. Actually, as table 4 shows, the variable $\lambda(t)$ has no significant effect on it. The last result may stand opposed to our theoretical prediction in that old people demand life insurance even though their bequest motives play no role. However, taking into account the fact that quite a few people in Japan demand endowment or whole life contracts having large cash values, the result still possibly holds.

As shown in the model section, the main purpose of life insurance is to insure against the loss in the expected lifetime (permanent) income incurred by the death of the insured. Furthermore, as is indicated in figure 2, the necessity for such an insurance eventually decreases with age. Consequently, the effect of annual permanent income, *PIncome,* should have a positive effect on the demand for life insurance, while the age, *Age,* should have a negative effect on it. Indeed, irrespective of age groups, the coefficient of *PIncome* is significantly positive. The coefficient of *Age* is also significantly negative for the young age group although it is not significant for the old age group.

The effect of annual transitory income (*TRIncome*) is negatively significant for the young age group. This may be due to the liquidity constraints faced by the young respondents. The same effect is negative but insignificant for the old age group. As figure 3 shows, most transitory incomes are acquired just after 55 years of age in the present samples. Thus, a large part of these incomes come in the form of huge severance pay at the time of (manda-

TABLE 4. Estimation Result of Life Insurance–Demand Equation (for Male Samples of > 50 years of Age)

Dependent Variable[a]	Amemiya's Two-step GLS		Nelson & Olsen's 2SLS		(Simple Tobit) (quasi-t-value)
	coefficient	t-value	coefficient	t-value	
Lambda	5.5059	(0.13)	6.3987	(0.15)	(0.43)
Constant	103.257	(0.80)	104.538	(0.81)	(2.21)**
Age	−1.6605	(−0.78)	−1.6581	(−0.78)	(−2.17)**
D_SelfE	4.9251	(0.86)	5.7280	(0.97)	(1.01)
D_NJob	1.1112	(0.16)	1.0990	(0.16)	(0.16)
EduYears	−0.1259	(−0.15)	−0.3090	(−0.34)	(−0.38)
PIncome	2.4125	(5.03)*	2.4838	(4.40)*	(5.31)*
TRIncome	−0.2490	(−1.30)	−0.2480	(−1.30)	(−1.29)
TAsset	0.0655	(4.86)*	0.0636	(4.55)*	(4.73)*
D_ARetire	−2.8485	(−0.68)	−2.0915	(−0.48)	(−0.50)
D_HLoan	2.8450	(0.58)	3.7362	(0.71)	(0.76)
N			356		
(Simple Tobit:)	$R^2 = 0.2652$;	Std. Error of Regr. $= 36.23$;		Likelihood $= -1738.9$	

Level of Significance: (*) = 1%, (**) = 5%, (***) = 10%
[a] Dependent Variable = Face Value of Life Insurance Protection

tory) retirement, which could reduce the necessity for the life insurance. Then it is possible that the effect for the old age group becomes negative.

From the viewpoint of human capital theory, those with higher education, on the average, tend to have higher lifetime earnings, to retire later, and to live longer. Thus, the coefficient of *EduYears* must be positive. The result, however, shows that it is insignificant and negative for both age groups.

The effects of job characteristics on the demand for life insurance are represented by the coefficients of *D_SelfE* (self-employment dummy, including the family worker) and *D_NJOB* (non–job holder dummy). The default group for job characteristic is that of the wage earners. The coefficient of *D_SelfE* is significantly positive for the young age group, while that of *D_NJob* is insignificant even for this group. For the old age group, neither *D_SelfE* nor *D_NJob* is significant even though the coefficient of *D_SelfE* is positive. It is quite possible that, when an individual (male here) is self-employed, his death results in serious difficulties for the survivors' livelihood. If so, even with other things being equal, the death would require a larger future income to be compensated compared with that of the wage earner.[18] The negative (for the young age group) coefficient value of *D_NJob* also suggests that the death of an individual with no job does not particularly affect the demand for life insurance. The same logic might be applicable to the insufficiency of after-retirement income (*D_ARetire*). Its effect, however, is insignificantly negative.

The total asset (*TAsset*) has a significant positive effect on the demand for life insurance for the young age group while it is insignificant for the old age group. Such a result suggests that the value of $\lambda(t)$ in equation 17 is greater than unity for the young age group and not so different from unity for the old age group. The effect of *D_HLoan* (home loan dummy) is positive and significant especially for the young age group. This might reflect the fact that in Japan, owning a home purchased through a loan forces a consumer to buy a life insurance contract against default risks caused by his or her death.

Determinants of Savings

Let us first of all examine the relationship between savings and intended bequest motives. The estimation result indicates that for both the young and old age groups (see tables 5 and 6), the effect of intended bequest motive, $\lambda(t)$, on savings is insignificant using any estimation methods. In the previous section, we have confirmed that the intended bequest motive has a positively significant effect on the demanded life insurance especially for the young age

---

18. It is well known that in Japan, luxurious life insurance contracts such as "keyman plans," which guarantee more than 1.0 billion yen of life insurance, are very popular among owners of medium- or small-scale firms.

group. Thus, at least the young respondents should have intended bequest motives, yet such motives do not significantly influence their savings. We also note that *Age* effects in tables 5 and 6 are both insignificant. Hence, it is hard to maintain that the unexplained part of intended bequest motives has a significant positive effect on savings.

The above results suggest that the hypotheses that emphasizes the positive relationship between savings and intended bequest motives is hard to justify even based on the cross-section data in which the positive relationship between age and savings is spuriously observed (see fig. 3). Judging from these results, the other hypotheses that do not emphasize intended bequest motives must be relevant in explaining this spurious relation.

Sign and Statistical Significance of Other
Explanatory Variables
Textbooks teach us that the rich normally save more than the poor. Also, according to the permanent income hypothesis, the propensity to consume from permanent income is greater than that from transitory income. Conforming to this prediction, the effect of both *PIncome* and *TRIncome* is positively significant for both age groups, where both the effect on savings and the significance of the latter is very much stronger than those of the former. The level of education, *EduYears,* also generally increases an individual's perma-

TABLE 5. Estimation Result of Savings Equation
(for Male Samples of ≤ 50 years of Age)

Dependent Variable[a]	Amemiya's Two-step GLS		Nelson & Olsen's 2SLS		(Simple OLS) (quasi-*t*-value)
	coefficient	*t*-value	coefficient	*t*-value	
Lambda	0.3645	(0.95)	0.3595	(0.93)	(1.05)
Constant	1.7566	(1.04)	1.7412	(1.03)	(1.52)
Age	−0.0301	(−1.09)	−0.0299	(−1.08)	(−1.21)
D_SelfE	0.3920	(2.21)**	0.3911	(2.20)**	(2.24)**
D_NJob	−0.1154	(−0.17)	−0.1153	(−0.17)	(−0.18)
EduYears	0.0081	(0.29)	0.0081	(0.28)	(0.29)
PIncome	0.0932	(4.55)*	0.0933	(4.55)*	(4.62)*
TRIncome	0.4179	(33.39)*	0.4178	(33.37)*	(33.87)*
TAsset	0.0015	(3.02)*	0.0015	(3.02)*	(3.06)*
D_ARetire	0.2035	(1.74)***	0.2035	(1.74)***	(1.78)***
D_HLoan	−0.2537	(−1.88)***	−0.2533	(−1.88)***	(−1.91)***
N			773		
(Simple OLS:)	$R^2 = 0.6503$		Std. Error of Regr. = 1.5733		

Level of Significance: (*) = 1%, (**) = 5%, (***) = 10%
[a] Dependent Variable = Savings.

**TABLE 6. The Estimation Result of Savings Equation
(for Male Samples of > 50 Years of Age)**

Dependent Variable[a]	Amemiya's Two-step GLS		Nelson & Olsen's 2SLS		(Simple OLS) (quasi-*t*-value)
	coefficient	*t*-value	coefficient	*t*-value	
Lambda	−0.8388	(−0.62)	−0.8384	(−0.62)	(−0.80)
Constant	−3.8113	(−0.90)	−3.6748	(−0.86)	(−1.10)
Age	0.0643	(0.93)	0.0634	(0.92)	(1.17)
D_SelfE	−0.0192	(−0.05)	−0.0195	(−0.05)	(−0.05)
D_NJob	−0.0076	(−0.02)	−0.0126	(−0.03)	(−0.03)
EduYears	−0.0762	(−1.31)	−0.0804	(−1.38)	(−1.38)
PIncome	0.3108	(9.29)*	0.3065	(9.08)*	(9.19)*
TRIncome	0.7981	(60.84)*	0.7980	(60.82)*	(60.21)*
TAsset	0.0007	(0.70)	0.0007	(0.73)	(0.73)
D_ARetire	−0.3667	(−1.25)	−0.3667	(−1.25)	(−1.24)
D_HLoan	−0.5168	(−1.49)	−0.5118	(−1.47)	(−1.48)
N			356		
(Simple OLS:)	$R^2 = 0.9169$		Std. Error of Regr. = 2.8028		

Level of Significance: (*) = 1%, (**) = 5%, (***) = 10%
[a]Dependent Variable = Savings.

nent income, retirement age, or longevity so that its effect must be positive. The result, however, indicates that it is insignificant for both age groups.

As long as an individual has to pay a certain amount of home loans, he or she cannot afford to save too much. The negatively significant effect of *D_HLoan* for the young age group is then quite reasonable. The same effect is insignificant for the old age group, which might reflect the fact that the burden of the home loan is less serious for the aged than for young people.[19]

As was mentioned, the rich tend to save more than the poor so that it is expected that total wealth (*TAsset*) increases savings. In fact, the effect of *TAsset* is significantly positive for the young age group and insignificantly negative for the old age group. The negative effect for the latter may reflect the fact that the ample total wealth (*TAsset*) may reduce, *ceteris paribus,* the necessity for savings. The (future) insufficiency of public and/or private annuity after retirement (*D_ARetire*) increases the necessity for saving so that its effect on savings must be positive. The result is significantly positive for the young age group and insignificantly negative for the old age group.

The self-employed do not have severance pay or private annuities (or pensions) and are guaranteed only for the less-than-average amount of public

---

19. About 30 percent of the young age group have home loans while the corresponding number for the old age group is about 26 percent.

annuities (in Japan). The positive significance of *D_SelfE* for the young age group is then reasonable. The same variable is negatively insignificant for the old age group. This may reflect the fact that their descendants are apt to succeed them.

Conclusion and Summary

My results indicate that for both the young and old age groups, the effect of intended bequest motive on savings is insignificant. Moreover, as will be summarized, the intended bequest motive has a positive significant effect on the demanded life insurance for the young age group, whereas that motive has no significant effect on such a demand for the old age group. Hence, it is concluded that the respondents have intended bequest motives at least over the relatively young stage of life, whereas such motives do not significantly increase or decrease savings over the old stage.

The preceding results also suggest that the saving hypothesis that emphasizes the positive relationship between savings and intended bequest motives is hard to justify even based on the cross-section data. As far as the determinants of savings are concerned, therefore, the implicit annuity hypothesis (Kotlikoff and Spivak 1981) or the strategic bequest motive hypothesis (Bernheim, Shleifer, and Summers 1985) must be much more relevant in explaining the spurious positive relationship between age and savings.

Concerning the degree of intended bequest motive per se, both males' and females' bequest motives are significantly influenced by their age (except for the female old age group). This result is a little bit disappointing in that intended bequest motives are likely to depend on whether or not an individual has descendants about whom he or she cares. Such a result is partly due to the limitation of the utilized data in that the variable *D_Kids* in that Nikkei Radar cannot be literally defined as the presence of children but only as the presence of *dependent* children.

Regarding family characteristics, only the effect of being single on the intended bequest motive is negatively significant for the male young age group, while only the effect of a spouse having no job is significant for the male old age group. Regarding the female groups, only the effect of having dependent kids is negatively significant for the female old age group.

The results also confirm that the individual's demand for life insurance is significantly influenced by the intended bequest motive and by such factors as permanent and transitory income, age, job status, total asset balance, and the presence of a home loan. The last result for life insurance demand, however, is fairly different from the one for the old age group. In fact, for such a group, the intended bequest motives do not matter at all in determining the desired amount of life insurance. For the old age group, the only significant variables are permanent income and total asset balance.

APPENDIX: VARIABLES

D_BQ: having a plan to bequeath financial and/or real assets for children or spouse
I(t): life insurance coverage (million yen)
S(t): amount of yen specified in answer to: "How much did you keep for savings or investment from your annual (permanent and transitory) income?"
Age: respondent's age—The variable *Age* actually used here is created by subtracting the mean age of samples from each observed age.
PIncome: normal household annual permanent income (million yen)—The raw data are given in 20 categorical values. Here we take a middle value in each interval. For the samples whose income is greater then 50 million yen (the greatest category), however, the value is set to be the minimum within that category.
TRIncome: normal household annual transitory income (million yen)—The raw data are given in 20 categorical values. Here we take a middle value in each interval. For the samples whose income is greater than 100 million yen (the greatest category), however, the value is set to be the minimum within that category.
TAsset: the financial and real asset balance (10 million yen)—The raw data are given in 23 categorical values. Here we take a middle value in each interval. For the samples whose balance is greater than 10 million yen (= the greatest category), however, the value is set to be 10 million yen.
λ: degree of bequest motives created by Probit estimation
D_SelfE: self-employment (including family workers)
D_NJob: non–job holder
EduYears: years of education—The graduate school educated respondent is treated as a university graduate.
D_Living: living together with dependent parents
D_Kids: having dependent children
D_Single: the unmarried (including the separated by death or divorce)
D_SNJob: spouse having no job
D_ARetire: insufficiency of public and/or private pension after retirement
D_HLoan: homeowner with home loans

REFERENCES

Amemiya, T. 1979. "The Estimation of A Simultaneous Equation Tobit Model." *International Economic Review* 20:169–81.
Arrow, K. 1974. *Essays in The Theory of Risk Bearing*. Amsterdam: North Holland.
Becker, G. S., and N. Tomes. 1986. "Human Capital and the Rise and Fall of Families." *Journal of Labor Economics* 4 (July): S1–S39.
Bernheim, B. D. 1991. "How Strong Are Bequest Motives? Evidence Based on Estimates of the Demand for Life Insurance and Annuities." *Journal of Political Economy* 99, no. 5:899–927.
Bernheim, B. D., A. Shleifer, and L. Summers. 1985. "Strategic Bequest Motives." *Journal of Political Economy* 93, no. 6:1045–76.
Chuma, H. 1987. "Life Insurance Savings, Life Protection and Inflation." *Finance Ken-Kyu*, no. 6 (January):31–53.

———. 1990. "Why Do People Demand Life Insurance Savings?" *Economic Studies Quarterly* (The Journal of the Japan Association of Economics and Econometrics) 41, no. 4 (December):317–25.

Chuma, H., and S. Asano. 1993. "Isan-Doki to Seimei-Hoken Jyuyo" (Bequest motives and life insurance demand). Forthcoming in *Keizai Kenkyu.*

Hayashi, F. 1986. "Why is Japan's Saving Rate So Apparently High?" In *NBER Macroeconomics Annual 1986,* ed. S. Fischer, 145–210. Cambridge, Mass.: MIT Press.

Horioka, C. Y. 1984. "Applicability of the Life-Cycle Hypothesis of Saving to Japan." *Kyoto University Economic Review* 54, no. 2 (October):31–56.

———. 1991. "Saving in Japan." Discussion Paper, no. 248. Osaka, Japan: The Institute of Social and Economic Research, Osaka University.

Hurd, M. 1989. "Mortality Risk and Bequest." *Econometrica* 57, no. 4:779–813.

Kotlikoff, L. J. 1989. "Estimating the Wealth Elasticity of Bequests from a Sample of Potential Descendents." In *What Determines Savings?* by L. J. Kotlikoff, chap. 16. Cambridge, Mass.: MIT Press.

Kotlikoff, L. J., and A. Spivak. 1981. "The Family as an Incomplete Annuities Market." *Journal of Political Economy* 89, no. 2 (April):372–91.

Kotlikoff, L. J., and L. Summers. 1981. "The Role of Intergenerational Transfer in Aggregate Capital Accumulation." *Journal of Political Economy* 89, no. 4 (August):706–32.

Lee, L. F. 1981. "Simultaneous Equation Models with Discrete and Censored Variables." In *Structural Analysis of Discrete Data with Econometric Applications,* ed. C. F. Manski and D. McFadden, 346–64. Cambridge, Mass.: MIT Press.

Lord, W., and P. Rangazas. 1991. "Savings and Wealth in Models with Altruistic Bequests." *American Economic Review* 81, no. 1 (March):289–96.

Modigliani, F. 1988. "The Role of Intergenerational Transfers and Life Cycle Saving in the Accumulation of Wealth." *Journal of Economic Perspectives* 2, no. 2: 15–40.

Nelson, F. D., and L. Olsen. 1978. "Specification and Estimation of a Simultaneous Equation Model with Limited Dependent Variables." *International Economic Review* 19:695–709.

Ohtake, F. 1991. "Bequest Motives of Aged Households in Japan." Discussion paper, no. 249. Osaka, Japan: The Institute of Social and Economic Research, Osaka University.

Richard, S. F. 1975. "Optimum Consumption, Portfolio and Life Insurance Rule for an Uncertain Lived Individual in a Continuous-Time Model." *Journal of Financial Economics* 2:187–203.

Sato, K. 1989. *Macro Keizaigaku Senka* (Advanced macroeconomics). Nihon Hyoron-Sha.

Yaari, M. E. 1965. "Uncertain Lifetime, Life Insurance and the Theory of the Consumer." *Review of Economic Studies* 32:137–50.

CHAPTER 3

Cost of Care and Bequests

Tadashi Yagi and Hirohisa Maki

In this essay, we analyze the wealth accumulation process and bequeathing behavior in an economy where the annuity system is readily available. There is an abundance of literature that analyzes the issues of wealth accumulation. Many researchers have focused on the effect of death probability and bequests on wealth accumulation (Hurd 1989). Only a small amount, however, have analyzed wealth accumulation by incorporating the behavior of choice between private annuities and bequeathable wealth into the model. Since the rate of return of annuities is larger than the rate of return of bequeathable wealth, holding bequeathable wealth generates certain costs. One of our purposes in this essay is to clarify the costs and benefits of holding bequeathable wealth in an economy where death is uncertain.

The importance of considering the wealth accumulation process that incorporates an annuity is evident when the recent rapid increase in privately managed homes for the aged in Japan is viewed. Different from public homes for the aged, many of these privately managed homes are fully equipped with a care system for the bedridden elderly. By paying a huge amount of money up front when the elder person enters the home, everything including accommodation, meals, and care is insured. In this sense, entering a privately managed home for the aged is the same as buying annuities, although the amount of money required is quite a bit larger upon entering the home. The entrance fee is usually financed by selling real estate.

As stated, the issue of care is significantly more important for the aged (see Boersch-Supan et al. 1990). Boersch-Supan et al. analyzed the provision

This paper was read at the International Conference on Savings and Bequests, which was held in Tokyo on March 17 and 18, 1992, under the sponsorship of the Japanese Institute for Posts and Telecommunications Policy (IPTP). This paper was also read at the annual meeting of the Japan Association of Economics and Econometrics that was held on Oct. 3 and 4, 1992, at Kyushu University. We are most grateful to Professors James B. Davies, Noriuki Takayama, and Toshiaki Tachibanaki, Fumio Otake, and to the participants of the symposium for their valuable comments.

of care by children empirically. There is a substitutability between the provision of care by children and buying care in the market. The privately managed home for the aged is a kind of institute that provides care in the market. If the possibility exists that the children's provision of time for the care is contingent on future bequests, changes in the relative price of care in the market affects the behavior of choice between the bequeathable wealth and annuities. We focus on this point and examine the consequences of changes in the cost of care on the wealth accumulation process.

Our essay consists of five sections. The second section investigates the motivation of saving and the relation between bequests and care by examining the 1990 Survey on Family and Savings Behavior (SFSB), which was compiled by the Institute of Posts and Telecommunications Policy (IPTP). The survey posed several questions to us on the validity of pure altruistic bequest motive and suggests the validity of the gift exchange model. The third section provides the model, and the fourth section examines the effect of changes in the cost of care on the wealth accumulation process. In the last section, the factors that affect the cost of care are discussed.

Posed Questions

Bequest Motive Theories

In inquiring about the saving behavior of the individual, the roles of bequests constitute one of the most important issues to be analyzed. A study on the factors that determine the amount of bequest is important to undertake. Much of the literature on this subject stresses the altruistic behavior of the parent to their children (Barro 1974; Becker 1974). The Ricardian neutrality theorem heavily depends on the existence of altruistic utility from the welfare of descendants. The fact that a relatively large proportion of individuals hold their monetary wealth in bequeathable monetary wealth even when an annuity is available seems to provide us with firm evidence for the existence of the bequest motive (Friedman and Warshawsky 1988, 1990).

Contrary to the approach that stresses the bequest motive, there is a group that stresses the strategic motivation of holding bequeathable wealth. According to Bernheim, Shleifer, and Summers (1985), the reason parents hold bequeathable wealth is that they expect a gift from their children. In addition, it is worthwhile noting that primogeniture is not consistent with utility maximization in the case where the utility function of the bequest motive is a concave function. That is, it is hard to explain the rationality of the system by using the bequest motive approach above, and another explanation is needed.

The empirical evidence for bequeathing behavior is witnessed in an accumulation of research. Kotlikoff and Summers (1981) presented a rigid methodology for estimating the intergenerational transfers and suggested the importance of intergenerational transfers in capital accumulation. Hayashi (1986) and Hayashi, Ando, and Ferris (1988) studied the saving behavior in the Japanese case, and demonstrated the importance of bequest and intergenerational transfer. There is, however, no specific evidence that the bequests are generated from altruistic motivation as Horioka (1991) pointed out. Additionally, a series of research stresses the precautionary savings and unintended bequest (Davies 1981; Skinner 1988; Caballero 1991).

Saving and Bequeathing Behavior Shown in SFSB Data

Our first task in this essay is to examine whether the empirical facts can be explained consistently from the theories stated here. Before investigating the econometric analysis on the bequeathing behavior, we look closely at the facts shown in the SFSB. We focus especially on the consciousness of the individual in saving and bequeathing. Although we admit that the consciousness does not match the behavior, it is also true that it is difficult to infer the true intention from the behavior. In this sense, it is worthwhile to examine the survey data that describes not only the results of behavior but also the consciousness behind the behavior.

From tables 1 to 5 we can infer that most of the individuals consider that the wealth accumulated before retirement would not be enough for financing the cost of the retirement period. Most individuals are anxious about their retirement period, and earnings income remains the main source of income for 35 percent of the retired elderly. This result is consistent with the result derived in Hayashi, Ando, and Ferris 1988.

As is shown in table 6, around 70 percent of individuals save even during the retirement period. Table 7 suggests that preparation for unintended expenditure is a major driving force for saving, and more than 30 percent save to have enough to pay for the cost of living. It is also shown that only a few save for bequest during the retirement period, while 60 percent of individuals have some intention to bequeath as is shown in table 8.

TABLE 1. Anxiety about the Future

Anxiety	1	2	3	4	Total
Count	448	1,547	638	134	2,767
Percent	16.2	55.9	23.1	4.8	100

Source: Institute for Posts and Telecommunications Policy 1990.

Note: 1. No anxiety. 2. A little anxiety. 3. Have anxiety about the future. 4. Have serious anxiety about the future.

TABLE 2. Feasibility of Financing Retirement Period by Public Pension

Financing	1	2	3	4	Total
Count	42	548	1,005	752	2,347
Percent	1.8	23.3	42.8	32.0	100

Source: Institute for Posts and Telecommunications Policy 1990.
Note: 1. All consumption and cost can be financed by public pension. 2. A large proportion of consumption and cost can be financed by public pension. 3. Around half of consumption and cost can be financed by public pension. 4. Only a small portion of consumption and cost can be financed by public pension.

TABLE 3. Financial Sources for the Retirement Period (Excluding Public Pension)

Source	1	2	3	4	5	6	7	8	Sample Size
Count	1,630	165	1,267	931	962	218	299	100	2,724
Percentage	59.3	6.0	46.5	34.2	35.3	8.0	11.0	3.7	100

Source: Institute for Posts and Telecommunications Policy 1990.
Note: The question permits multiple answers. The percentage is calculated by dividing the count by sample size. 1. Wealth. 2. Liquidate real property such as land and house. 3. Insurance and private annuity. 4. Retirement allowance. 5. Working after retirement age. 6. Capital income. 7. Gift from children. 8. Others.

TABLE 4. Current Income (Questions Given to Elderly over 60)

Income	1	2	3	4	5	6	7	8	Sample Size
Count	621	195	72	402	111	109	6	25	862
Percent	72.0	22.6	8.4	46.6	12.9	12.6	0.7	2.9	100

Source: Institute for Posts and Telecommunications Policy 1990.
Note: The question permits multiple answers. The percentage is calculated by dividing the count by sample size. 1. Public pension, corporate pension. 2. Savings. 3. Private annuity. 4. Earnings income. 5. Capital income. 6. Gift from children. 7. Public transfer. 8. Others.

TABLE 5. Main Income in Table 4

Income	1	2	3	4	5	6	7	8	Total
Count	390	17	11	260	22	27	2	7	736
Percent	53.0	2.3	1.5	35.3	3.0	3.7	0.3	1.0	100

Source: Institute for Posts and Telecommunications Policy 1990.

TABLE 6. Are You Still Saving Now?
(Questions Given to Elderly over 60)

Saving	1	2	3	Total
Count	264	380	212	856
Percent	30.8	44.4	24.8	100

Source: Institute for Posts and Telecommunications Policy 1990.
Note: 1. Still saving regularly. 2. Still saving, but irregularly. 3. Not saving.

TABLE 7. Reasons for Saving
(Questions Given to Elderly over 60)

Reason	1	2	3	4	5	Total
Count	284	472	39	61	25	881
Percent	32.2	53.6	4.4	6.9	2.8	100

Source: Institute for Posts and Telecommunications Policy 1990.
Note: 1. Prepare for living cost. 2. Prepare for unintended expenditure. 3. Prepare for bequests. 4. No items to consume. 5. Others.

TABLE 8. Form of Bequests

Bequest	1	2	3	4	Sample Size
Count	1,811	859	59	1,488	3,601
Percent	50.3	23.9	1.6	41.3	100

Source: Institute for Posts and Telecommunications Policy 1990.
Note: The question permits multiple answers. The percentage is calculated by dividing the count by sample size. 1. House or land. 2. Monetary wealth. 3. Other form. 4. No intention to bequeath.

TABLE 9. Was the Provision of Care the
Condition for Inheriting Bequests?

	Yes	No	Total
Count	426	379	994
Percent	42.9	38.1	100

Source: Institute for Posts and Telecommunications Policy 1990.
Note: The sample size of 994 is the number of individuals who inherited bequests.

Table 9 provides us with the most interesting fact concerning the relation between care and bequests. According to the table, 43 percent of individuals who inherited a bequest answered that provision of care was the condition for inheriting a bequest. This percentage is larger than the proportion of individuals who answered that care was not the condition for inheriting a bequest.

It is hard to conclude that the pure bequest motive explains satisfactorily the survey facts. There is a large possibility that most individuals behave in the same manner as the altruistic individual, though their main concern is their own consumption. The fact suggested in table 9 implies that the gift exchange approach more suitably explains these facts. The monetary exchange, however, cannot be seen by the survey because only around 10 percent of individuals expect monetary transfer from their children, and around 10 percent of the aged actually receive monetary transfer from their children as is shown in tables 3 and 4. In addition, table 5 shows that only 3 percent of the aged answer that a gift from their children is their main income.

Care and Bequest

In the following, we construct our hypothesis with careful attention given to the facts presented in tables 7 and 9. Table 7 suggests that preparation for unintended expenditure is a major driving force behind saving. The typical example of unintended expenditure for the aged is the expenditure for the cost of care. That is, the cost of care is a crucial matter for the aged, and some explanation must be given to the relation between the wealth accumulation process, cost of care, and bequests.

There are two ways to obtain care: one is to obtain it from children, the other is to buy it on the market. One example of care provision in the marketplace is the privately managed home for the aged. The cost of care is defined as the direct expenditure necessary to obtain care. It is possible, however, to consider the case where the expenditure for the care can be reduced by receiving the care from children rather than buying it on the market because the compensation needed for the caring relatives may be smaller than that required for care by others.

Recalling the relationship between care provision and inheriting bequests (see table 9), in our model we incorporate the possibility that bequeathable wealth reduces the expenditure for care by inducing children to care for their parents. In the following section, we investigate the optimal portfolio selection between annuities and bequeathable wealth, and between optimal wealth accumulation process and optimal bequest level, by considering the possibility that owing bequeathable wealth induces children to take care of their parents.

Optimal Allocation of Wealth

Model

In this model, we consider the optimal choice behavior in allocating the wealth of an individual who considers that the cost of living during a retirement period depends on the amount of bequeathable wealth holdings. The individual seeks to maximize his or her lifetime utility, as given by

$$U = \int_0^T u(c_{1t})e^{-\rho t}a_t dt + \int_0^T \phi(B_t)e^{-\rho t}m_t dt, \tag{1}$$

where u is a strictly increasing concave utility function, c_{1t} is consumption at time t, ρ is the constant rate of time preference, a_t is the probability that the individual will be alive at time t, m_t is the instantaneous mortality rate at t, ϕ is the utility from bequeathing wealth to descendants, and ϕ is assumed to be a strictly increasing concave function. T is the maximum age one can live. The formulation of altruistic utility permits us to deal with the unintended bequest (Hurd 1989).

The relationship between the life rate a_t and the instantaneous mortality rate m_t is given by

$$a_t = 1 - \int_0^t m_s ds, \tag{2}$$

such that $m_t = -da_t/dt$.

In this model, we assume there exists an uncontrollable consumption at time t that is denoted by c_{2t}. Since it is uncontrollable to each individual, it is assumed that this consumption is included in the utility function separate from the utility of controllable consumption c_1. The typical example of c_2 is consumption of care at the time of illness. Especially for the aged, the consumption of care is expected to be large and uncontrollable. The assumption of uncontrollability implies that the level of care that is necessary for an individual is given exogenously.

Since the death period is stochastic for the individual, the introduction of the annuity market makes it possible for the individual to earn a higher rate of return by holding resources in an annuity rather than by holding them in bequeathable wealth. Without a bequest motive and uncontrollable consumption that is independent from bequeathable wealth, it is easily shown that the

optimal allocation of wealth between the annuities and bequeathable wealth
is holding the whole wealth in annuities. In the case where the level of
bequeathable wealth changes the price of living (i.e., cost of one unit of care),
the possibility of holding bequeathable wealth arises as a mean of improving portfolio selection. That is, the determination of optimal allocation
of wealth between annuities and bequeathable wealth becomes an unsettled
problem.

The optimizing behavior of the individual is to maximize the utility
function (1) by controlling consumption, a share of the annuities in the wealth
and a share of consumption financed by the annuities subject to the following
dynamic equations:

$$\frac{dA}{dt} = r_{at}A_t + \alpha_t(w_t + r_tB_t + B_t) - \beta_t[c_{1t} + p(\pi_tB_t, w_t^k)c_{2t}], \tag{3}$$

$$\frac{dB}{dt} = w_t + r_tB_t - \alpha_t(w_t + r_tB_t + B_t) - (1 - \beta_t)[c_{1t} + p(\pi_tB_t, w_t^k)c_{2t}], \tag{4}$$

where α is a share of wealth invested in the annuities at each period, β is a
share of consumption financed by the annuities, A is a stock in the annuities, B
is bequeathable wealth, and $p(\cdot)$ is the price of uncontrollable consumption.
We assume that the price of uncontrollable consumption is a function of the
expected bequests and wage rate of a child. The rate of return of bequeathable
wealth is r, r_a is the rate of return of the annuities, and w^k is the wage rate of a
child.

The actuarial rate of return is given by

$$r_{at} = r_t + \frac{m_t}{a_t} = r_t + \pi_t, \tag{5}$$

where π_t is the instantaneous mortality probability on the condition that the
individual lives until time t. (See Yaari 1965.)

We assume that factor prices w, w^k, and r are given exogeneously, and
that α and β are within [0, 1] for institutional reasons. One example of
institutional reasons is that an insurance company prohibits an aged annuity
owner from surrendering an insurance policy. This example restricts the sign
of α to be nonnegative.

Given π and w^k, the first derivative of $p(\pi B, w^k)$ with respect to B is
assumed to be negative and the second derivative of $p(\pi B, w^k)$ with respect to
B is assumed to be positive. The rationale of this assumption is based on the
fact that 43 percent of individuals bequeath their wealth to their children on

the condition that their children take care of them. That is, bequeathable wealth provides an incentive for the children to take care of their parents. This incentive, however, decreases as the wage rate of a child, w^k, increases, because the opportunity cost of child's caregiving increases.

One of the reasons why it is possible that p'_B is negative stems from the fact that the compensation required for caring for an individual's parents is less than the compensation required for caring for others.

Finally, we require an additional assumption that restricts the individual to borrow money and invest it in annuities. That is, we assume that

$$A_t \geq 0 \text{ and } B_t \geq 0 \text{ for all } t. \tag{6}$$

Without this assumption it is possible to earn money by investing in annuities with borrowed money as long as the rate of return on the annuities is larger than the interest rate on borrowing.

Optimality Conditions

To derive the optimality conditions of the problem, we define the following current value Hamiltonian function:

$$H = u(c_{1t})a_t + \phi(B_t)m_t$$

$$+ \lambda_{1t}\{r_{at}A_t + \alpha_t(w_t + r_tB_t + B_t) - \beta[c_{1t} + p(\pi_tB_t, w_t^k)c_{2t}]\}$$

$$+ \lambda_{2t}\{w_t + r_tB_t - \alpha_t(w_t + r_tB_t + B_t)$$

$$- (1 - \beta_t)[c_1 + p(\pi_tB_t, w_t^k)c_2]\} \tag{7}$$

where λ_{1t} and λ_{2t} are the current value costate variables. These two variables represent the marginal contribution of state variables to the objective function at each time. Thus, these two variables are nonnegative all the time unless the annuities and bequeathable wealth are invaluable. In the following discussion, we call these two costate variables as the "shadow prices" of the annuities and bequeathable wealth.

The optimality conditions are given by

$$\frac{\partial H}{\partial c_1} = u'(c_1)a_t - \beta\lambda_1 - (1 - \beta)\lambda_2 = 0, \tag{8}$$

$$\frac{\partial H}{\partial \alpha} = (w + rB + B)(\lambda_1 - \lambda_2), \tag{9}$$

$$\frac{\partial H}{\partial \beta} = [c_1 + p(\pi B, w^k)c_2](\lambda_2 - \lambda_1), \tag{10}$$

$$\frac{d\lambda_1}{dt} = \rho\lambda_1 - r_a\lambda_1, \tag{11}$$

$$\frac{d\lambda_2}{dt} = \rho\lambda_2 - \phi'(B)m_t - [(1 + r)\alpha - \beta\pi p'_B(\pi B, w^k)c_2]\lambda_1$$

$$- [r - (1 + r)\alpha - (1 - \beta)\pi p'_B(\pi B, w^k)c_2]\lambda_2, \tag{12}$$

and the transversality conditions when one lives until time T are derived as

$$\lambda_{1T} = 0, \tag{13}$$

and

$$\lambda_{2T} = \phi'(B_T)m_T. \tag{14}$$

From equation (8), it is shown that

$$c^*_{1t} = u^{-1}\left[\frac{\beta^*_t\lambda_{1t} + (1 - \beta^*_t)\lambda_{2t}}{a_t}\right]. \tag{15}$$

From equations (9) and (10), it is shown that the model exhibits a bang-bang feature. When

$$\lambda_1 > \lambda_2, \tag{16}$$

then

$$\alpha^* = 1, \tag{17}$$

and

$$\beta^* = 0 \tag{18}$$

as far as $B > 0$. On the other hand, in the case where

$$\lambda_2 > \lambda_1, \tag{19}$$

then

$$\alpha^* = 0, \tag{20}$$

and

$$\beta^* = 1, \tag{21}$$

as far as $A > 0$.

Optimal Path When the Cost of Care Depends on Bequeathable Wealth and the Consumption of Care is Positive

To solve the optimal trajectory, we start from the transversality conditions (13) and (14). Since the shadow price of the annuities must be nonnegative, $d\lambda_1/dt$ must be negative from a certain period of time to satisfy the transversality condition (13). This implies that $\rho - r_a$ must be negative before the terminal time T. From the transversality condition (14) and the strict concavity of utility function ϕ, bequeathable wealth B_T and the shadow price λ_{2T} must be positive. Transversality conditions (13) and (14) result in $\lambda_{2T} > \lambda_{1T}$. That is, $\alpha_T^* = 0$.

When $\lambda_1 > \lambda_2$ holds, then $\alpha^* = 1$ is derived from condition (17). Since all of the wealth is held in the form of annuities, consumption is financed by these annuities. That is, β^* is equal to 1 because of the nonnegative constraint of the wealth holdings.[1]

Thus, the relative speed of the shadow price is given by

$$\frac{d\lambda_2}{dt} - \frac{d\lambda_1}{dt} = \rho(\lambda_2 - \lambda_1) + (r_a\lambda_1 - r\lambda_2) + (1 + r)(\lambda_2 - \lambda_1)$$

$$+ \pi p_B'(0, w^k)c_2\lambda_1 - \phi'(0)m_t. \tag{22}$$

Recalling that both $p(\pi B, w^k)$ and $\phi(B)$ are concave functions with respect to B, it is expected that $\pi p_B'(0, w^k)$ and $\phi'(0)$ dominate other terms. Especially when the uncontrollable consumption c_2 is large, λ_2 decreases faster than λ_1 decreases. Thus, the relative size of shadow prices never switches until the terminal time. This implies that once $\lambda_1 > \lambda_2$ holds, the switch of the relative size of shadow prices never occurs. That is, no bequeathable wealth is accumulated until the terminal time, and this violates the transversality condition (14).

---

1. The value of β^* does not essentially change the argument. The term that includes $\pi p_B'(\pi B, w^k)c_2$ is written as $[\beta^*\lambda_1 + (1 - \beta^*\lambda_2)]\pi p_B'(\pi B, w^k)c_2$ generally, and is always nonpositive.

When $\lambda_1 < \lambda_2$ holds, then $\alpha^* = 0$ is derived from condition (20). Thus, the relative speed of the shadow price is given by

$$\frac{d\lambda_2}{dt} - \frac{d\lambda_1}{dt} = \rho(\lambda_2 - \lambda_1) + (r_a\lambda_1 - r\lambda_2) + [\beta^*\lambda_1$$

$$+ (1 - \beta^*)\lambda_2] \pi p_B'(\pi B, w^k)c_2 - \phi'(B)m_t. \qquad (23)$$

Since $\lambda_2 > \lambda_1$, the second term of the r.h.s. of equation (23) can be negative. Thus, it is more probable that λ_2 decreases faster than λ_1 decreases. To satisfy the transversality condition, λ_2 must be large enough so the relative size of shadow prices does not switch until the terminal time.

The Case When the Private Annuity Is Demanded

In the preceding subsection, the terms $\pi p_B'(\pi B, w^k)c_2$ and $\phi'(B)m_t$ have a negative effect on the sign of $d\lambda_2/dt - d\lambda_1/dt$. If $d\lambda_2/dt - d\lambda_1/dt$ is positive when $\lambda_1 > \lambda_2$, then it is possible that the switch of wealth allocation occurs. In other words, holding annuities until a certain time can be consistent with both optimality conditions and transversality conditions.

To highlight the effect of bequeathable wealth on the cost of care, we reconsider the relative speed of shadow prices when $\lambda_1 > \lambda_2$ holds. When $\pi p_B'(\pi B, w^k) = 0$ or $c_2 = 0$, equation (22) is rewritten as

$$\frac{d\lambda_2}{dt} - \frac{d\lambda_1}{dt} = \rho(\lambda_2 - \lambda_1) + (r_a\lambda_1 - r\lambda_2)$$

$$+ (1 + r)(\lambda_2 - \lambda_1) - \phi'(0)m_t. \qquad (24)$$

When neither the bequest motive nor death probability is large, there is a possibility that the relative speed of the decrease in shadow prices is larger in λ_1 than that of λ_2. This implies that the switch from allocating the whole wealth to annuities to holding bequeathable wealth may occur, even when no bequeathable wealth is accumulated. In this case, the possibility of demanding annuities arises without violating the transversality conditions.

After the relative size of shadow prices switches from $\lambda_1 > \lambda_2$ to $\lambda_2 > \lambda_1$, the relative speed is given by

$$\frac{d\lambda_2}{dt} - \frac{d\lambda_1}{dt} = \rho(\lambda_2 - \lambda_1) + (r_a\lambda_1 - r\lambda_2)$$

$$- \phi'(B)m_t. \qquad (25)$$

Since $\lambda_2 > \lambda_1$, the value of $r_a\lambda_1 - r\lambda_2$ can be negative. Thus, $d\lambda_2/dt - d\lambda_1/dt$ can be negative even when the cost of care is independent of the amount of bequeathable wealth and the death probability is quite small. That is, the relative size of shadow prices may switch again before the terminal time. In conclusion, the switch of allocation may arise several times until the terminal time when the utility from the bequest motive is not dominant and the cost of care is independent of the amount of bequeathable wealth.

The Case of Nonrestriction for Surrender

To examine whether the above results come mainly from the assumption of prohibition of surrender or not, we consider the case where it is possible to cancel the insurance contract without incurring any cost. Wealth accumulation equations (3) and (4) are thus modified:

$$\frac{dA}{dt} = r_{at}A_t + \alpha_t(w_t + r_tB_t + B_t) - \beta_t[c_{1t} + p(\pi_tB_t, w_t^k)c_{2t}]$$

$$- \gamma_t(r_{at}A_t + A_t), \tag{26}$$

$$\frac{dB}{dt} = w_t + r_tB_t - \alpha_t(w_t + r_tB_t + B_t) - (1 - \beta_t)[c_{1t} + p(\pi_tB_t, w_t^k)c_{2t}]$$

$$+ \gamma_t(r_{at}A_t + A_t), \tag{27}$$

where γ_t is a share of the annuities surrendered at time t.

Defining the following current value Hamiltonian function, we have

$$H = u(c_t)a_t + \phi(B_t)m_t$$

$$+ \lambda_{1t}\{r_{at}A_t + \alpha_t(w_t + r_tB_t + B_t) - \beta[c_{1t} + p(B_t)c_{2t}]$$

$$- \gamma_t(r_{at}A_t + A_t)\}$$

$$+ \lambda_{2t}\{w_t + r_tB_t - \alpha_t(w_t + r_tB_t + B_t)$$

$$- (1 - \beta_t) \times [c_{1t} + p(\pi_tB_t, w_t^k)c_{2t}] + \gamma(r_{at}A_t + A_t)\}. \tag{28}$$

The optimality conditions are given by

$$\frac{\partial H}{\partial c_1} = u'(c_1)a_t - \beta\lambda_1 - (1 - \beta)\lambda_2 = 0, \tag{29}$$

$$\frac{\partial H}{\partial \alpha} = (w + rB + B)(\lambda_1 - \lambda_2), \tag{30}$$

$$\frac{\partial H}{\partial \beta} = [c_1 + p(\pi B, w^k)c_2](\lambda_2 - \lambda_1), \tag{31}$$

$$\frac{\partial H}{\partial \gamma} = (r_a A + A)(\lambda_2 - \lambda_1), \tag{32}$$

$$\frac{d\lambda_1}{dt} = \rho\lambda_1 - [r_a - (1 + r_a)\gamma]\lambda_1 - (1 + r_a)\gamma\lambda_2, \tag{33}$$

$$\frac{d\lambda_2}{dt} = \rho\lambda_2 - \phi'(B)m_t - [(1 + r)\alpha - \beta\pi p_B'(\pi B, w^k)c_2]\lambda_1 \tag{34}$$

$$- [r - (1 + r)\alpha - (1 - \beta)\pi p_B'(\pi B, w^k)c_2]\lambda_2,$$

and the transversality conditions when one lives until time T are derived as

$$\lambda_{1T} = 0, \tag{35}$$

and

$$\lambda_{2T} = \phi'(B_T)m_T. \tag{36}$$

Our task is to examine how the optimal allocation policy changes. Optimality conditions (30), (31), and (32) suggest that the optimal solution exhibits a bang-bang feature. From the transversality conditions (35) and (36), a positive amount of bequeathable wealth must be accumulated at the terminal time, and $\lambda_{2T} > \lambda_{1T}$ must hold.

When $\lambda_1 > \lambda_2$ holds, $\alpha^* = 1$ and $\gamma^* = 0$ are derived from optimality conditions (30) and (32). The relative speed of the decrease in shadow prices is given by

$$\frac{d\lambda_2}{dt} - \frac{d\lambda_1}{dt} = \rho(\lambda_2 - \lambda_1) + (r_a\lambda_1 - r\lambda_2)$$

$$+ (1 + r)(\lambda_2 - \lambda_1) + [\beta^*\lambda_1$$

$$+ (1 - \beta^*)\lambda_2]\pi p_B'(0, w^k)c_2 - \phi'(0)m_t. \tag{37}$$

This is the same with equation 22. This implies that once $\lambda_1 > \lambda_2$ holds, the switch of the relative size of shadow prices never occurs. This violates the transversality condition (14).

When $\lambda_2 > \lambda_1$, $\alpha^* = 0$ and $\gamma^* = 1$ are derived from optimality conditions (30) and (32). The relative speed of the decrease in shadow prices is given by

$$\frac{d\lambda_2}{dt} - \frac{d\lambda_1}{dt} = \rho(\lambda_2 - \lambda_1) + (r_a\lambda_1 - r\lambda_2)$$

$$+ [\beta^*\lambda_1 + (1 - \beta^*)\lambda_2]\pi p'_B(\pi B, w^k)c_2$$

$$+ (1 + r_a)(\lambda_2 - \lambda_1) - \phi'(B)m_t. \tag{38}$$

The relaxation of the assumption on the possibility of insurance policy cancellation does not essentially influence the results in this subsection. The difference in this subsection is the relative speed of the shadow prices. The difference is partly caused by the inclusion of the fourth term on the R.H.S. of equation (38) and is partly caused by the changes in the value of β^*. When $\lambda_2 > \lambda_1$, all the wealth is held in bequeathable wealth. In this case, $\beta^* = 0$ from the nonnegativity condition of A. When the insurance company prohibits the surrendering of the insurance policy, β^* can be positive, and this lessens the speed of decrease in λ_2.

From the result of this subsection, we retain our initial assumption that an insurance company prohibits the individual from surrendering the insurance policy in the following discussion.

Effect on Savings

Consumption Stream and Path of Wealth Accumulation

In this section, we consider the effect of care cost changes on saving behavior. We restrict the analysis to the case where the surrender of the insurance policy is prohibited. The preceding arguments showed us that the shadow price of bequeathable wealth must always be greater than that of the annuities so that one bequeaths a desired amount of wealth after the consumption of care becomes significant. We denote the time when the consumption of care becomes positive by t_1. We assume that the retirement period starts from time t_2 and that the wage earnings during the working period are constant. The probability of life is a decreasing function of age as is shown in figure 1a. At the terminal time, the shadow price of the annuities is zero and the shadow price of the bequeathable wealth is positive. This requires that the relative size

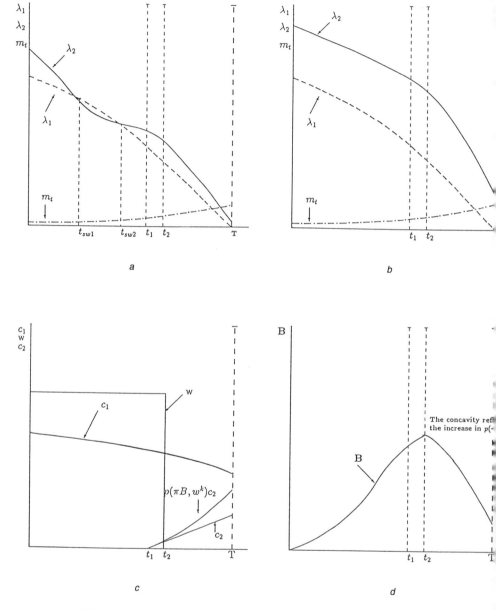

Fig. 1. Paths of: *a* and *b,* shadow prices; *c,* consumption; and *d,* bequeathable wealth

of the shadow price of bequeathable wealth must be larger than that of the annuities at least from a certain period during t_1 and T.

In figure 1a, we depict the paths of shadow prices. It is possible that the shadow price of bequeathable wealth is initially larger than that of the annuities. This does not contradict the transversality conditions. Until time t_1, the consumption of care is zero. Since $\lambda_2 > \lambda_1$ at initial time, $\alpha^* = 0$ at initial time from condition (20). Recalling that $\lambda_2 > \lambda_1$ and $\phi'(B) > 0$, the speed of the decrease in shadow price λ_2 can be larger than that of λ_1 from equation (23). Thus, it is possible that the relative size of shadow prices switches at time, for example, t_{sw1}. At the time of switching, α^* changes from zero to one. This is shown in equation (12).

After all the bequeathable wealth is converted to annuities, the speed of the decrease in shadow price of bequeathable wealth is smaller than that of the annuities as long as the death probability is small. In this case, the relative size of shadow prices can be switched again before the consumption of care becomes positive.

We suppose that this switching time is t_{sw2}. When $\lambda_2 > \lambda_1$, accumulation of bequeathable wealth begins again. Whether or not the relative size of the shadow price switches again before time t_1 depends on the relative size of r_a, r, and $\phi'(B)m_t$.

As is shown in equation (12), the speed of the decrease in shadow price of bequeathable wealth increases as the effect of bequeathable wealth on the decrease in the cost of care increases. When $r_a - r$ is large and $\phi'(B)m_t$ is small, there is a possibility that the gap between the two shadow prices is large enough at time t_1 that the increased speed of the decreases in bequeathable wealth does not violate the transversality conditions after time t_1. This situation, however, may not arise when $\pi p'_B(\pi B, w^k)$ is large.

When $\pi p'_B(\pi B, w^k)$ is large and the bequest motive is large, it is more natural to consider the case where no switching occurs during the lifetime as is shown in figure 1b.

The consumption stream is derived from the optimality condition (15). Recall that the utility function is strictly concave, c_1^* is a decreasing function of the weighted average of shadow prices and is an increasing function of the death probability. In figure 1c, the consumption stream that corresponds to the path of the shadow prices in figure 1a is depicted.

Given the income stream, the amount of bequeathable wealth is derived from wealth accumulation, equation (4). In depicting the path of bequeathable wealth accumulation, $\alpha^* = 0$, $A = 0$, $\beta^* = 0$ is substituted into equation (4). As stated, we assume that consumption of care (c_2) becomes positive from time t_1 and increases until terminal time. As c_1 decreases dB/dt increases and dB/dt decreases as c_2 increases. Since $p(\pi B, w^k)$ is a decreasing function of B, the cost of care decreases as the bequeathable wealth increases. From these arguments, the path of bequeathable wealth is depicted as in figure 1d.

Changes in the Effect of Bequeathable Wealth on the Price of Care

In this subsection, we consider how the changes in the effect of bequeathable wealth on the price of care affect the consumption stream and path of wealth accumulation. Here, suppose that the wage rate of a child decreases, then $\pi p'_B$ $(\pi B, w^k)$ decreases (i.e., $|\pi p'_B(\pi B, w^k)|$ increases) for a given π and B. This case arises when the spouse of a child quits his or her regular job. The reason for this is that quitting the job decreases the opportunity cost of caring for parents. When the opportunity cost of caring for parents decreases, the incentive for caring parents increases for a given level of B.

When $\pi p'_B(B)$ decreases for a given B, the speed of the decrease in λ_2 increases as is shown in optimality condition (12). The increase in speed of a decrease in the shadow price after c_2 becomes positive is depicted in figure 2a. In this case, the cost of care decreases as the effect of bequeathable wealth increases, which is represented by the downward shift from $p(\pi B, w^{k,1})c_2$ to $p(\pi B, w^{k,2})c_2$ as is shown in figure 2b.

The increase in the effect of bequeathable wealth on a decrease in the cost of care increases the marginal value of bequeathable wealth at least one certain period during the whole life. From optimality condition (12), λ_2 decreases faster as $|p'(\cdot)|$ increases, and λ_2 must be larger than λ'_2 after c_2 becomes positive. From these two facts, the slope of the path of λ_2 becomes steeper, and possibly the path of λ_2 shifts up in the individual's early period of life and shifts down in his or her later period of life as is shown in figure 2a.

The changes in the consumption stream are given by (15), corresponding to the changes in the path of λ_2. A larger value of λ_2 decreases consumption and a smaller value of λ_2 increases consumption when λ_1 and the death probability are not affected by the changes in $|p'(\cdot)|$. This shift in the consumption stream is depicted in figure 2b. The shift in the consumption stream is interpreted as follows. The increases in the marginal value of bequeathable wealth drives the individual to consume less and save more. The decrease in the cost of care, however, permits the individual to consume more after c_2 becomes positive.

The smaller consumption incurred during the early period of life and the larger consumption during the later period of life shifts the wealth accumulation path as is shown in figure 2c. Since the value of bequeathable wealth increases as the effect of bequeathable wealth on the reduction of cost of care increases, it is more efficient to accumulate the bequeathable wealth before c_2. Thus, the bequeathable wealth becomes larger before time t_1 when $p(\cdot)c_2$

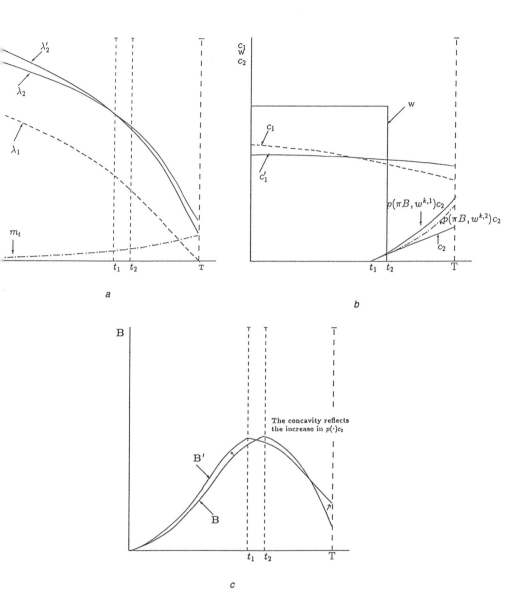

Fig. 2. Paths of: *a,* shadow prices; *b,* consumption; and *c,* bequeath-able wealth

TABLE 10.   Changes in the Number of Privately Managed Homes for the Aged

Type of owner	1975	1980	1985	1991
Corporation	11	14	24	106
Nonprofit corporation	35	34	44	36
Social welfare organization	9	12	11	21
Others	18	16	18	65
Total	73	76	97	228

Source: Ministry of Welfare 1985a.
Note: Others include the organization managed by public pension system, postal insurance, individual owner, and so on.

shifts down. The decrease in the cost of care allows the individual to consume more and bequeath more. The increase in bequest is consistent with the smaller value of λ_2 at the terminal time. This story is represented by the flattened path of B' after time t_1 in figure 2c. When the wage rate of children increases, which is represented by an increase in w^k, we will get results opposite to those previously mentioned.

Implications for the Aged Society

When we look at the movement of the number of privately managed homes for the aged, we are surprised by the rapid increase in the number of these homes. According to the statistics compiled by the Ministry of Welfare, privately managed homes for the aged doubled during the most recent six-year period as is shown in table 10. Especially distinctive is the increase in the number of homes for the aged managed by corporations. For example, life insurance companies are expanding this type of business by including lifelong care insurance.

Our analysis provides one explanation for this movement. In a society like Japan, where the working place of women is expanding and their earnings income is increasing, the opportunity cost of taking care of parents increases.

TABLE 11.   Financial Source of Entrance Fee for the Home

Source	1	2	3	4	5	6	7	Total
Count	1,142	1,005	98	140	152	56	365	2,958
Percent	38.6	34.0	3.3	4.7	5.1	1.9	12.3	100

Source: Ministry of Welfare.
Note: 1. Real estate. 2. Deposit. 3. Stock or bond. 4. Retirement allowance. 5. Assistance from children. 6. Others. 7. No answer.

TABLE 12.   Portion of the Aged Who Have Children

Among the aged who are in the home	0.544
Among all aged	0.937

Source: Ministry of Welfare 1985c.

In the preceding model, the increase in women's wage is represented by the increase in w^k. The increase in w^k weakens the force of bequeathable wealth in inducing care from children. This decreases the value of $|p'(B)|$, and drives the individual to demand annuities.

The empirical facts support our theory. The rapid increase in the number of homes mentioned above is consistent with the recent advancement of women in the labor market. Around 38 percent of residents in the home entered the home by selling real estate as is shown in table 11. This constitutes a dramatic shift in the wealth component from bequeathable wealth to annuities. Table 12 shows that more than half of the residents in the privately managed homes for the aged have children. This tells us that not only the individual who does not have children but also the individual who has children enters the privately managed home. Coupled with the fact that the portion of the aged who live with their children decreased from 1985 to 1988 (see table 13), the recent development in the number of privately managed homes for the aged reflects an increase in the aged who leave their children's family and enter one of these homes.

The surveys thus far conducted on privately managed homes for the aged provide us with the evidence confirming that the provision of care for the bedridden by the home is the crucial motivation for entering the home, as is shown in tables 14–18.

Table 14 shows that 56.4 percent answered that the most important reason why they entered the home was the fear of contracting an illness. The portion of the residents who are thinking that they will continue to stay in the home at the time of being bedridden is largest as is shown in table 15. Only a small amount answered that they will return to their family's house. The

TABLE 13.   Portion of the Aged Who Live with Their Children

1985	0.69
1989	0.586

Sources: Ministry of Welfare 1985b, 1989.

TABLE 14. Reasons Why the Individual Entered the Privately Managed Home for the Aged

Ranking	1985	1988
1	Anxiety over expected illness (56.2%)	Anxiety over expected illness (56.4%)
2	Difficulty in doing housework (15.6%)	Difficulty in doing housework (15.3%)
3	Recommendation of friends (5.9%)	To live separately from children (9.8%)

Sources: Ministry of Welfare 1985c, 1988.
Note: The sample size of the 1985 survey was 3,246, and that of 1988 was 3,423. The question was given to the aged who are living in a privately managed home for the aged.

TABLE 15. Place Where the Individual Lives at the Time of Being Bedridden

Ranking	1985	1988
1	The privately managed home for the aged where the individual lives now (20.8%)	The privately managed home for the aged where the individual lives now (23.3%)
2	Publicly managed special home for the aged (20.8%)	Publicly managed special home for the aged (23.3%)
3	Family's house (5.1%)	Family's house (3.0%)

Source: Ministry of Welfare 1985c.
Note: The sample size of the 1985 survey was 3,246, and that of 1988 was 3,423. The question was given to the aged who are living in a privately managed home for the aged.

TABLE 16. Factors Given Large Importance in Selecting a Privately Managed Home for the Aged

Ranking	Factor
1	Whether the individual can receive care at the time of being bedridden
2	Level of medical equipment
3	Stability of the home management
4	Kindness of the home's staff

Source: Kokumin Seikatsu Center 1988.
Note: The sample size was 1,331. The question was given to the residents in the privately managed home for the aged.

TABLE 17.   Status of Care System in the Privately Managed Home for the Aged

Portion of homes having a care system	84.1%
Portion of homes including the cost of care in the entrance money or monthly maintenance cost	60.0%
Portion of homes collecting the cost of care separately from the entrance money or monthly maintenance cost	22.0%
Portion of homes requiring the residents to pay for their helper	18.0%

Source: Kokumin Seikatsu Center 1988.
Note: The sample size was 1,331. The question was given to the residents in the privately managed home for the aged.

importance of the care system in the home for the aged is reflected in table 16, indicating that the most important factor in selecting a privately managed home for the aged is the treatment at the time of being bedridden. Most of the homes' managers recognize the need of the care system, and 84 percent of the homes provide care service as is shown in table 17. Among them, 60 percent of the homes include the cost of care as part of the entrance money or in the monthly maintenance cost. Finally, importance of the care system in the home does not differ according to the state of health condition (see table 18). It is worth noting that 57.4 percent of healthy residents in the home are anxious about the care system. This suggests that the concern of the aged about the care system is very strong even though they are presently healthy.

Currently, in Japan, the portion of the aged in the population is increasing. At the same time, advancement of women in the workplace is significant. These two movements have led to an increase in the number of aged who cannot receive care from their children. This has stimulated the demand for the privately managed home for the aged and has brought about the huge shift from bequeathable wealth to annuities. The decrease in bequeathable wealth seriously affects the capital accumulation of the economy as well as the economic growth over the long run.

TABLE 18.   Portion of Residents Having Some Anxiety over the Care System

Among healthy residents	57.4%
Among slightly weak or frail residents	65.0%
Among weak or frail residents	67.3%

Source: Kokumin Seikatsu Center 1988.
Note: The sample size was 1,331. The question was given to the residents in the privately managed home for the aged.

REFERENCES

Barro, R. J. 1974. "Are government bonds net wealth?" *Journal of Political Economy* 82:1095–1117.
Becker, G. 1974. "A theory of social interactions." *Journal of Political Economy* 82:1063–91.
Bernheim, B. D., A. Shleifer, and L. H. Summers. 1985. "The strategic bequest motive." *Journal of Political Economy* 93(6): 1045–76.
Boersch-Supan, A., J. Gokhale, L. J. Kotlikoff, and J. Morris. 1990. "The provision of time to the elderly by their children." NBER Working Paper, no. 3363.
Caballero, R. J. 1991. "Earnings uncertainty and aggregate wealth accumulation." *American Economic Review* 81 (4): 859–71.
Davies, J. B. 1981. "Uncertain lifetime, consumption, and dissaving in retirement." *Journal of Political Economy* 89:561–78.
Friedman, B. M., and M. J. Warshawsky. 1988. "Annuity yields and saving behavior in the United States." In *Pensions in the U.S. Economy,* ed. Z. Bodie, J. Shoven, and D. Wise. Chicago: NBER and University of Chicago Press.
———. 1990. "The cost of annuities: Implications for saving behavior and bequests." *Quarterly Journal of Economics* 105:135–54.
Hayashi, F. 1986. "Is Japan's saving rate so apparently high?" In *NBER Macroeconomics Annual 1986,* ed. Stanley Fischer, 147–210.
Hayashi, F., A. Ando, and R. Ferris. 1988. "Life cycle and bequest saving." *Journal of Japanese and International Economics* 2(4): 450–91.
Horioka, C. Y. 1991. "Savings in Japan." Osaka University Discussion Paper, no. 248.
Hurd, M. D. 1989. "Mortality risk and bequests." *Econometrica* 57(4): 779–813.
Institute for Posts and Telecommunications Policy. 1990. "Survey on Family and Savings Behavior."
Kokumin Seikatsu Center. 1988. "Yuryo Rojin Houmu Nyuukyosha no Jitsujyo" (State of the residents in the privately managed home for the aged).
Kotlikoff, L., and L. H. Summers. 1981. "The role of intergenerational transfers in aggregate capital accumulation." *Journal of Political Economy* 89(3): 706–32.
Ministry of Welfare. 1985a. "Shakai Fukusi Sisetsu Chousa" (Survey on social welfare organization).
———. 1985b. "Rojin Jittai Chousa Kekka No Gaiyo" (Survey on the state of the aged).
———. 1985c. "Yuryo Rojin Houmu Nyuukyosha Jittai Chousa Kekka no Gaiyo" (Survey on the state of residents in the privately managed home for the aged).
———. 1988. "Yuryo Rojin Houmu Nyuukyosha Jittai Chousa Kekka no Gaiyo" (Survey on the state of residents in the privately managed home for the aged).
———. 1989. "Rojin Jittai Chousa Kekka no Gaiyo" (Survey on the state of the aged).
Skinner, J. 1988. "Risky income, life cycle consumption, and precautionary savings." *Journal of Monetary Economics* 22:237–55.
Yaari, M. 1965. "Uncertain lifetime, life insurance, and the theory of the consumer." *Review of Economic Studies* 32:137–50.

CHAPTER 4

Storing the Option and Saving
for Retirement in Canada

Anil K. Gupta, Steven F. Venti, and David A. Wise

Registered Retirement Saving Plans (RRSPs) were first introduced in Canada in 1957. Under this program an individual can make contributions to a retirement plan and deduct the contributions from income for tax purposes. Interest accrues tax-free until withdrawal, when taxes are paid. The contribution limits were increased substantially in the early 1970s and RRSPs were widely promoted. Since then, they have become a prominent form of saving. Contributions grew from $225 million in 1970 to almost $3.7 billion in 1980 to $12 billion by 1989. Since 1977 annual RRSP contributions have exceeded contributions to employer-provided pension plans. In 1989 about 23 percent of all tax filers contributed to an RRSP, with an average contribution of $2,869. Some analysts have concluded that the divergence in the personal saving rates between the United States and Canada that occurred in the early seventies can be attributed to the widespread promotion and adoption of RRSPs.[1] The effect of limit changes on RRSP contributions and their tax cost was analyzed by Wise (1984).[2] In particular, that analysis considered the tax cost of several options for increasing the RRSP limits. Since that time, the limits have been progressively increased; the highest limit is now $11,500 per year and will increase to $15,500 by 1995. Thereafter the limit will be indexed to the average wage.

More recently, interest has focused on a carry-forward plan that will

The authors wish to thank Keith Horner, Richard Laliberté, and other members of the Department of Finance, Government of Canada, for their help and comments. Vicky Bolton and Ben Benoit of the Department of Finance provided programming assistance. All errors remain the responsibility of the authors and any views expressed in the paper are those of the authors and do not necessarily represent the views or policies of the Government of Canada.

1. See Summers and Carroll 1987.

2. A later report by Wise (1985) distinguished the determinants of the decision to contribute from the determinants of the amount of the contribution and compared RRSP contributions with contributions to individual retirement accounts (IRAs) in the United States.

come into effect in 1992. The carry-forward plan allows a foregone contribution in one year to be made in a subsequent year. For example, a person who made no contributions over the past three years, but was eligible to contribute $2,000 in each of the three years, could contribute $8,000 in the subsequent year—$2,000 plus $6,000 in carry-forward from the previous three years. In 1992 a carry-forward from the previous year only will be allowed. The number of years of carry-forward permitted will be increased by one year each year through 1998. Thereafter, the carry-forward will be limited to seven years. Further, the limit on the carry-forward of unused RRSP contribution room will be subject to a minimum value of 3.5 times the money purchase limit for the year. This guarantees a positive contribution limit for retirees and for persons who leave the labor force for other reasons. The primary question addressed in this paper is the effect of the carry-forward provision on RRSP contributions.

What about bequests? We do not consider bequests directly; but of course bequests are of little interest if there is no accumulation of assets. Possibly 70 percent of U.S. households accumulate virtually no bequeathable financial assets and thus for this group bequests must necessarily be in the form of housing, which for most is also small. In addition, our reading of the data suggests that even households that do accumulate significant financial assets do not deplete these systematically after retirement, which could be due to a bequest motive. But the evidence, in the United States at least, that depletion of financial assets or housing wealth does not depend on whether the elderly household has children seems to us presumptive evidence against the bequest hypothesis. It appears more likely that assets are maintained after retirement in anticipation of possible medical or long-term care costs. In this event, some fraction—and we guess a large fraction—of households that accumulate significant financial wealth will die with a substantial portion of that wealth unspent, even with no bequest motive.

Thus any special saving program, like the RRSP and the new carry-forward provisions, that affects the accumulation of financial assets for retirement is also likely to affect the magnitude of financial assets left as bequests. Although we do not address bequests directly, an implication of our analysis is that the RRSP program has had a substantial effect on personal saving in Canada and will have a large effect on the distribution of wealth at retirement. The carry-forward provisions are likely to further increase the accumulation of financial assets. Thus it is also likely to increase the wealth that will be passed to heirs in the form of bequests. The analysis can also be used to demonstrate how special saving programs can change the prevalence and magnitude of bequests. Personal financial asset saving is much larger in Canada than in the United States, for example. This is apparently due in part to the Canadian

RRSP program—and the carry-forward plan will magnify the difference. Thus, empirically, incentives to accumulate assets are likely to be closely linked to bequests.

The essay follows a somewhat nontraditional approach. First, we attempt to detail not only formal results but the process that was used to "get a feel for the data," to reveal the basic empirical regularities exhibited by RRSP contributions. The results are presented essentially in the order in which they were developed. Second, the goal of our analysis is to use simple but robust methods, with properties that can be readily understood and interpreted. One implication of this goal is that structural models with strong behavioral assumptions—that impose important restrictions on the data—are ruled out. As the subsequent discussion will show, this approach carries with it some limitations. Finally, we attempt to use procedures that are practical in a modern government finance or treasury department. Our analysis, however, may have exceeded this bound in some respects. In general, our essay is of the form: "How might one go about it?"

Descriptive evidence on individual contribution patterns over time is then explored in the third section. The major question is the extent to which some tax filers continue to make contributions year after year while others never contribute. The effect of carry-forward provisions on contributions is considered in the next three sections, beginning with a simple model and progressing to more complex formulations. The key results are in the form of simulations based on alternative models of RRSP contributions. The effect of the carry-forward provisions on RRSP assets at age 65 and comparison of RRSP assets to financial assets in the United States is discussed in the seventh section. The final section is a summary and discussion of the results.

Background

The amount that can be contributed each year to an RRSP depends on whether the person is covered by an employer-provided pension plan. In 1990, persons without employer plans could contribute 20 percent of earned income up to a limit of $7,500. An employee covered by an employer plan could contribute 20 percent of earned income up to a limit of $3,500, less employee contributions to the pension plan. The limits have been increased periodically since the inception of the program in 1957. The highest limit is now $11,500 per year and will increase to $15,500 by 1995. Thereafter the limit will be indexed to the average wage.

Both the proportion of persons making RRSP contributions and the amount of the contributions have increased dramatically in the past two decades. The average contribution (right axis) of all filers is shown in figure 1a together with the contribution limits (left axis).[3] Beginning in the early 1970s the contribution limits were increased and the program was widely promoted. Anecdotal evidence suggests that the promotion has accelerated in the past decade and the rapid increase in average contributions since the early 1980s is apparently due in part to the increased promotion. Now, the Minister of National Revenue sends a special letter to every tax filer each year advising the person of the RRSP amount that can be contributed. The implication is that each filer should be aware of and take advantage of the saving opportunity. It can be seen that even during periods when the limits did not change, the average contribution continued to increase. The proportion of filers that contributed increased from about 10 percent in 1976 to 22 percent in 1989.

Total RRSP contributions relative to contributions to employer-provided "registered pension plans" (RPP) provide a measure of the growing importance of RRSPs in retirement planning. RRSP contributions have exceeded RPP contributions since 1976 and are now more than twice as large.

RRSP contributions in 1989 were almost 3 percent of total earnings, as shown in figure 1b.

Conceptual Issues

The conceptual discussion has two purposes: the first is to set forth the framework that has guided the empirical analysis. The second is to highlight two issues that are not fully addressed in the analysis and thus must be kept in mind when drawing conclusions from the results. The first of these is that the analysis is based on an important assumption: the opportunity to carry forward foregone RRSP contributions from this year to the next will not affect how much is contributed this year. Or, under the current provisions—without a carry-forward—the fact that the tax-free RRSP contribution for this year must be made now or never has no effect on whether a contribution is made, or on how much is contributed. It seems likely, however, that the "now-or-never" provision does provide an incentive—in addition to the tax advantage—to save now rather than later. If this is true, eliminating this provision by introducing a carry-forward provides an incentive to postpone saving. The question then is whether saving that is "postponed" *ex ante* will turn out *ex post* to have been postponed or, instead, delayed indefinitely. The second issue is that the higher contribution limits generated by accumulated carry-forwards may increase the probability that a contribution is made, not just the amount of

---

3. The lower limit pertains to persons with an employer provided registered pension plan (RPP) and the upper limit to persons without an employer plan. Between 1965 and 1990 the allowable contribution could not exceed 20 percent of earnings, in addition to the limit restriction. Before 1965, the contribution could not exceed 10 percent of earnings. Beginning in 1991, the contribution was limited to 18 percent of earnings.

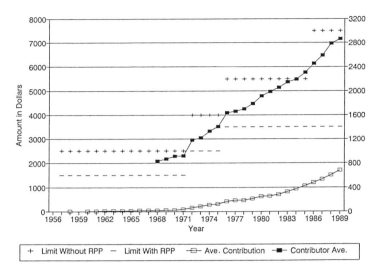

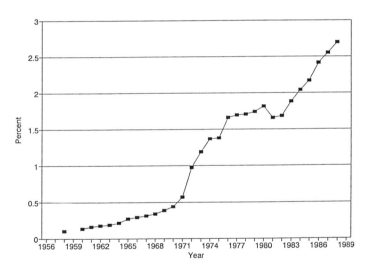

Fig. 1. Trend in RRSP contributions: *a,* limits and average contribution, 1956–89; *b,* percent of total earnings, 1956–89

positive contributions. It may be that some persons facing low contribution limits find that gaining the tax advantage on a small contribution is not worth the effort, but it would be worthwhile if the allowable contribution were larger. This "transaction cost" effect is addressed only in a preliminary manner in the analysis.

The Independence Assumption

The tabulation below helps to summarize the issues. Suppose for simplicity that there are two possible saving periods, one and two, that the contribution limit is L in each period, and that all contributions are at the limit. Because the current system limits the options of potential savers, it is useful to think of the current system as imposing a constraint—the now-or-never choice—relative to the more flexible carry-forward plan. Then it is natural to think of saving behavior under the no-carry-forward constraint. Suppose that there are four possible saving patterns under the constraining provisions of the current system. Assume that they represent four saver types. For example, type one savers in table 1 would contribute each period under the constrained provisions; type four savers would contribute in neither period without the carry-forward. The fourth column gives the period two limit under the carry-forward scheme, based on the period one contribution, for each contributor type. The expected result of the carry-forward is summarized in the last column of table 1.

Type three savers are the apparent target of the carry-forward provision. This saver type is constrained by the second period limit and thus would contribute more under the carry-forward provision that raises the limit to $2L$. The typical type three saver would not contribute $2L$ in period two, however. That is $E(R|2L) < 2E(R|L)$. If the limit is doubled, the contribution will typically not be doubled. This is a property of the distribution of desired contributions. Fewer people will want to contribute at L than at $2L$, given age

TABLE 1.   The Carry-Forward Plan and Savings Outcomes

| Type | Constrained Contribution | | Carry-forward | |
	Period 1	Period 2	Period 2 Limit	Outcome
(1)	L	L	L	Could save less than $2L$
(2)	L	0	L	Could save less than L
(3)	0	L	$2L$	Will save more than L
(4)	0	0	$2L$	May save if the higher period 2 limit induces a contribution

and income. On the other hand, because the desired contribution increases with age and income, it is likely that desired contributions will be higher next year than this year. The model and the simulations account for these two effects.

Type four savers may be affected to the extent that persons in this group do not save because the single-year limit is too low but the accumulated second period limit under the carry-forward is large enough to induce a contribution. This situation is also addressed in the model, although not as carefully as it could be with a more appropriate specification.

But the model does not properly account for the effect of the carry-forward on type one savers. It is clear that the carry-forward will not increase the saving of type one savers. The carry-forward provision relaxes the now-or-never constraint, but does not affect the total contribution permitted over the two-year period. Thus the timing but not the total contribution limit is affected. Type one savers could save less, however. Some save L in period 1 because they are constrained by the now-or-never offer; they don't want to lose the tax-advantaged saving opportunity. Were it not for the prospect of losing the opportunity, some would put off saving if the same tax advantage would still be available in period two, as under the carry-forward program. But saving "put off" in period one will not necessarily be saving realized in period two. By period two *ex ante* expected circumstances may have changed and they may no longer want to save the amount L postponed in period one. Or, the now-or-never provision may provide the chain of discipline that one would like to have seen in oneself when looking back even though it is hard to insure that this year's link is put in place. The constraint may serve as a means of self-control.

Type two savers may also postpone period one saving for the same reason and then may not save L in period two. Thus the carry-forward cannot increase and is likely to decrease the saving of type one and type two savers. The question is how much of the contribution increase of type three and type four savers will be offset by the reduced contributions of type one and type two savers. To answer this question requires a model with more behavioral assumptions than are incorporated in the analysis presented here. To the extent that the analysis accurately captures other effects of the carry-forward, the estimates presented here exaggerate the contribution increase that may be expected from the new carry-forward provisions.

The Transactions Cost Effect

Another limitation of the analysis is the treatment of the effect of the "contribution room" on whether a contribution is made, as may be the case with type four savers discussed above. The issue is addressed in a preliminary way by including the limit as a variable in a probit equation predicting the probability that a contribution will be made. Extrapolation of the probit model results to situations with large accumulated limits under the carry-forward plan undoubtedly exaggerates the transactions cost effect—that with higher limits more people will find it worthwhile to make contributions. Indeed, the simulation results that ignore this effect are very likely to be more accurate than those that account for it. A better formulation would explicitly allow for a minimum contribution below which a person would not find it worthwhile to make a contribution. The minimum could be random across individuals. This approach would not allow the accumulating limit to continue to increase the contribution probability after it had surpassed the minimum necessary to induce a contribution.

Descriptive Data on RRSP Contributions

Two characteristics of RRSP contributions are emphasized. First, once a person begins to contribute, he or she is likely to continue to contribute in subsequent years. The persistence is greater for older than for younger persons and is greater for higher income than for lower income persons. Second, the likelihood of contributing increases with age and with income. These patterns help to gage the potential responses to the carry-forward plan of the saver types discussed in the previous section on conceptual issues. These implications are discussed at the end of this section.

The descriptive data are based largely on two longitudinal files: the first is a sixteen-year file reporting data for the years 1967 through 1982. The advantage of this file is the long time period that is covered. The data available for analysis from this file, however, are limited. In particular, the age of respondents is unknown. The second data source is a six-year file, presenting data for the years 1978 through 1983. This file contains each individual's age and other information not contained in the sixteen-year file. The sixteen-year file provides a broad overview of RRSP contribution patterns. The extended overlap in time periods allows the conclusions based on the sixteen-year file to be directly compared with results from the 1978–83 six-year file. The descriptive conclusions based on the two files are very similar. The formal analysis presented in the subsequent sections of the paper is based on a later six-year file covering the period 1982 through 1987. To demonstrate comparability, some descriptive data is presented from this file as well.

The Sixteen-Year File

There are several ways in which one might view data over time. First, it is useful to have in mind the nature of the data. This is described in table 2.

TABLE 2. Illustration of Years of Data for Persons in Sixteen-Year File

Person	1967	1968	1969	1970	1971	1972	1973	1974	1975	1976	1977	1978	1979	1980	1981	1982
1	X	X	X	X	X	X	X	X	X	X	X	X	X	X	X	X
2	X	X	X	X	X	X	X									
3							X	X	X	X	X	X	X	X	X	X
4					X	X	X	X								
5			X	X	X	X	X	X	X	X	X	X				
6	X	X	X	X	X	X	X	X	X	X	X	X	X	X	X	X

Calendar years are listed across the top of the table and each row represents an individual. The Xs in each row indicate that the person filed a tax return in that year and thus data is available for the year. Individuals one and six, for example, filed in each of the sixteen years. For many persons, however, data are available only for a subset of the sixteen years. In many instances data for an individual are available for 1967 and some number of subsequent years, say through 1973, but not thereafter. This pattern might reflect the returns of a person who died or for some other reason did not file after some age. Others would not have filed returns for the first years of the file, but would begin, say, in 1973 and file returns in each of the subsequent years. This would be the case, for example, for younger persons who were not old enough to file returns in 1967. A few persons file in a subset of years in the middle of the sixteen-year period, although this is a less common pattern. Others could file in all but one or two of a consecutive string of years.

Many persons begin to make contributions in a year and then continue to make contributions in subsequent years. For example, they may not file while younger but begin to file at an older age. Others contribute over a continuous string of years, then quit and make no subsequent contributions. This would be a typical pattern, for example, for persons who do not make contributions after retirement. For example, of persons who filed in each year of a five-year subset of the sixteen-year file, from 1978–82, about 20 percent of filers made RRSP contributions in at least one of these years. Of this group, 62 percent either contributed in each of the five years or contributed in each of the years after they began to contribute (as illustrated by persons two through five in table 2). An additional 14 percent contributed in some consecutive number of years in the beginning of the five-year period and once they quit making contributions made no further contributions thereafter.

These patterns suggest that an informative representation of the data is to consider the probability that a person who contributes in one year will also contribute in subsequent years. Such calculations are presented in table 3. It shows the probability that a person who contributed in one of the sixteen years also contributed in each of the other years, given that the person filed a tax return in the other year under consideration. For example, of persons who made RRSP contributions in 1972, 81.0 percent also made contributions in 1973, 74.9 percent contributed in 1974. Five years later in 1977, 66.2 percent made RRSP contributions, while 54.5 percent made contributions ten years later in 1982.

Table 3 indicates several features of RRSP contributions. First, persons who contribute in one year are likely to contribute in the next year as well. The proportion is typically about 80 percent, judging by the entries to the right of the 100.0 diagonal. The first shaded diagonal in the northeast part of the

TABLE 3. Probability of Contributing in Year j, Given a Contribution in year i, 1967–82

	1967	1968	1969	1970	1971	1972	1973	1974	1975	1976	1977	1978	1979	1980	1981	1982
1967	100.0	73.5	68.5	64.6	62.3	64.4	62.6	60.6	60.1	58.0	56.1	55.0	54.7	54.6	50.5	48.8
1968	63.3	100.0	74.5	70.2	68.3	71.2	69.2	64.1	62.5	62.7	59.4	58.4	55.5	56.8	53.5	49.8
1969	48.9	63.2	100.0	73.2	69.7	70.6	70.6	67.9	65.5	63.9	62.1	59.7	57.6	57.8	53.9	52.3
1970	38.6	49.5	60.8	100.0	79.2	79.1	76.2	71.8	69.8	68.0	66.4	62.7	61.6	59.3	57.0	53.0
1971	27.3	34.7	41.9	56.8	100.0	84.6	79.4	75.0	71.5	70.8	67.3	64.6	62.2	62.0	59.0	55.2
1972	18.3	23.1	27.1	36.2	54.1	100.0	81.0	74.9	71.3	70.1	66.2	64.0	61.3	60.9	57.6	54.5
1973	13.5	16.9	20.1	25.4	36.8	59.0	100.0	78.7	73.2	70.4	68.0	65.4	62.6	62.1	59.0	54.8
1974	10.4	12.4	15.4	19.3	27.9	43.2	62.5	100.0	75.1	67.5	61.2	53.9	52.4	51.5	49.1	46.0
1975	9.4	11.1	13.5	16.8	23.9	36.8	51.4	68.8	100.0	82.8	75.4	71.5	68.8	65.7	62.2	58.2
1976	7.8	9.5	11.2	14.0	20.3	30.6	41.9	53.7	69.7	100.0	80.5	74.7	70.9	67.5	63.6	59.8
1977	7.1	8.3	10.0	12.5	17.7	26.5	36.8	45.3	57.4	72.8	100.0	81.5	75.5	71.5	66.8	62.5
1978	6.4	7.6	8.9	10.9	15.6	23.5	32.1	38.6	48.9	60.3	72.6	100.0	81.6	74.9	68.8	64.6
1979	5.9	6.6	7.9	9.9	13.9	20.7	28.4	34.0	43.2	52.4	61.8	74.5	100.0	80.3	72.3	67.2
1980	5.4	6.2	7.3	8.9	12.6	18.9	25.8	30.0	37.4	45.3	52.9	61.7	72.6	100.0	78.2	70.9
1981	4.9	5.7	6.6	8.3	11.7	17.3	23.7	27.3	34.0	41.0	47.4	54.5	62.7	75.1	100.0	78.3
1982	3.9	4.4	5.4	6.7	9.4	14.1	19.5	22.1	28.7	35.5	41.9	47.6	54.0	62.9	72.7	100.0

Note: The estimate in each cell is based only on persons who filed in each of the two years.

table marks the percent contributing five years after an earlier contribution. The average is 65.3 percent. The second diagonal line marks the percents who contributed ten years later. The average is 57.5 percent. Thus there is considerable persistence in contribution status.

Second, the proportion contributing to an RRSP increased over time. The shaded diagonal line in the southwest part of the table marks the percent of those who contributed in a given year that also contributed five years earlier. These numbers reveal a marked increase over time, reflecting the increase in proportions of people who made RRSP contributions in the later years. For example, of those who contributed in 1972, only 18.3 percent had contributed in 1967, whereas 41.9 percent of those who contributed in 1982 had contributed in 1977.

Third, although the proportion who contributed increased over time, persistence did not. That is, the likelihood that contributions once started would continue did not change much. For example, 56.1 percent of those who contributed in 1967 also contributed in 1977 and 54.5 percent of those who contributed in 1972 also contributed in 1982. A similar pattern is revealed by the five-year intervals.

The data may appear to suggest "state dependence": that the experience of being a contributor may itself affect future saving behavior and thus the likelihood of contributing in subsequent years. The evidence comes from comparing the probability of contributing the year after observing a contribution with the probability of contributing the year before. These are the percentages just to the right and the left of the 100.0 diagonals. For example, of persons who contributed in 1972, 81 percent also contributed in 1973, but only 54.1 percent contributed in 1971. If the propensity to contribute were constant over time for each person, one might expect to see similar percentages in 1973 and 1971; having contributed in 1972 would have no effect on subsequent contributions, so, on average, the 1971 and 1973 probabilities would be the same. This reasoning is not complete, however, because contributions increase with age. Thus, for example, the percents would tend to be larger five years after contributing than five years before because the contributors were ten years older in the later period. This issue is discussed further below.

In summary: table 3 reveals substantial consistency. Once a person begins to make RRSP contributions, it is quite likely that the person will also contribute in subsequent years.

The Six-Year File

An advantage of the six-year file is that data are available on the age and the income of the tax filer. Not only does the likelihood of an RRSP contribution increase with age and with income, but the likelihood that once contributions start they will continue also increases with age and income.

Probability matrices like the one in table 3 are shown for the six-year file by age in table 4. Comparing the first and the third panels of the table shows that only about 50 percent of persons 20 to 24 years old at the beginning of the six-year period contributed three years after making an initial contribution,

TABLE 4. Probability of Contributing in Year *j*, Given a Contribution in Year *i*, 1978–83, Selected Age Groups

	1978	1979	1980	1981	1982	1983
			20–24 Years Old			
1978	100.00	68.24	58.85	50.58	42.95	40.52
1979	50.48	100.00	66.67	55.76	51.29	47.25
1980	32.49	48.90	100.00	67.64	56.60	52.37
1981	23.71	35.14	57.35	100.00	68.60	59.38
1982	15.12	24.05	35.88	51.55	100.00	69.54
1983	11.42	17.64	26.48	35.41	55.44	100.00
			25–29 Years Old			
1978	100.00	74.29	65.17	56.29	52.89	50.21
1979	63.51	100.00	73.23	61.52	56.05	53.79
1980	48.22	63.46	100.00	70.47	62.34	58.55
1981	39.61	50.30	66.52	100.00	72.11	65.46
1982	33.29	40.97	52.99	64.88	100.00	75.10
1983	27.19	33.78	42.38	50.47	64.31	100.00
			55–59 Years Old			
1978	100.00	86.10	81.70	74.82	68.80	66.56
1979	81.80	100.00	86.27	78.04	70.99	68.04
1980	70.33	78.27	100.00	82.14	74.44	69.79
1981	64.62	71.06	82.43	100.00	80.11	73.21
1982	59.15	64.55	74.67	80.65	100.00	80.69
1983	56.34	60.85	69.00	72.85	80.30	100.00
			All Age Groups			
1978	100.00	81.63	75.00	68.50	63.37	60.95
1979	74.88	100.00	80.84	72.14	66.24	63.44
1980	61.92	72.75	100.00	78.10	70.06	66.43
1981	54.79	62.79	75.39	100.00	77.97	71.28
1982	47.57	53.90	63.21	73.04	100.00	78.69
1983	41.33	46.56	54.00	60.18	71.10	100.00

Note: The estimate in each cell is based only on persons who filed in each of the two years.

whereas approximately 70 percent of persons 55 to 59 did. It is clear that persistence increases with age.

Probability matrices by income are shown in table 5. Comparing the first and second panels shows that between 45 and 52 percent of persons who contributed in a given year also contributed three years later if they had incomes less than $10,000. On the other hand, over 80 percent of persons with incomes greater than $70,000 contributed three years after having made a contribution. These tables do not distinguish between the effects of age and income. Persons who are older also typically earn more, and vice versa. Thus the separate tables on age and income confound these two effects.

The persistence matrices by age and income help to distinguish state dependence from the effect of age. Referring to table 4: for persons 25 to 29,

TABLE 5. Probability of Contributing in Year *j*, Given a Contribution in Year *i*, 1978–83, Selected Income Ranges

	1978	1979	1980	1981	1982	1983
			$1–$10,000			
1978	100.00	68.35	49.75	45.27	41.38	39.98
1979	64.28	100.00	59.97	50.93	45.72	43.69
1980	49.27	62.03	100.00	67.21	57.10	52.71
1981	37.05	43.60	55.13	100.00	70.19	61.62
1982	27.81	31.54	37.45	56.81	100.00	71.08
1983	21.46	24.05	27.57	39.98	57.35	100.00
			$70,001 and Over			
1978	100.00	89.55	88.42	83.05	81.95	78.65
1979	91.09	100.00	92.82	86.21	83.87	79.34
1980	88.17	90.22	100.00	87.99	84.66	80.17
1981	88.82	90.09	94.31	100.00	88.52	84.21
1982	88.00	87.20	90.85	89.60	100.00	88.05
1983	88.49	86.89	90.16	89.18	92.11	100.00
			All Income Ranges			
1978	100.00	81.63	75.00	68.50	63.37	60.95
1979	74.88	100.00	80.84	72.14	66.24	63.44
1980	61.92	72.75	100.00	78.10	70.06	66.43
1981	54.79	62.79	75.39	100.00	77.97	71.28
1982	47.57	53.90	63.21	73.04	100.00	78.69
1983	41.33	46.56	54.00	60.18	71.10	100.00

Note: The estimate in each cell is based only on persons who filed in each of the two years. Earned income is in 1980 dollars.

over 56 percent contributed three years after making a prior contribution, but fewer than 42 percent were making contributions three years before, when they were six years younger. The percents before and after are not very different for persons 55 to 59, however. The effect of age is not as important for the older age group and the data for this group do not give the appearance of state dependence. Indeed, comparing the percents just to the right with those just to the left of the diagonal reveals almost no difference on average for persons 55 to 59. The matrices by income in table 5 show a similar pattern. Persons with low incomes in a given year are likely to have higher incomes later and thus the probability of contributing three years later would tend to be higher than three years earlier when incomes were likely to have been lower. On the other hand, the average income of high-income persons was probably not changing much over time, and indeed may have been lower three years later than it was three years earlier. Thus the probability of contributing three years later would be lower than it was three years earlier, as the data in the second panel of table 5 show.

State Dependence versus Heterogeneity: Age and Income

A simple diagram helps to understand the observed differences in persistence by age and income and to understand how the data may appear to suggest state dependence when the appearance of state dependence is in fact due to increases in age or income. The relationship between age and the likelihood of contributing is represented in figure 2. Assume that on average the propensity to contribute increases up to age 55 and then remains approximately constant, as shown by the heavy solid line. At each of the ages there is a distribution of propensities to contribute. That is $RRSP = f(Age) + \epsilon$, where ϵ is the random term that generates the distribution around the mean. Assume that these random terms are independent from age to age.[4] A contribution occurs if the propensity is greater than 0. A small proportion of persons who are age 30 contributes (represented by the proportion of the distribution that is above zero). Five years later at age 40 a much larger proportion contributes, while five years earlier a much smaller proportion contributes. The data may give the appearance of state dependence, but the pattern is due instead to the increase in the contribution propensity with age. On the other hand, at age 55 the probability of contributing five years later is about the same as five years earlier.

---

4. Alternatively, if one assumes that individuals have saving propensities that persist over time, the mean function may be thought of as the expected saving for a given individual over time, with actual saving governed in part by independent random occurrences represented by ϵ.

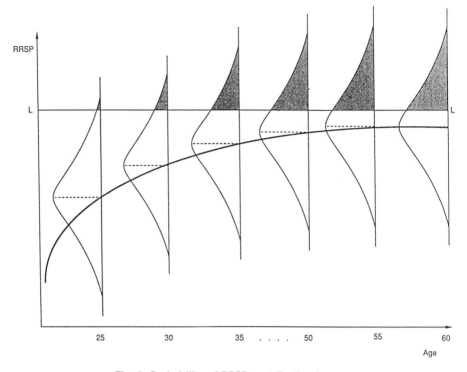

Fig. 2. Probability of RRSP contribution by age

Six- versus Sixteen-Year Panels

The first five years of the 1978–83 six-year file can be compared to the last five years of the sixteen-year file. These numbers correspond to those in the southeast corner of the sixteen-year probability matrix shown in table 3. The numbers are extremely close. For example, based on the sixteen-year file, 64.64 percent of those who contributed in 1978 also contributed in 1982. Based on the six-year file, 63.37 percent of those who contributed in 1978 also contributed in 1982.

The 1982–87 Six-Year File

The formal results presented subsequently are based on the 1982–87 six-year file (table 6). In general, the probabilities are rather similar to those for the 1978–83 time period, shown in tables 4 and 5. However, when the same estimate can be calculated, the results differ to some extent. For example, 78.47 percent of 1982 contributors also contributed in 1983 based on the 1982–87 file; 78.69 percent contributed based on the 1978–83 file. The differences by age are larger, however.

TABLE 6.   Probability of Contributing in Year j, Given a Contribution in Year i, 1982–87, Selected Age Groups

	1982	1983	1984	1985	1986	1987
			20–24 Years Old			
1982	100.00	59.86	51.23	49.05	51.05	52.50
1983	40.63	100.00	65.20	56.32	56.22	56.37
1984	21.85	40.79	100.00	66.45	60.45	57.84
1985	15.68	26.23	49.22	100.00	71.72	64.87
1986	11.91	19.21	33.08	52.79	100.00	72.17
1987	10.20	16.04	26.27	39.82	59.95	100.00
			25–29 Years Old			
1982	100.00	70.64	63.15	63.17	62.80	61.22
1983	59.08	100.00	72.54	68.14	65.72	63.55
1984	42.20	57.99	100.00	74.45	69.14	65.96
1985	35.65	45.97	62.71	100.00	76.32	70.28
1986	30.34	37.78	49.33	64.99	100.00	76.05
1987	26.61	32.89	42.59	53.90	68.26	100.00
			55–59 Years Old			
1982	100.00	84.39	78.25	73.38	68.92	66.81
1983	79.48	100.00	82.26	76.39	70.57	67.55
1984	71.61	80.34	100.00	81.91	75.39	70.68
1985	66.49	74.02	81.99	100.00	80.52	73.77
1986	63.03	68.84	75.90	81.29	100.00	79.74
1987	61.70	66.69	71.89	75.20	80.95	100.00
			All Age Groups			
1982	100.00	78.47	72.68	69.06	66.96	65.12
1983	70.96	100.00	79.03	73.07	69.75	67.12
1984	57.76	69.54	100.00	78.50	73.10	69.66
1985	50.09	58.59	71.55	100.00	79.31	73.40
1986	43.78	50.41	59.85	71.32	100.00	78.94
1987	39.79	45.15	53.00	61.14	72.96	100.00

Note: The estimate in each cell is based only on persons who filed in each of the two years.

Summary and Discussion

The descriptive data show that once a person makes an RRSP contribution, it is very likely that person will continue to make contributions in subsequent years. The likelihood is substantially greater for older persons and for those with higher incomes. In addition, the likelihood that a contribution is made increases with age and income. (These data, together with the description in figure 2, illustrate that the effect of age and income on RRSP contributions can be confounded with state dependence—the effect on subsequent contributions of an initial contribution itself.) These findings have qualitative implications for the effect of the carry-forward, in particular for the effect on type one savers discussed in the previous section. Persons who now contribute in successive years tend to be older and thus may be less inclined to put off saving—when the now-or-never constraint is removed—than younger persons might be. This tends to limit the reduction in the saving of type one savers. On the other hand, persons who don't contribute when they are young but begin when they are older, will now be able to contribute much more. They will have stored seven years worth of RRSP contribution options and many of these contributors will now contribute more than the old one-year limit. Noncontributors tend to be young and to have low incomes. Most of these type four savers probably would not be more likely to contribute if their limits were raised. They are noncontributors because they are young and have low incomes, not because the limit is too low to make the gain from a contribution worth the effort. Thus it may be that increasing the limit will not raise the overall contribution probability. Nonetheless, we will present some estimates that assume such an effect.

Estimation and Simulation Based on Single-Year Models

The goal of the RRSP analysis is to estimate how carry-forward provisions are likely to affect individual RRSP contributions and ultimately the tax cost of the carry-forward provision. The approach followed here is to consider how actual contributions in a given year would have changed had there been a carry-forward from one or more previous years. As many as five prior years can be considered with the six years of data. Allowing a carry-forward from previous years may be thought of as increasing the limit that would have pertained in a given year had it not been for the carry-forward from previous years. To estimate the effect on contributions of increasing the limit, it is first necessary to estimate a model of RRSP contributions. Estimates and simulations based on the single-year models are presented first. Simulations based on a more general model are presented in the third section. And "lifetime" simulations to determine the long-run effects of the program are presented in the fourth section. Two basic distinctions are made as the discussion develops:

> Single-year estimates—obtained for each year separately—versus estimates based on a random effects panel model that combines all of the data and that allows for individual-specific saving effects.
> Whether the increasing limits that accrue as carry-forwards accumulate are allowed to affect (increase) the probability that a contribution is made.

The implications of these distinctions are shown through the simulations. At least two key issues are not fully addressed in the analysis and they are discussed in the last section.

The Data

The data represent a random sample of approximately 30,000 tax filers from each year in the six-year file for 1982 through 1987. In some instances, estimation is based on a random subsample of the larger sample.

Estimates

The Model

Because the RRSP contributions are zero, between zero and the limit *L,* or at the limit, a two-limit Tobit specification would seem to be a natural way to describe them. This model was used initially. But the Tobit model did not fit the data well. Thus a second specification that estimates separately the probability of contributing and the amount of the contribution was ultimately used. It is informative, however, to understand the nature of the two-limit Tobit failure and it is described first.

Two-Limit Tobit

It is assumed that "desired" RRSP contributions are related to age and income according to the specification

$$R_i = \alpha + BA_i + Y_i^\delta + \eta_i Y_i + \epsilon_i, \tag{1}$$

where i indexes individuals, R represents RRSP saving, A represents age, and Y income. The random component of the equation is $\eta_i Y_i + \epsilon_i$, where η_i and ϵ_i have mean zero and variances σ_η^2 and σ_ϵ^2 respectively. Thus given age and income the variation in desired RRSP contributions increases with income and is given by $\sigma^2 = \sigma_\eta^2 Y^2 + \sigma_\epsilon^2$. The functional form was adopted after prior experimentation with alternative specifications. In particular, a model with a heteroskedastic variance improved the model fit substantially. The functional form Y_i^δ was also chosen to fit the data; it approximates a log-linear (constant elasticity) specification but can be used in this situation where the "desired" contribution could be negative. According to this representation RRSP data may be described by a two-limit Tobit model, with observed contributions, denoted by r, given by

$$r = 0, \text{ if } \quad R < 0;$$

$$r = R, \text{ if } 0 < R < L;$$

$$r = L, \text{ if } L < R;$$

where L is the contribution limit.[5]

The Tobit specification assumes that the effect of a variable on whether a person contributes is the same as the effect on the amount of the contribution if it is positive; a one-year increase in age, for example, will increase the mean *desired* contribution by the same amount whether the desired level is less than or greater than zero, if the regression function R_i in equation 1 is linear in parameters.

A Two-Equation Model: Probit and One-Limit Tobit

An alternative to the two-limit Tobit single equation is two separate relationships: one describing the probability that a contribution will be made and the other describing the amount of the contribution given that it is positive. The relationships between these specifications is explained in more detail in the Appendix. The two-limit Tobit model described in the previous section uses both contributor and noncontributor observations. Under the two-equation specification, the contribution probability is estimated with a probit model that uses only information on whether the contribution is zero or positive. The amount contributed is estimated using only data on contributors, accounting for the fact that persons with zero contributions are not included in the data (adjusting for the "truncation" caused by deleting observations with $R < 0$). As explained in the Appendix, constraining the parameter estimates in the two equations to be the same yields the two-limit Tobit specification.

Actual versus Pseudolimits

The model description above and the details in the Appendix are explained with reference to the contribution limit L, with the implication that actual

---

5. The limit varies from person to person depending on income and the provisions of the person's firm or government pension plan.

limits would be used in estimation. In practice, however, it is apparent from the data that a large proportion of people contribute very close to but not at the calculated limit. Thus it seems apparent that many are constrained by the limit even though they contribute below the limit. Using 1987 data for illustration, figure 3 compares the proportion of people at the calculated limit with the proportion who are within 5 percent of the actual limit, called the pseudolimit. On average there are twice as many contributions within 5 percent of the limit as at the actual limit itself. Depending on the income interval, there are up to 2.77 times as many at or above the pseudolimit as at the actual limit. Thus the pseudolimit is used in estimation, assuming that persons who are within 5 percent of the limit in fact intended to contribute at the limit and thus were constrained by the limit.[6] The percentage contributing within and at the pseudolimit is shown by income interval in figure 4.

Parameter Estimates and Model Fit

Parameter Estimates

Parameter estimates based on the two-limit Tobit and the two-equation (probit and one-limit Tobit) specifications are shown in table 7. The specifications are estimated separately for each of the years 1982 through 1987. If the Tobit specification is an accurate representation of the data, the three sets of parameter estimates should be similar. The probit and the one-limit Tobit are the component parts of the two-limit Tobit and all three are alternative ways to estimate the same parameters.[7] It is clear from table 7 that the estimated parameters are very different, thus rejecting the two-limit Tobit specification.[8] For example, the coefficient on age in the one-limit Tobit equation is three or four times as large as the coefficient in the probit equation. As estimated and reported in table 7, however, this "test" is not strictly appropriate because the probit equation includes the limit level as a variable, which is not included in the two-limit Tobit specification. The limit is included to reflect the possibility that making an RRSP contribution is only worthwhile if the amount that can be contributed is large enough—say to cover the "transaction" costs of making the contribution.

---

6. To obtain maximum likelihood estimates, it is assumed that given income and age contributions are normally distributed, up to the limit. The expectation is that there would be a mass point at the limit, consistent with a censored normal distribution. The concentration of points just below the limit, however, is not consistent with a normal distribution. Assuming censoring at the pseudo instead of the actual limit solves the problem by inducing a distribution that is closer to a censored normal distribution.

7. Except for the variance parameter, which, in the probit equation, is fixed at the one-limit Tobit estimated value.

8. The difference in the other variables, however, is not attributable to the inclusion of the limit in the probit equation.

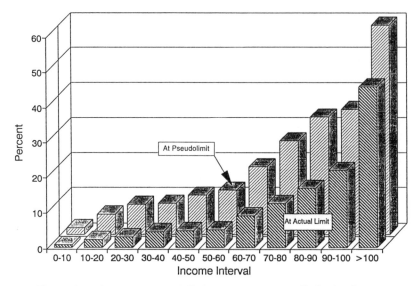

Fig. 3. Actual versus pseudolimit: percentage at limit, by income interval

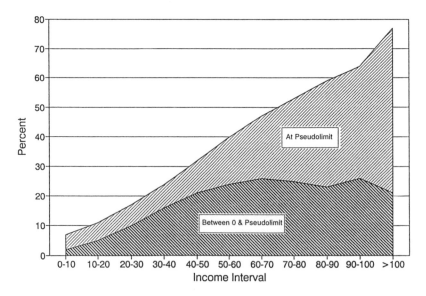

Fig. 4. Percentage contributing to RRSP: at and below the pseudolimit, by income

Whether the limit level should be included as a determinant of whether a contribution is made is open to question. On the one hand, the idea that the limit has to be large enough to make a contribution worth the effort seems qualitatively correct. On the other hand, the limit tends to be large for persons who are not covered by an employer-provided registered pension plan—an RPP. Given age and income, the self-employed, for example, may be more inclined to save through an RRSP than an employee who has employer-provided saving through an RPP. Indeed, the different limits for the two groups were chosen to provide "comparable" tax-advantaged saving opportunities for persons with and without employer-provided pension plans. Thus the estimated coefficient on the limit could reflect the saving propensity of persons without employer pensions rather than the effect of the size of the possible contribution. Estimates in Wise 1985, however, show that neither RPP nor self-employed status is significantly related to whether an RRSP contribution was made in 1981.

But even if the limit level does matter, it would be more plausible to model the effect as a lower threshold that must be exceeded if a contribution is to be worthwhile. As estimated, the predicted probability of contributing increases continuously as the limit is raised, in particular through accumulated carry-forwards. The discussion of the simulations will suggest that accounting for transaction costs in this way is not completely satisfactory. It is nonetheless instructive to consider more fully the effect of this specification. Thus the simulated effects of the carry-forward are reported with and without an increase in the *contribution probability* as the carry-forward accumulates. The average contribution of contributors increases of course as the accumulating carry-forward raises the limit.

Model Fit

Because parameter estimates are to be used to simulate the effects of changes in contributions provisions, it is particularly important that the model predict well the outcomes under the current provisions, that it fit the data on which it was estimated. Thus some attention is given to practical indicators of model fit. The 1987 estimates are used for illustration.

Several graphs help to show the nature of the mismatch between actual contributions and the model predictions based on the two-limit Tobit specification. It is revealing to consider actual versus predicted values by income interval, beginning with the expected contribution $E(R)$, which may be decomposed into six series: (i) the probability of a contribution greater than zero; (ii) the average contribution, given that R is greater than zero; (iii) the probability of a contribution between zero and the limit; (iv) the average contribution given that it is between zero and the limit, (v) the probability of contribution at the limit, and (vi) the average contribution given that it is at the

TABLE 7. Parameter Estimates (and Standard Errors) by Year and by Specification

	1982	1983	1984	1985	1986	1987
			Two-Limit Tobit			
Income	0.736	0.738	0.735	0.735	0.743	0.746
	(0.002)	(0.002)	(0.002)	(0.002)	(0.002)	(0.002)
Age	70.95	64.99	56.10	51.40	45.39	43.31
	(2.27)	(2.11)	(1.83)	(1.69)	(1.63)	(1.60)
σ_η	0.019	0.017	0.015	0.014	0.021	0.020
	(0.001)	(0.001)	(0.001)	(0.001)	(0.001)	(0.001)
σ_ϵ	2,353.0	2,373.8	2,245.7	2,223.3	2,190.9	2,171.5
	(51.1)	(49.2)	(40.8)	(36.7)	(36.4)	(35.4)
Constant	−7,682.0	−7,269.5	−6,471.4	−6,104.1	−5,923.6	−5,852.5
	(164.5)	(151.8)	(125.7)	(114.9)	(108.2)	(106.9)
Likelihood Number	−36,451.0	−39,298.4	−44,936.7	−47,933.2	−52,301.9	−53,768.3
			Probit			
Income	0.820	0.826	0.830	0.832	0.847	0.850
	(0.002)	(0.002)	(0.002)	(0.002)	(0.002)	(0.002)
Age	220.45	204.51	190.42	173.12	157.27	151.21
	(6.49)	(6.29)	(6.19)	(5.84)	(6.28)	(6.19)

Limit	480.60	490.98	554.21	609.00	482.91	540.57
	52.34	(51.75)	(51.10)	(49.43)	(43.45)	(44.14)
σ_η	0.073	0.067	0.067	0.066	0.068	0.082
σ_ϵ	7,090.6	7,346.6	7,643.5	7,471.7	8,296.0	8,059.7
Constant	−23,741.4	−22,940.9	−22,344.2	−21,162.0	−21,438.6	−21,259.1
	(333.6)	(323.2)	(324.8)	(308.5)	(329.0)	(327.9)
Likelihood Number	−10,794.0	−11,643.8	−12,937.0	−13,784.6	−14,591.7	−14,915.3

One-Limit Tobit

Income	0.853	0.865	0.872	0.872	0.883	0.869
	(0.012)	(0.009)	(0.006)	(0.007)	(0.006)	(0.007)
Age	587.14	598.74	640.98	602.00	705.62	745.19
	(27.08)	(30.76)	(23.95)	(33.17)	(27.43)	(25.65)
σ_η	0.073	0.067	0.067	0.066	0.068	0.082
	(0.008)	(0.007)	(0.006)	(0.007)	(0.006)	(0.007)
σ_ϵ	7,090.6	7,346.3	7,643.5	7,471.7	8,296.0	8,059.7
	(315.2)	(307.8)	(253.4)	(300.3)	(269.7)	(259.0)
Constant	−51,944.4	−53,175.5	−57,848.4	−53,623.7	−62,767.2	−62,875.8
	(2,170.6)	(2,513.0)	(1,730.9)	(2,788.3)	(2,151.7)	(1,932.7)
Likelihood Number	−27,991.1	−30,202.4	−35,012.6	−37,481.7	−41,347.0	−42,809.7

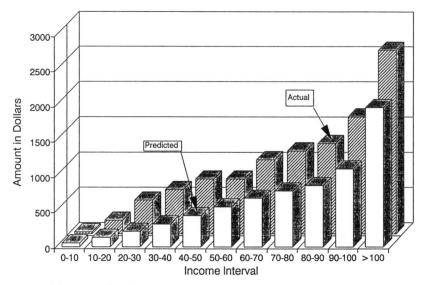

Fig. 5. Predicted versus actual contribution: two-limit Tobit—$E(R)$

limit. Each series may be described as a function of income. The decomposition may be written as

$$E(R) = \underset{\text{(i)}}{Pr(R < 0) \times 0} + \underset{\text{(ii)}}{Pr(R > 0) \times E(r|R > 0)}$$

$$= \underset{\text{(iii)}}{Pr(R < 0) \times 0} + \underset{\text{(iv)}}{Pr(0 < R < L) \times E(R|0 < R < L)}$$

$$+ \underset{\text{(v)}}{Pr(R > L)} \times \underset{\text{(vi)}}{E(R|R > L)}. \tag{2}$$

By considering each of the components, the nature of the failure of the Tobit model can be seen. The predicted values of each of the components is compared graphically with the actual values. The 1987 data and estimates are used for illustration; the results are similar for the other years. First, figure 5 shows that the two-limit Tobit specifications consistently underestimates the average contribution, $E(R)$. Overall, the average of observed contributions is $639; the average of predicted contributions is $401. As shown in figure 6, the two-limit Tobit model accurately predicts the probability of contributing. But it underestimates the contributions of contributors, $E(R|R > 0)$, as shown in figure 7. Even though the overall probability of contributing is predicted well, as

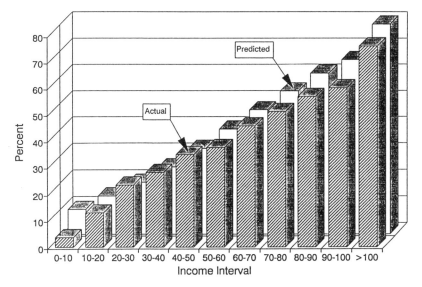

Fig. 6. **Predicted versus actual percentage contributing: two-limit Tobit—** $Pr(R > 0)$

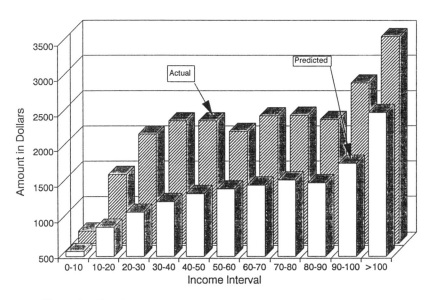

Fig. 7. **Predicted versus actual contributor amounts: two-limit Tobit—** $E(R|R > 0)$

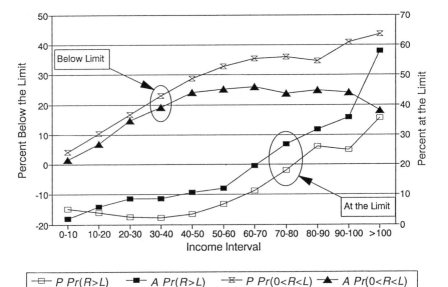

Fig. 8. Predicted versus actual percentage contributing: two-limit Tobit—
Pr(0 < R < L) and Pr(R > L)

shown in Figure 6, the components—the probabilities within and at the limit—are not. This can be seen in figure 8. The model consistently over-predicts the *probability* of contributing below the limit and consistently under-predicts the probability of contributing at the limit. The predicted versus actual contributions within and at the limit are shown in figure 9. The model consistently underpredicts *contributions* below the limit and consistently over-predicts contributions at the limit. Combining the contributor status probabilities and the contributions (fig. 8 and 9), there are more people at the limit than the model predicts and their limits are somewhat lower than the expected limits of limit contributors based on the model predictions. There are fewer people below the limit than the model predicts and their contributions are larger than the expected contributions based on the model predictions. On balance, the expected contribution based on the model is much too low, as shown for all contributors in figure 7.

The two-equation model fits the data quite well, however. Again, the decomposition in equation 2 serves as a guide and several graphs show the fit. First, the average predicted contributions, $E(R)$, closely match the actual averages, by income interval, as shown in figure 10. The actual overall average is $639 and the average of predicted values is $602, a difference of 5.8 percent. Decomposing the average into the probability of a positive contri-

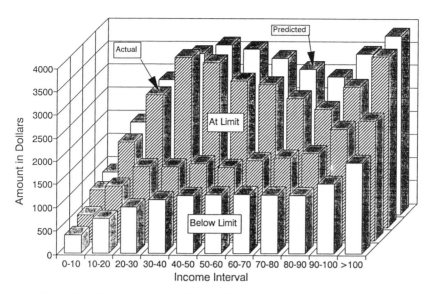

Fig. 9. Predicted versus actual contributor amounts: two-limit Tobit—
$E(R|0 < R < L)$, $E(R/R > L)$

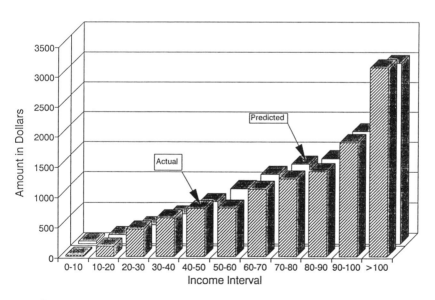

Fig. 10. Predicted versus actual contribution: noncontributors and contributors—$E(R)$

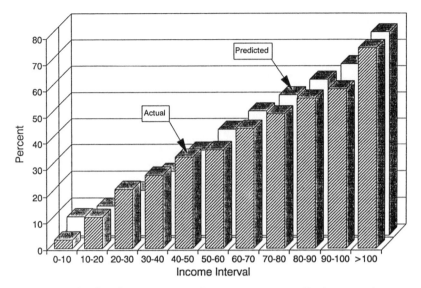

Fig. 11. Predicted versus actual percentage contributing: total—
Pr(R > 0)

bution and the expected contribution given that it is positive, figures 11 and 12 show that both of these predicted components closely accord with their actual counterparts. Considering the more detailed decomposition, figure 13 shows that the predicted probabilities of contributing within the limit and at the limit closely match their actual counterparts. Finally, the predicted amounts contributed conditional on being within and at the limit also correspond rather closely to the actual amounts, although there are some points of divergence, as shown in figure 14. The model slightly overestimates the amounts for persons at the limit in the income intervals above $50,000 and slightly underestimates the amounts in the higher income intervals for persons within the limit. About 40 percent of contributors have incomes in this range. Overall the fit is very close.

Simulations
Consider the effect of a carry-forward from 1982 to 1983. Suppose that, instead of the actual 1983 limit, the limit had been increased by the amount of the unused 1982 contribution, sometimes referred to as the unused "room." Thus, for example, a person who had a limit of L_{82} in 1982 but made no contribution in that year would have a limit of $L_{83} + L_{82}$ in 1983.

Simulated contributions one, two, . . . , and six years after the introduction of the carry-forward plan are shown in tables 8 and 9. Table 8 does not

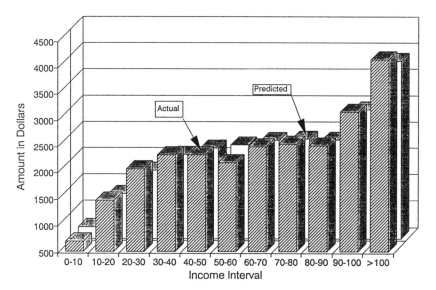

Fig. 12. Predicted versus actual contributor amounts: all—$E(R|R > 0)$

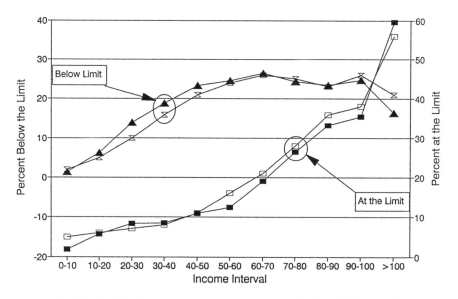

Fig. 13. Predicted versus actual percentage contributing: $Pr(0 < R < L)$, $Pr(R = L)$

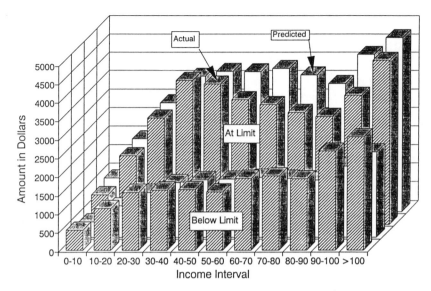

Fig. 14. Predicted versus actual contributor amounts: $E(R|0 < R < L)$, $E(R|R = L)$

TABLE 8. Simulated Effects of Carry-Forward Provisions, 1982–87 Two-Equation Model, Without Contribution Probability Effect of Limit Increase

	1982	1983	1984	1985	1986	1987
			Average Contributions			
Without Carry-Forward	405	433	491	545	618	620
With Carry-Forward From:						
1986						779
1985					767	864
1984				699	860	927
1983			620	784	924	976
1982		560	694	843	974	1017
			Index without Carry-Forward = 100			
Without Carry-Forward	100	100	100	100	100	100
With Carry-Forward From:						
1986						126
1985					124	139
1984				128	139	150
1983			126	144	150	157
1982		129	141	155	158	164

allow the *contribution probability* to increase as the carry-forward increases the contribution limit, described as "without the contribution probability effect of the limit increase." The simulations reported in table 8 incorporate an increase in the contribution probability as accumulating carry-forwards increase the limit, using the estimated effect of the limit *variable* in the probit equation (table 7). Without the carry-forward, the average 1983 simulated contribution would have been $433. With the carry-forward from 1982, the average simulated contribution is $560 without and $717 with the limit effect on the contribution probability. The simulated average under the actual 1983 limits was obtained by predicting the contribution of each person under the 1983 limits, based on the model estimates. To obtain the average with the carry-forward, the predictions were repeated for each person but with each

TABLE 9. Simulated Effects of Carry-Forward Provisions, 1982–87 Two-Equation Model, with Contribution Probability Effect of Limit Increase

	1982	1983	1984	1985	1986	1987
			Average Contributions			
Without Carry-Forward	413	433	492	543	623	629
With Carry-Forward From:						
1986						974
1985					944	1,194
1984				912	1,168	1,363
1983			801	1,178	1,341	1,498
1982		717	1,038	1,394	1,490	1,616
			Index without Carry-Forward = 100			
Without Carry-Forward	100	100	100	100	100	100
With Carry-Forward From:						
1986						155
1985					151	190
1984				168	187	217
1983			163	217	215	238
1982		166	211	257	239	257
			Probability of Contributing			
Without Carry-Forward	0.183	0.198	0.229	0.252	0.270	0.274
With Carry-Forward From:						
1986						0.333
1985					0.325	0.381
1984				0.328	0.374	0.423
1983			0.293	0.395	0.416	0.459
1982		0.254	0.354	0.456	0.456	0.491

person's limit raised by the carry-forward from 1982. The two estimates are shown in the second column of the first panel in tables 8 and 9; the ratio of the two is shown in the second panel.

Comparable calculations have been made for 1984 through 1987, but assuming that the carry-forward program began one year earlier, two years earlier, . . . , back to 1982. For example, for 1985, the top row shows the prediction with no carry-forward; below are shown the predictions assuming that the carry-forward program began one year earlier in 1984, two years earlier in 1983, and three years earlier in 1982. If the program began in 1982, the unused 1982 room is carried over to 1983, establishing the 1983 limit, including the carry-forward. The unused room from this 1983 limit is carried forward to 1984 to establish the 1984 limit, including the carry-forward. And so forth. Again, the corresponding ratios are shown in the second panel. One year of carry-forward increases the average contribution by 24 to 28 percent without and 51 to 66 percent with the limit effect, depending on the year.

The last panel in table 9 shows the effect of the accumulated carry-forward on the probability of contributing. The effect, based on the probit parameter estimates in table 7, is very large. For example, the average 1987 contribution probability with no carry-forward is .27; with a carry-forward plan introduced 1982 the 1987 contribution probability is .49.[9]

To show the effect of the carry-forward by income, the estimates are shown for 1987 by income interval in Table 10. Compared to no carry-forward, a carry-forward plan introduced in 1982 raises 1987 contributions the most for low and high income filers and the least for middle income persons: by 130 percent for persons with incomes below $10 thousand, by 89 percent for persons with incomes above $100 thousand, and by 40 percent for those with incomes between $30 and $40 thousand.

The simulations suggest the ultimate effect of the carry-forward could be very large. For example, the 1987 estimates show that carry-forward from five previous years would increase the 1987 average contribution by 64 percent without and 157 percent with the limit effect.

A More General Random Effects Panel Model

The estimates and simulations above are based on the assumption that contributions are independent from year to year, given income, age, and the contribution limit. It is likely, however, that saving in one year is related to saving in other years, that there is an individual-specific saving effect that influences individual saving in each year. Some people typically save more than others.

---

9. The estimation sample excludes all persons with no income or with a zero contribution limit, and includes only persons aged 18 to 65.

TABLE 10.   Simulated Effects of Carry-Forward Provisions by Income Interval for 1987, without Contribution Probability Effect of Limit Increase

	0–10	10–20	20–30	30–40	40–50	50–60	60–70	70–80	80–90	90–100	100+
						Income Interval					
Without Carry-Forward	47	157	318	507	717	934	1,180	1,355	1,449	1,913	3,126
With Carry-Forward From:											
1986	71	215	398	614	874	1,150	1,442	1,677	1,813	2,340	3,819
1985	87	248	437	666	954	1,273	1,613	1,906	2,093	2,645	4,449
1984	97	265	456	689	995	1,337	1,720	2,074	2,326	2,898	4,964
1983	104	275	466	701	1,017	1,377	1,797	2,200	2,519	3,114	5,478
1982	108	281	472	708	1,029	1,404	1,850	2,298	2,680	3,298	5,904
					Index: Without Carry-Forward = 100						
Without Carry-Forward	100	100	100	100	100	100	100	100	100	100	100
With Carry-Forward From:											
1986	151	137	125	121	122	123	122	124	125	122	122
1985	185	158	137	131	133	136	137	141	144	138	142
1984	206	169	143	136	139	143	146	153	161	151	159
1983	221	175	147	138	142	147	152	162	174	163	175
1982	230	179	148	140	144	150	157	170	185	172	189

To account for this possibility, a probit model with an individual random effect is estimated. With reference to figure 2, the random effect shifts the average contribution propensity, the heavy solid line, up or down. A positive random effect means that the person is more likely than the typical person to contribute in each year (at each age) and a negative term means that the person is less likely than the typical person to contribute.

The probit specification is of the form

$$R_{it} = \alpha + \beta A_{it} + Y_{it}^{\delta} + \lambda_i + \epsilon_{it}, \tag{3}$$

where λ_i is the random individual effect for the ith person, with variance σ_λ^2 and mean zero.

The random components of the contribution equations of contributors are still assumed to be independent from year to year. Again the contribution equation is a one-limit Tobit specification, in this case estimated on pooled 1982–87 data. Both equations include year dummy variables, to allow for the substantial increase in contribution probabilities over this time period. To facilitate comparison of the contributor and contribution parameters, the probit estimates are normalized by setting the variance of ϵ such that $\sigma_\lambda^2 + \sigma_\epsilon^2$ equals the one-limit Tobit variance, evaluated at mean income over both contributors and noncontributors.

Why should it matter that the individual effect is accounted for? Recall that the simulated carry-forward in a given year is based on *predicted* contributions in previous years. Recall also that the higher limit that results from the accumulating carry-forwards may increase the probability of contributing. The individual effect changes both the predicted carry-forward and the predicted contribution probability and one tends to offset the other. The range of carry-forwards is increased but the probability of contributing when the carry-forward is large is reduced. Consider a person age A with income Y and with limits L_{82} and L_{83}, who does not contribute in 1982 or 1983, based on the two-equation year-by-year model. Thus his total 1984 limit is $LT_{84} = L_{82} + L_{83} + L_{84}$. As the limit increases, the probability of contributing is assumed to increase as well. Under the independent random term assumption the probability that he will contribute in 1984 is the same as any other person with limit LT_{84} (and age A with income Y). But under the random effects specification, this person would be assumed to have a relatively low individual-sepcific saving term—an important determinant of the choice not to contribute in 1983 and 1984. And this same individual effect would be used to predict the contribution probability in 1984. The probability would be lower than the average probability for persons with limit LT_{84}.

In general, persons with low saving propensity will accumulate the largest carry-forwards. Because of the individual effect, these persons will also be the least likely to contribute, even with the large carry-forward. Thus in this respect the individual effect tends to reduce the simulated effect of the carry-forward. On the other hand, the individual effect increases the likelihood that a person who does not contribute in one year will also not contribute in successive years, yielding larger carry-forwards than would be predicted without the individual effect. The higher limits increase the contribution probability for persons with low saving propensity. Thus if the probability of contributing increases with the higher limit it tends to offset the fact that higher accumulated limits are associated with persons with low propensities to save.

Estimates

The parameter estimates are shown in Table 11. The individual coefficients are very similar to the estimates based on the year-by-year two-equation models (table 7). The variance estimates suggest that the random effect variance σ_λ^2 is more than twice as large as the variance of ϵ. Thus the random effect accounts for over two-thirds of the total variance in RRSP contributions given age and income.

TABLE 11. Parameter Estimates (and Standard Errors) for Panel Random Effects Model

	Probit	One-Limit Tobit
Income	0.818	0.867
	(0.001)	(0.003)
Age	171.20	614.19
	(7.36)	(12.80)
σ_λ	6,606.9	—
	(92.7)	—
σ_η	—	0.067
	—	(0.003)
σ_ϵ	4,294.2	7,388.1
	—	(130.0)
Constant	−24,125.0	−55,206.0
	(409.7)	(1,037.6)
1983	305.56	471.95
	(219.86)	(438.13)
1984	1,355.79	246.86
	(191.91)	(439.06)
1985	1,740.58	1,730.22
	(179.82)	(491.58)
1986	1,941.90	2,016.51
	(177.60)	(486.98)
1987	2,319.38	2,777.58
	(169.52)	(486.46)
Likelihood Number	−11,257.6	−158,961.5

Simulations

The simulated effects of the carry-forward based on the random effects panel model are shown without and with the effect of the limit increase on the contribution probability in tables 12 and 13 respectively. If the accumulating limit is not allowed to affect the contribution probability, the random effect reduces the effect of the carry-forward, in conformance with the previous conceptual explanation. Compared to no carry-forward, for example, the average 1987 contribution is 47 percent higher with carry-forwards beginning in 1982. Based on the year-by-year two-equation model the comparable increase is 64 percent, as shown in Table 8.

But incorporating the effect of the accumulating limit on the contribution probability, the relationship is the reverse. The increase based on the random effects model is 196 percent, whereas the increase based on the year-by-year model is 157 percent.

"Lifetime" Simulations

The simulations above provide estimates of the effect of the carry-forward plan through the first six years following its introduction, assuming the plan was introduced in 1982. The long-run effect of the carry-forward may also be

TABLE 12. Simulated Effects of Carry-Forward Provisions, 1982–87 Random Effects Model, without Effect of Limit Increase

	1982	1983	1984	1985	1986	1987
			Average Contributions			
Without Carry-Forward	370	366	429	463	532	559
With Carry-Forward From:						
1986						684
1985					639	740
1984				578	693	775
1983			530	636	728	801
1982		453	578	672	753	822
			Index: without Carry-Forward = 100			
Without Carry-Forward	100	100	100	100	100	100
With Carry-Forward From:						
1986						122
1985					120	132
1984				125	130	139
1983			124	137	137	143
1982		122	135	145	142	147

important with respect to the tax cost of the program and is probably even more important than the short-run effect with respect to individual saving. To give an indication of the longer term implications of the program, the "lifetime" contributions of 1987 tax filers are simulated with and without the carry-forward provision. For each 1987 filer in the sample, contributions through age 65 are simulated. The simulations are based first on the single-year two-equation model for 1987 and then on the random effects panel model. For each person in the 1987 sample, future expected income is estimated based on the relationship between age and income in previous years, using a variance components specification that distinguishes transitory income variation. The simulated income stream of a person is obtained by adding a random term to expected income. The random term is drawn from a normal distribution with

TABLE 13. Simulated Effects of Carry-Forward Provisions, 1982–87 Random Effects Model, with Effect of Limit Increase

	1982	1983	1984	1985	1986	1987
			Average Contributions			
Without Carry-Forward	370	366	429	463	532	559
With Carry-Forward From:						
1986						897
1985					836	1,137
1984				785	1,085	1,334
1983			729	1,051	1,289	1,495
1982		646	986	1,279	1,464	1,632
			Index: without Carry-Forward = 100			
Without Carry-Forward	100	100	100	100	100	100
With Carry-Forward From:						
1986						157
1985					157	203
1984				170	204	239
1983			170	227	242	267
1982		175	230	276	275	292
			Probability of Contributing			
Without Carry-Forward	0.156	0.159	0.193	0.207	0.220	0.231
With Carry-Forward From:						
1986						0.300
1985					0.287	0.359
1984				0.277	0.351	0.413
1983			0.262	0.345	0.400	0.459
1982		0.225	0.334	0.410	0.461	0.500

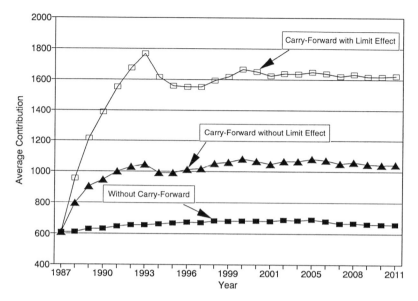

Fig. 15. Contributions of 1987 filers for 1987 to 2011: two-equation model

variance equal to the transitory component of variance of unexplained earnings in previous years. The simulations are carried through the year 2011, dropping persons who reach age 65 before then.

The Two-Equation Model

The average contribution of persons still in the sample (i.e., under age 65) in each year through 2011 are shown in figure 15. Without the limit effect on the contribution probability, contributions with the carry-forward peak five years after the introduction of the program at about twice the no-carry-forward level. Thereafter, the contributions decline to about 1.8 times the no-carry-forward amount and remain at approximately that level through 2011. Allowing the accumulating limit to increase the contribution probability, the contributions with the carry-forward peak six years after the introduction of the program at about three times the no-carry-forward amount. Thereafter the average contribution declines to about 2.6 times the no-carry-forward amount.

Total contributions through age 65 of the 1987 tax filers—based on the two-equation model—are estimated to be $110 million without the carry-forward. They are $168 million with the carry-forward without the limit effect on the contribution probability and $254 million with the effect on the contribution probability.

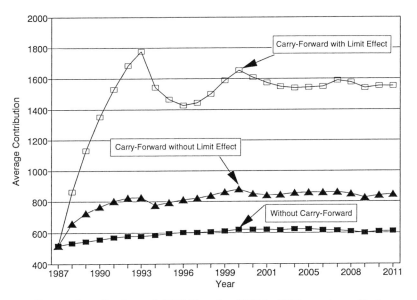

Fig. 16. Contributions of 1987 filers for 1987 to 2011: random effects model

The Random Effects Panel Model

The simulations based on the panel model are shown in figure 16. In the long run the average contribution under the carry-forward plan without allowing the contribution probability to increase is about 1.65 times the average under the no-carry-forward plan, compared to about 1.80 based on the single-year two-equation specification. Allowing the estimated increase in the contribution probability, the long-run average with the carry-forward is about 2.6 times the no-carry-forward average, about the same as the ratio based on the single-year model. In both cases, the contributions peak six or seven years after the introduction of the program and then decline to a relatively stable lower level. The relationship between the single-year two-equation model and the panel model results—with and without the limit effect on the contribution probability—is summarized in figure 17.

Effect on Age 65 Assets

This volume emphasizes savings and bequests. Although this paper does not consider bequests directly, the accumulation of savings through the RRSP program may have a substantial effect on the size and prevalence of bequests. The effect of the carry-forward program on RRSP assets at age 65 is consid-

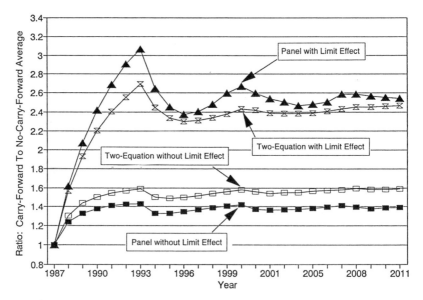

Fig. 17. Two-equation and panel results: with and without limit contributor effect

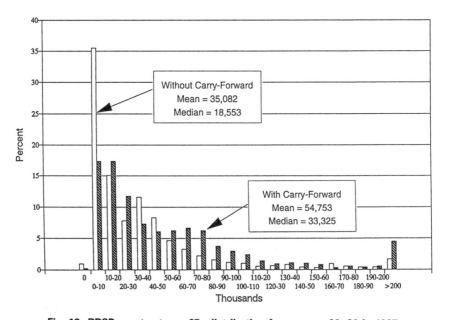

Fig. 18. RRSP assets at age 65: distribution for persons 20–30 in 1987

ered first. To help to put the data in context, financial assets in Canada and the United States are compared.

RRSP Assets at Age 65

RRSP savings are intended primarily for retirement. Thus one important measure of the potential impact of the carry-forward program is its effect on assets at retirement age. The simulated distribution of the RRSP assets at 65 of persons 20 to 30 in 1987 is shown in figure 18, with and without the carry-forward. The results are based on the two-equation model for 1987 without a limit effect on the contribution probability. A 3 percent real interest rate is assumed. Median RRSP assets are increased by 80 percent, from \$18,553 to \$33,325. The proportion of persons with RRSP assets less than \$20 thousand is reduced very substantially, from about 37 percent to about 18 percent. The proportion with assets in the \$50 thousand to \$150 thousand range is increased substantially. Thus the carry-forward plan may have a noticeable effect on the financial well-being of the elderly. And, to the extent that financial assets are not completely depleted before death, and they are unlikely to be, the carry-forward plan may have a very substantial effect on bequests.

Financial Assets in Canada and the United States Compared

The low saving rate in the United States is often noted. Summers and Carroll (1987) have emphasized the divergence between the personal saving rate in Canada and the United States and have attributed the divergence to the Canadian RRSP program. Personal financial assets are much higher in Canada than in the United States. Indeed the simulated RRSP assets alone of individuals age 65 in Canada are greater than total financial assets—including individual retirement account and Keogh saving—of households with heads 60 to 70 in the United States. The distribution of these assets is shown in figure 19. The Canadian numbers do not include the new carry-forward provisions, which will further magnify the difference in financial asset saving in Canada and the United States. Thus special saving programs like the RRSP are likely to have a very substantial effect on bequests when compared across countries.

Discussion and Summary

As we emphasized at the outset, our analysis is based on one important "independence" assumption: that allowing foregone RRSP saving to be made up later does not affect current saving. In our view this assumption is unlikely to be true. In addition, the model undoubtedly exaggerates the potential effect

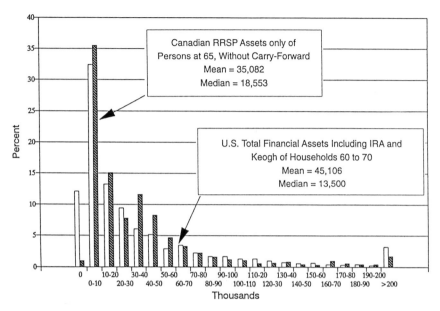

Fig. 19. U.S.-Canadian comparison: RRSP versus total financial assets in the United States

of the accumulating limit on the probability of contributing, when that effect is considered. This is called the transaction cost effect.

Ignoring the decline in the saving of type one and type two savers—those who are likely to violate the independence assumption—leads to simulation results that exaggerate the increase in contributions under the carry-forward plan. Ignoring the effect of the accumulating limits on the contribution probability yields simulated effects of the carry-forward that are too low. The results that account for this effect are surely too large. Thus it seems most reasonable to rely on the simulations that do not allow for the limit increases to increase the contribution probabilities. In addition, the results based on the random effects panel model should be more reliable than the results based on the year-by-year two-equation model. Based on the lifetime simulations the carry-forward will raise average contributions by 60 to 70 percent in the long run, with a peak increase of almost 100 percent occurring six or seven years after the introduction of the program. In addition, the carry-forward will increase RRSP assets at 65 by a large amount, possibly on the order of 80 percent, according to the simulations. The lifetime simulations estimate the effect of the carry-forward assuming that the underlying propensity to contribute remains at the 1987 level. But contributions have increased dramatically since 1982 in the absence of the carry-forward, and indeed since 1987. This underlying trend could continue. None of the results allow the popularity of RRSPs to increase as it has over the past several years.

The three models discussed in the text are described. The first is a single-equation two-limit Tobit specification, estimated for each year separately. The second is the two-equation specification, also estimated for each year separately. The first equation is a probit specification of contributor status. The second equation is a one-limit Tobit specification of the RRSP contributions of contributors. The third model also includes two equations, but is based on pooled data for the period 1982–87. The first equation in this model is a probit specification with a time invariant random effect. The second equation is a one-limit Tobit specification estimated on pooled data.

The basic relationship underlying all three models is:

$$R_i = \alpha + \beta X_i + Y_i^\delta + \eta_i Y_i + \epsilon_i, \tag{A.1}$$

where R_i is the desired RRSP saving of individual i, X_i is age, and Y_i is income. The disturbances η_i and ϵ_i are assumed to be independently distributed with mean zero and variances σ_η and σ_ϵ respectively.

The Two-Limit Tobit Model

Three outcomes are possible: (*a*) no contribution, (*b*) a positive contribution but less than the limit, and (*c*) a contribution at the limit. The observed contribution is denoted by r_i and the contribution limit by L_i. The three outcomes and associated likelihoods are:

$$(a) \; r_i = 0, \qquad \Phi\left(\frac{-z_i}{\sigma_i}\right);$$

$$(b) \; 0 < r_i < L_i, \qquad \frac{1}{\sigma_i}\, \phi\left(\frac{R_i - z_i}{\sigma_i}\right);$$

$$(c) \; r_i = L_i, \qquad 1 - \Phi\left(\frac{L_i - z_i}{\sigma_i}\right); \tag{A.2}$$

where $z_i = \alpha + \beta X_i + Y_i^\delta$, $\sigma_i = \sqrt{\sigma_\eta^2 Y_i^2 + \sigma_\epsilon^2}$ is the standard deviation of the composite disturbance, and $\phi(\bullet)$ and $\Phi(\bullet)$ denote the standard normal density and distribution functions respectively.

Two-Equation Model: Probit and Truncated One-Limit Tobit

The two equations are estimated independently. The one-limit Tobit equation is estimated using contributors only, with a correction for the selection. Contributions may be below or at the limit. The likelihood of each outcome is as described for the two-limit Tobit except for the truncation adjustment to account for the exclusion of noncontributors—by dividing each component by the probability of a positive contribution and thus being in the sample, $\Phi(z/\sigma_i)$. The outcomes and associated likelihoods are:

$$(a)\ 0 < r_i < L_i, \qquad \frac{1}{\sigma_i}\ \Phi\left(\frac{R_i - z_i}{\sigma_i}\right) \Big/ \Phi\left(\frac{z_i}{\sigma_i}\right);$$

$$(b)\ r_i = L_i, \qquad \left[1 - \Phi\left(L_i - \frac{z_i}{\sigma_i}\right)\right] \Big/ \Phi\left(\frac{z_i}{\sigma_i}\right). \qquad (A.3)$$

The probit equation is estimated separately and is based only on contributor status. Since the variance in the probit equation is not identified, to facilitate comparison, σ_ϵ and σ_η are fixed at the values estimated from the one-limit Tobit. This normalization ensures that the probit and one-limit Tobit coefficients will have the same scale.

The limiting case of the two-equation model, with the parameters in each constrained to have the same values, is the two-limit Tobit specification—if the same variables are used in each. Without this constraint, the two equations are allowed to imply different contribution probabilities, since the denominator in the one-limit Tobit likelihood terms in equation A.3 is the probability of a positive contribution.

Panel Data: Random Effects Probit and Pooled One-Limit Tobit

The one-limit Tobit specification for contributors is estimated on pooled data for 1982–87. The estimated variance from this model is used to fix the variance in the random effects probit specification. The specification is the same as in equation A.1 except that the error structure is homoskedastic and a random individual effect, denoted by λ_i, is introduced. Both the probit and the one-limit Tobit includes year dummies. Desired RRSP contributions are given by:

$$R_{it} = \alpha + \beta X_{it} + Y_{it}^\delta + \lambda_i + \epsilon_{it}, \qquad (A.4)$$

where the subscript t indexes the year. Let $z_{it}(\lambda_{it}) = \alpha + \beta X_{it} + Y_{it}^\delta + \lambda_i$. As above, let σ_ϵ denote the standard deviation of ϵ. The two variance components, ϵ_{it} and λ_i are independent. The variance of the composite disturbance is normalized using the estimated variances from the pooled one-limit Tobit, $\hat{\sigma}_\epsilon^2$ and $\hat{\sigma}_\eta^2$. The random effects probit variance ($\sigma_\lambda^2 + \sigma_\epsilon^2$) is set equal to $\sigma_\epsilon^2 + \bar{y}^2\sigma_\eta^2$ where $\bar{y}$ is mean income evaluated over both contributors and noncontributors.

In each period there are two outcomes: $R_{it} < 0$ and $0 < R_{it}$. Let P_{it} denote the likelihood for period t. Then

$$
P_{it}(\lambda_{it}) = \begin{cases} \Phi\left(\dfrac{-z_{it}(\lambda_i)}{\sigma_{it}} \right) & \text{if } R_{it} \le 0, \\[2ex] 1 - \Phi\left(\dfrac{-z_{it}(\lambda_i)}{\sigma_{it}} \right) & \text{if } R_{it} \ge 0. \end{cases} \tag{A.5}
$$

The likelihood over T periods—the probability that a sequence of T outcomes will be realized—is given by:

$$
\int_{-\infty}^{\infty} \left[\prod_{t=1}^{T} P_t(\lambda) \right] f(\lambda) d\lambda, \tag{A.6}
$$

where $f(\bullet)$ denotes the (nonunit) normal density function and the individual subscript has been dropped for notational convenience.

The above likelihood function, although complete, cannot be readily evaluated without further manipulation. Let u be the standardized individual-specific random term: $u = \lambda/\sigma_\lambda$. Then $\lambda = \sigma_\lambda u$. Substituting into equation A.6 and writing out the normal density $f(\bullet)$ yields:

$$
\int_{-\infty}^{\infty} \left[\prod_{t=1}^{T} P_t(\sigma_\lambda u) \right] \frac{1}{\sqrt{2\pi}} \exp\left(\frac{1}{2} u^2 \right) du.
$$

Let $v^2 = 1/2u^2$, so $u = \sqrt{2}\, v$ and $du = \sqrt{2}\, dv$. This yields:

$$
\int_{-\infty}^{\infty} \left[\prod_{t=1}^{T} P_t(\sigma_\lambda \sqrt{2}\, v) \right] \frac{1}{\sqrt{\pi}} \exp\left(-v^2 \right) dv
$$

$$
= \int_{-\infty}^{\infty} A(v)\exp(-v^2)dv.
$$

In this form the integral can readily be evaluated using the technique of Gaussian quadrature. (See, for example, Butler and Moffitt 1982.)

REFERENCES

Butler, John S., and Robert Moffitt. 1982. "A Computationally Efficient Quadrature Procedure for the One-Factor Multinomial Probit Model." *Econometrica* 50:3.
Summers, Lawrence H., and Chris Carroll. 1987. "Why is U.S. National Saving So Low?" *Brookings Papers on Economic Activity* 2:607–35.
Wise, David A. 1984. "The Effects of Policy Change on RRSP Contributions." Prepared for the Tax Policy and Legislation Branch of the Canadian Department of Finance. Mimeo.
————. 1985. "Contributors and Contributions to Registered Retirement Saving Plans." Prepared for the Tax Policy and Legislation Branch of the Canadian Department of Finance. Mimeo.

CHAPTER 5

Measuring the Bequest Motive: The Effect of Children on Saving by the Elderly in the United States

Michael D. Hurd

According to the life-cycle hypothesis of consumption (LCH) the link be-tween generations is weak: the older generation provides the younger genera-tion with human capital, but after the younger generation begins to work, the link is broken except through transactions in the marketplace. Bequests are accidental, the result of uncertainty about the date of death and a weak or nonexistent market for annuities.

The LCH makes the strong prediction that the retired elderly will dissave, although the age at which they begin to dissave depends on unknown utility function parameters. However, some early empirical results indicated that the elderly do not seem to dissave as they age (Mirer 1979; Danziger et al. 1982; Kotlikoff and Summers 1988). These findings have been taken to be partic-ularly damaging to the LCH. Other results found only a small role for life-cycle savings. In simulations of lifetime earnings and consumption trajecto-ries, "reasonable" utility function parameter values lead to savings that are considerably smaller than observed household wealth (White 1978; Darby 1979). This implies that a good deal of household wealth has been inherited, not saved during the working life. Kotlikoff and Summers (1981) found from estimated earnings and consumption paths that as much as 80 percent of household wealth is inherited. Although large inheritances are not necessarily inconsistent with the life-cycle hypothesis, many people would think they indicate that at least part of bequests are intentional. These kinds of result have stimulated empirical and theoretical research on models of intentional or desired bequests.

The magnitude of bequests and how they vary with changes in the

Presented at the International Conference on Savings and Bequests, organized by the Japanese Institute for Posts and Telecommunications Policy (IPTP), in Tokyo on March 17 and 18, 1992.

environment are important from the point of view of economic policy. For example, the effects of financing government expenditures through taxation rather than through borrowing will depend on the strength of the bequest motive (Barro 1974). Bequests are also important for economic analysis because intergenerational links change the nature of the utility maximizing problem of individuals and, therefore, the analysis of their decisions.

My goal in this essay is to present a model that allows, within certain assumptions, the separation of accidental bequests from desired bequests. Simulations of the estimated model give estimates of desired bequests from which the effect of the bequest motive on the saving rate of the elderly can be calculated. This will show how much of saving is life-cycle saving and how much is intended for bequests.

Implications of a Bequest Motive for Saving

Because the date of death is uncertain, bequests can be either intended (desired) or unintended (accidental). A bequest is intended if it would be made even if the date of death were known with certainty. If all bequests are unintended, it would seem that an individual could increase his lifetime utility by buying annuities with all his bequeathable wealth. However, in the United States almost no one purchases annuities. This has been taken as evidence that bequests are intended, but there are several other good explanations. The transactions cost of annuity purchases have been so high that often the rate of return on annuities (including the mortality premium) has been lower than on long-term government bonds.[1] This means that bonds have a higher cash flow than annuities and in addition they have wealth value. Furthermore, other kinds of uncertainty faced by the retired elderly make annuity purchases unattractive: they are not indexed, which makes their income flow vulnerable to inflation; because of moral hazard, annuities cannot be converted to cash if needed for medical care. A final reason is due to the Social Security system. In the United States the Social Security system provides indexed annuities to about 95 percent of the retired. Social Security benefits are a large fraction of total resources of many retired people; so many retired may be overannuitized. Because the consumption stream cannot be chosen independently from the annuity stream, people may value an increment to annuities at less than the fair market price of annuities and, therefore, would not purchase annuities even if there were no load factor (Bernheim 1987; Hurd 1987a). For these reasons and possibly others, even childless single persons, who proba-

---

1. Friedman and Warshawsky (1988) estimate that the load factor on annuities was about 35 percent. Someone would have to be quite old before the mortality premium would offset such a high load factor.

bly have only a weak desire to leave a bequest, rarely purchase annuities in the United States.

According to the LCH the consumption path will vary with variation in mortality risk; but because the magnitude of the variation depends on unknown parameters such as the risk aversion parameter, intended bequests cannot be identified in consumption and wealth data simply from the variation in their paths as mortality risk varies. In particular, very slowly declining wealth paths could be consistent with the LCH. However, some authors, while admitting that the elderly dissave, say that rate of dissaving is too low to be consistent with the LCH (Bernheim 1987; Modigliani 1986, 1988; Kotlikoff 1988; Kotlikoff and Summers 1988). I find it difficult to assess what the appropriate rate of dissaving should be in the LCH model. Suppose for example that the instantaneous utility function is

$$u(c) = \frac{1}{1 - \gamma} c^{1 - \gamma}.$$

Then, in a common formulation, the optimal consumption path satisfies

$$\frac{dc_t}{dt} \frac{1}{c_t} = \frac{1}{\gamma} (r - \rho - h_t),$$

where r is the real rate of interest, ρ is the subjective time rate of discount and h_t is mortality risk. If γ, the risk aversion parameter, is large, consumption will be practically flat. Take that extreme case, and assume a real interest rate of 3 percent and a maximum age of 105. Then, wealth at age 85 would be about 65 percent of wealth at age 65, an average rate of dissaving of about 2 percent per year. This is certainly consistent with observed rates of dissaving.[2]

Because the rate of wealth decumulation does not by itself provide any evidence about the importance of a bequest motive for saving, additional information is necessary to identify its importance. In particular, identification of intended bequests must come from a specification that the consumption path fluctuates with some observable variables, and that the variation represents intended bequests. For example, in previous work, I specified that the difference in the consumption paths of retired parents and of retired nonparents was a measure of the strength of the bequest motive (Hurd 1987b, 1989). I used this specification to find the increment to bequests that comes from having children. Only the increment can be found by this method be-

---

2. The rate of wealth decumulation increases with age. With less risk aversion than the extreme case, the rate of decumulation predicted by the LCH could be rather small at the younger ages observed in the Retirement History Survey (RHS) and in other panel data sets.

cause any base level of desired bequests among the childless elderly cannot be separated from their unintended bequests. It is not a reasonable empirical goal to find the base level of desired bequests.

The Effect of a Bequest Motive on Consumption and Wealth

The framework is that of a retired individual who wants to maximize lifetime utility, but the date of death is uncertain. Utility depends on consumption each time period and on any bequests he or she might leave upon death. Economic resources are initial bequeathable wealth, w_0, and on the path of annuities, (A), which include Social Security, Medicare and Medicaid (the U.S. medical insurance system for the elderly), and private pensions.

Following Yaari (1965), I assume that individuals maximize in the consumption path (c_t) lifetime utility

$$\int_0^N u(c_t)e^{-\rho t}a_t dt + \int_0^N V(w_t)e^{-\rho t}m_t dt. \tag{1}$$

The first term in lifetime utility is the expected discounted utility from consumption: $u(\bullet)$ gives the utility flow from consumption; ρ is the subjective time rate of discount; a_t is the probability of being alive at t; N is the maximum age to which anyone can live, so that $a_N = 0$. The second term in the lifetime utility function is the expected discounted utility of bequests. $V(\bullet)$ is the utility from bequests; w_t is bequeathable wealth at t; and m_t is the probability of dying at t.

Because in this formulation utility does not depend on leisure, the model is only valid after retirement. Furthermore, it is only valid for a single person: a utility model for couples is much more complicated because it should include the utility flows for when both spouses are alive and for when only one spouse is alive, as well as a utility from bequests. Such a model for couples is given below.

The constraints on the maximization of utility are a given level of initial wealth, a borrowing constraint that will be discussed subsequently, and the equation of motion of wealth:

$$\frac{dw_t}{dt} = rw_t - c_t + A_t$$

in which r, the real interest rate, is constant and known and A_t is annuities at time t. Annuities differ from other economic resources in that they are not bequeathable: they are only paid when the annuitant is alive.

Utility maximization implies that

$$u_t = u_{t+h} \frac{a_{t+h}}{a_t} e^{h(r-\rho)} + \int_t^{t+h} V_s e^{(s-t)(r-\rho)} \frac{m_s}{a_t} ds \qquad (2)$$

over an interval $(t, t + h)$ in which w_t is positive. V_s is the marginal utility of bequests.

If V_s were zero (no bequest motive),

$$u_t = u_{t+h} \frac{a_{t+h}}{a_t} e^{h(r-\rho)} \approx u_{t+h} e^{h(r-\rho-h_t)},$$

$h_t = m_t/a_t$ is the mortality hazard rate, which increases approximately exponentially at ages over, say, 60. If $\rho > r$, then $u_t < u_{t+h}$; that is, marginal utility will increase with age, which implies, under the usual assumption about the concavity of $u(\bullet)$ that consumption will fall with age. If $\rho < r$, the age at which marginal utility will begin to rise and consumption fall is found from

$$h_t = r - \rho.$$

For example, if $r = 0.03$ and $\rho = 0$, consumption will begin to fall at about age 66 for males and age 74 for females.

The path of wealth depends on the level of consumption, which depends on the entire annuity path. In this analysis (but not in the empirical work discussed later), I assume that $A_t = A$, a constant, which is a correct assumption for about 65 percent of the sample I use in the empirical work.[3] Under the assumption that $A_t = A$, if consumption declines with age, wealth must also decline. If dw_t/dt were positive and dc_t/dt negative, then

$$\frac{d^2w_t}{dt} = r\frac{dw_t}{dt} - \frac{dc_t}{dt} > 0.$$

This implies that dw_t/dt would remain positive for all future ages, violating a terminal condition that anyone who lives to the greatest age possible (age $= N$) will consume all of his bequeathable wealth; that is, $w_N = 0$. Therefore, the LCH makes the strong prediction that, in the absence of a bequest motive for saving, wealth should begin to fall at some age and that it will continue to fall at all greater ages. A reasonable guess would be that the wealth of retired single men would begin to fall by their 60s or possibly earlier, and of retired single women by their early 70s or earlier.

---

3. This is the percentage of the sample that has only indexed annuities, mainly Social Security. Even among the part of the sample that has nominal (not indexed) annuities, nominal annuities tend to be a small fraction of total annuities.

Many studies, however, have found that wealth seems to increase with age in cross-section (Lydall 1955; Projector and Weiss 1966; Mirer 1979; Blinder, Gordon, and Wise 1983; Menchik and David 1983). These results have been interpreted as particularly damaging to the LCH. For example: "Perhaps the most decisive attack on the life-cycle theory of savings came from the direct examination of the wealth-age profile itself" (Kurz 1985).

The cross-section findings have stimulated research in the bequest motive for saving. Equation 2 shows that for given u_{t+h}, u_t would be larger with a bequest motive for saving than without a bequest motive because V_s is positive. Therefore, a bequest motive will flatten a rising path of marginal utility, and the bequest motive will flatten a falling consumption path. A flatter consumption path leads to a flatter wealth path, and, depending on the form of the bequest utility function and the initial conditions, wealth could increase with age (Hurd 1989). Of course, because wealth enters utility function 1, it follows almost directly that more wealth will be held.

As an empirical matter, however, closer examination of cross-section data shows that wealth does decline with age as required by the LCH. The earlier findings were misleading because the highest age category was 65 or over; when finer categories were used it became clear that in cross-section wealth declines. Furthermore, direct examination of wealth change in panel data has consistently found that the bequeathable wealth of retired individuals and couples falls over time (Hurd 1990).

Empirical Model of Consumption by Singles

A falling wealth path is consistent with both the LCH and the LCH augmented with a bequest motive. Further specification is required to separate the two hypotheses.

Utility Maximization by Singles

As before, suppose a retired individual maximizes in the consumption path (c_t) lifetime utility

$$\int_0^N u(c_t)e^{-\rho t}a_t dt + \int_0^N V(w_t)e^{-\rho t}m_t dt,$$

and let

$$u(c_t) = \frac{c_t^{1-\gamma}}{1-\gamma}.$$

In this widely used utility function, γ is a measure of risk aversion.

I parametrize the bequest function by assuming that the marginal utility of bequests is constant.[4] This assumption may be defended in several ways. First, in other work I found that the strength of the bequest motive did not seem to depend on the wealth level (Hurd 1987b). Second, variations in the level of wealth cause only small variations in the level of the wealth of the heirs; therefore, the marginal utility of wealth to the heirs will roughly be constant over variations in wealth of the older generation, so we would expect the marginal utility of bequests to be constant. Third, the observed variation within a family in actual bequests suggests that parents do not bequeath according to the economic status of their children: the rule is that all children receive the same bequest (Wilhelm 1991). Apparently the marginal utility of bequests from the point of view of the parents does not depend on the economic status of the children. This is consistent with a constant marginal utility of bequests. And fourth, from a practical point of view, without such an assumption the model cannot be solved; yet, the estimation requires a model solution.

The Pontryagin necessary conditions associated with this utility maximization problem are

$$c_t = A_t, \text{ if } w_t = 0,$$

and

$$c_t^{-\gamma} a_t = c_{t+h}^{-\gamma} a_{t+h} \, e^{h(r-\rho)} + \alpha \int_t^{t+h} e^{(s-t)(r-\rho)} m_s ds$$

over an interval $(t, t + h)$ in which $w_t > 0$. The constant marginal utility of bequests is α.

These first-order conditions do not determine the level of consumption, just the relationship between consumption at t and at $t + h$. The complete solution depends on the parameters, initial wealth and the annuity path. A typical solution is shown in figure 1.

Unless initial wealth is very large or annuities very small, bequeathable wealth is eventually consumed. T is the age at which bequeathable wealth reaches zero. Then the solution is given by

$$c_t = A_T, \, t \geq T; \tag{3.1}$$

$$c_0^{-\gamma} = c_t^{-\gamma} a_t e^{t(r-\rho)} + \alpha \int_0^t e^{(r-\rho)s} m_s ds, \, t < T; \tag{3.2}$$

---

4. A more complete discussion of the material in this section is in Hurd 1989.

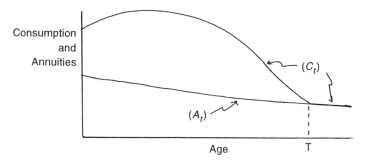

Fig. 1. Consumption path of a typical single

$$w_T = w_0 e^{rT} + \int_0^T (A_s - c_s) \, e^{(T-s)r} \, ds; \qquad (3.3)$$

$$w_T = 0. \qquad (3.4)$$

If initial wealth is very large, wealth will never go to zero, and the nature of the solution is different. Although these cases are taken care of in the estimation reported subsequently, I will not discuss them here because empirically they are not important.

In previous work I estimated the parameters of this model (Hurd 1989). Given the parameters, the model can be solved for the optimal consumption trajectory. The solution will depend on initial bequeathable wealth, the real annuity stream, the nominal annuity stream, actual mortality data, and the marginal utility of bequests.

In that the results depend on the parameter estimates of the model in equations 3.1–3.4, I outline the data and estimation methods on which they are based.

Estimation of a Model of Consumption by Singles

The data are from the Retirement History Survey (RHS), which was sponsored by the U.S. Social Security Administration. About 11,000 households whose heads were born in 1906–11 were interviewed every two years from 1969 through 1979. Detailed questions were asked about all assets (except for the cash value of life insurance), and the data were linked with official Social Security records, which permits an exact calculation of Social Security benefits. There are some data on consumption, but they are not complete, so I estimate the parameters of the model of singles over wealth data. Bequeathable wealth includes stocks and bonds, property, businesses, and savings accounts, all less debts. As suggested by King and Dicks-Mireaux (1982), I excluded housing wealth because the costs of adjusting housing consumption are substantial; therefore, people may not follow their desired housing consumption path. As long as the consumption of other goods follows its desired path, the parameters can be estimated over bequeathable wealth excluding housing wealth. Annuities include pensions, Social Security benefits, an estimated income value from Medicare and Medicaid, privately purchased annuities (which are very small), welfare transfers, and transfers from relatives. See Hurd and Shoven 1985 for a detailed description of the data.[5]

The estimation method is to use equations 3.1–3.4 to solve for the consumption path as a function of an initial choice of the parameter values. This requires numerical integration and a search for T, the age at which bequeathable wealth reaches zero. The solution will depend on initial wealth, the time paths of annuities and of mortality rates. Then wealth in the next survey, w_2, is predicted from the equation of motion of wealth, $dw_t/dt = rw_t - c_t + A_t$. Therefore, the necessary conditions and the boundary conditions, equations 3.1–3.4, implicitly define

$$w_2 = f[w_0, (A), (a), \theta],$$

in which w_0 is initial wealth, (A) is the annuity stream, (a) is the path of the probabilities of living, and θ is the parameter vector $(\gamma \rho \alpha)'$. The parameter space is searched to minimize a function of $(w_2 - f)$.

Although α is, in principle, identified through nonlinearities in the functional form, the identification is very weak, and entirely dependent on the validity of the assumed functional forms. Therefore, I specify that α is zero if a household has no living children.[6] The interpretation of α is the increase in the marginal utility of bequests across households according to whether or not they have living children.

Even casual study of the data suggests considerable observation error on wealth. Therefore, I estimate the parameters by nonlinear two-stage least squares (*NL2SLS*), in which the parameter estimates come from solving

$$\min_{\theta} \ [w_2 - f(\theta)]'X(X'X)^{-1} X'[w_2 - f(\theta)],$$

---

5. The RHS cannot be used to estimate total wealth holdings in the population because wealth entries are top-coded and because the very wealthy are not included in the sample. See Hurd 1990 for a discussion. Thus, the results here apply to the RHS sample, which will represent the behavior of the population except for the very wealthy.

6. The RHS has no information about the ages of the children, but almost all children would be in their 30s or early 40s, and will be living in their own households.

where w_2 and f are n-vectors of second period wealth and predicted second period wealth respectively and X is an $n \times 15$ matrix of observations on income from wealth; these data are not derived from the wealth data but come from separate questions in the RHS, so they should not be correlated with the observation errors in w.

The results from the *NL2SLS* are

γ	ρ	α
1.12	−0.011	6.0×10^{-7}
(.074)	(.002)	(32×10^{-7})

Number of observations = 5,452

The estimate of γ is much smaller than what has typically been assumed by other researchers. For example, Kotlikoff, Shoven, and Spivak (1987) and Kotlikoff and Spivak (1981) use a value of 4 in their simulations. Hubbard (1987) uses values of 0.75, 2, and 4, and Davies (1981) uses a range of values for his simulations with a best guess of 4. Large values of γ mean that the slope of the consumption trajectory is not sensitive to variations in mortality risk; my estimates imply that the consumption paths of the elderly will have substantial variation with mortality risk.

The marginal utility of bequests, α, is estimated to be very small, which is consistent with other estimates I have made in a model that is almost free of functional form restrictions.[7] The small estimate of α is caused by the fact that in the data there is little difference between the saving rates of households with children and households without children.

Model of Consumption by Couples

As with singles I assume that couples choose a consumption path (C_t) to maximize discounted expected lifetime utility, which may include utility from a bequest to the heirs of the couple.

Utility Maximization by Couples

Let the expected lifetime utility of a retired couple be given by

$$\int U(C_t)e^{-\rho t}a_t \, dt + \int M(C_t)e^{-\rho_m t}b_t \, dt + \int F(C_t)e^{-\rho_f t}f_t \, dt$$

$$+ \int V(w_t)e^{-\rho_b t}m_t \, dt. \tag{4}$$

---

7. See Hurd 1987b.

The first integral is the expected discounted utility of consumption by the household during the period when both spouses are alive. $U(\bullet)$ is the utility function of the couple; ρ is the subjective discount rate of the couple; and a_t is the probability that both spouses will be alive at t. The second integral gives the expected discounted utility of the widower following the wife's death. $M(\bullet)$ is the utility function of the widower. In general, we would not expect any relationship between U and M. The subjective discount rate of the widower is ρ_m and b_t is the probability that the widower only is alive at t. The third integral gives the expected discounted utility of the widow. $F(\bullet)$ is the utility function of the widow; ρ_f is the widow's discount rate; and f_t is the probability that the widow only is alive at t. The last integral is the utility the couples gets from contemplating leaving a bequest to its heirs. $V(\bullet)$ is the utility from bequests (here bequests refer to transfers following the death of the surviving spouse to someone outside the household, typically the couple's children). Bequeathable wealth is w_t at t; ρ_b is the subjective time rate of discount for bequests; and m_t is the probability (density) that the surviving spouse dies at t.

In this formulation assets transferred to the surviving spouse on the death of the other spouse are not bequests. The surviving spouse is simply the continuation of the household, and his or her welfare influences the consumption decisions of the couple through the second and third terms of the lifetime utility function of the household (eq. 4). Any desire to leave a true bequest influences consumption decisions through $V(\bullet)$ and through the consumption decisions the surviving spouse might make.

Suppose the couple maximizes expected lifetime utility (eq. 4) subject to the equation of motion of wealth

$$\frac{dw_t}{dt} = rw_t - C_t + A_t,$$

where r is the real rate of interest, assumed to be fixed and known, and A_t is annuities, including Social Security and other pensions. Other restrictions on the maximization are that initial bequeathable wealth, w_0, is given and that bequeathable wealth must be nonnegative. The nonnegativity condition means that the couple cannot die in debt.

The solution to the utility maximization problem at $t = 0$ when all couples are alive ($a_0 = 1$) satisfies the equation of motion of marginal utility,

$$\frac{dU_t}{dt} = U_t(h_t + \rho - r) - (M_t\phi_t + F_t\mu_t), \tag{5}$$

in which U_t is marginal utility; h_t is the couple's mortality risk (the probability density that one of them will die at t given that neither has died before t); M_t is the marginal utility of consumption by the widower; and F_t is the marginal utility of consumption by the widow. The mortality risk of the wife is ϕ_t and μ_t is the mortality risk of the husband. If the surviving spouse optimizes his or her lifetime utility, M_t will be put equal to the marginal utility of wealth by the widower and F_t will be put equal to the marginal utility of wealth by the widow.

The last term in equation 5 is composed of two parts: the marginal utility of the widower times the probability he becomes a widower (the wife dies), and the marginal utility of the widow times the probability she becomes a widow (the husband dies). Therefore, the last term is the expected marginal utility of the household in the event that one or the other of the spouses dies. This solution is similar to the solution of the single person's utility maximization problem. For example the equation of motion of marginal utility of the surviving widow is

$$\frac{du_t}{dt} = u_t(\phi_t + \rho_f - r) - \phi_t V_t.$$

V_t is the marginal utility of a bequest and ϕ_t is the probability (density) that the widow will die at t and leave the bequest. $\phi_t V_t$ corresponds to the last term of equation 5. In the case of the couple, the wealth goes to the surviving spouse; in the case of the widow, the wealth goes to the heir.

Because of time separability of utility, the couple maximizes equation 4 starting from any arbitrary date. That is, as long as the couple is alive, we can make $t = 0$ and solve the utility maximization problem forward from that date.

At a later time t, both spouses are alive, the husband only is alive, the wife only is alive, or both have died, so the probabilities of these outcomes must sum 1. That is,

$$a_t = 1 - b_t - f_t - \int_0^t m_s ds.$$

If t becomes small the probability that both will die between 0 and t goes to zero. Therefore, in a small interval of time a bequest takes place through the surviving spouse, not through the simultaneous deaths of both spouses: one spouse must die in order that the probability the other spouse will die and leave a bequest becomes positive. Typical trajectories of the probabilities a_t, b_t, f_t and the density m_t are shown in figure 2.

The relationship between h_t, ϕ_t, and μ_t can be found as follows. Let h_{t0} be the probability density that one spouse or the other or both die at t given that both are alive at $t = 0$. Thus,

$$a_t = 1 - \int_0^t h_{s0} ds.$$

Let ϕ_{t0} be the mortality risk of all females alive at $t = 0$, and μ_{t0} the mortality risk of males. Then

$$h_{t0} = -\frac{da_t}{dt} = \frac{db_t}{dt} + \frac{df_t}{dt} + m_t.$$

Under the assumption that the mortality risk of the husband and of the wife are independent, the probability that the husband only is alive at t is given by

$$b_t = \int_0^t \phi_{s0} \, ds \left(1 - \int_0^t \mu_{s0} \, ds \right).$$

Similarly,

$$f_t = \int_0^t \mu_{s0} \, ds \left(1 - \int_0^t \phi_{s0} \, ds \right).$$

Then,

$$\frac{db_t}{dt} = \phi_{t0} \left[1 - \int_0^t \mu_{s0} \, ds \right] - \mu_{t0} \int_0^t \phi_{s0} ds \to \phi_0 \text{ as } t \to 0.$$

This says that the rate of flow of husbands to widowers is given by the mortality risk of wives.

In a similar way

$$\frac{df_t}{dt} \to \mu_0.$$

Then,

$$m_t = \mu_t b_t + \phi_t f_t \to 0 \text{ as } t \to 0 \text{ because } b_t \text{ and } f_t \to 0.$$

Finally, $h_{t0} \to \phi_0 + \mu_0$ as $t \to 0$.

In equation 5, $h_t + \rho$ will be larger than r if the couple is sufficiently old because both ϕ_t and μ_t increase approximately exponentially. Therefore, in

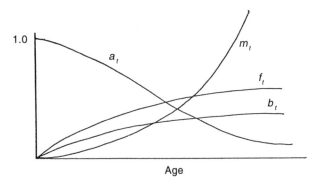

Fig. 2. Probabilities of living and mortality rates

the absence of the second term in equation 5, U_t would be increasing. The second term flattens the path of U_t and could even cause it to fall. Thus, with the usual assumption that $U(\bullet)$ is concave, the second term flattens the path of consumption, which would otherwise be declining, and could even cause the path to rise. This "bequest" motive (to leave wealth to the surviving spouse) has the same effect on the consumption path of a couple as it does on the consumption path of a single person. Beyond the fact that the consumption path is flattened, the path of marginal utility is not easy to analyze because neither M_t nor F_t could be expected to be constant as bequeathable wealth varies.

The equation of motion of marginal utility (eq. 5) can be integrated over a small interval $(0, t)$ to give

$$U_0 \approx U_t a_t e^{(\rho - r)t} + \int_0^t M_s \phi_s e^{(r - \rho_m)s}\, ds + \int_0^t F_s \mu_s e^{(r - \rho_f)s}\, ds. \qquad (6)$$

The interpretation of this equation is that the reallocation of consumption from $t = 0$ to t will result in a loss of utility at $t = 0$ of U_0. The offsetting gain is composed of three parts: the discounted increase in utility should the couple live, the discounted increase in utility should the wife die between 0 and t, and the discounted increase in utility should the husband die between 0 and t. The approximation ignores a second-order term, which is the utility from bequests should both spouses die between 0 and t, but this term goes to zero as t goes to zero much faster than the other three terms because the probability density goes to zero. Thus, the first-order conditions imply a Euler condition: marginal utility at $t = 0$ equals the expected discounted marginal utility in all future periods.

The true bequest motive (bequeathing to heirs outside of the household) operates through M_s and F_s: a bequest motive will increase the marginal utility of wealth of both the widower and the widow. This increases the right-hand side of equation 6, which requires that U_0 be increased. That, in turn, requires that C_0 be decreased with the result that more wealth will be held. Thus, the effect of a true bequest motive on a couple is the same as on a single: consumption will be lower and wealth higher.

Empirical Model of Consumption by a Couple

Estimation of a model of consumption by couples is work in progress. For this paper I estimate consumption by couples from the equation of motion of wealth:

$$C_t = -\frac{dw_t}{dt} + A_t + rw_t.$$

In the RHS the average rate of decumulation of nonhousing bequeathable wealth was 1.85 percent per year over couples with positive wealth (Hurd 1987b). Because the costs of moving are high, this may also be a good estimate of the desired rate of decumulation of housing wealth. Therefore, following the suggestion of King and Dicks-Mireaux (1982), I use this rate of dissaving to approximate the desired rate of dissaving of the total of housing and nonhousing bequeathable wealth. Then, from observed A_t and an assumed real rate of interest, r, of 0.03 I calculate C_t.

As with singles the identification of a bequest motive for saving by couples comes from the difference in the saving rates of parents and of nonparents. However, I found that the rate of dissaving by couples is, if anything, larger among parents than among nonparents, which gives no support for a bequest motive as an important determinant of saving behavior (Hurd 1987b). Therefore, in this paper I take the rate of dissaving to be the same for parents and nonparents.

This assumption can be justified in another way. According to the model for couples, any true bequest motive enters the consumption decision of couples through its effect on the marginal utility of wealth of widowers, M_t, and of widows, F_t. At the optimal consumption level of widowers, $M_t = C_{th}^{-\gamma}$, and similarly of widows. A bequest motive influences both the level and slope of the consumption paths of widowers and of widows as in equations 3.1–3.4. In particular, a bequest motive will decrease initial consumption and hence increase (algebraically) the rate of change of wealth. However, in previous work I found that whether a single person had a child did not influence his or her rate of wealth decumulation or rate of consumption (Hurd 1987b, 1989). Therefore, children should not influence the rate of wealth decumulation of couples or their rate of consumption. Indeed, in the RHS neither the rate of wealth decumulation nor the rate of consumption by couples is influenced by whether or not the couple has children (Hurd 1992).

Desired Bequests

By 1979 the respondents in the RHS were aged 68 to 74. Actual and desired bequests are found from forecasts of their future consumption and wealth paths. The calculations accumulate income and consumption as long as a couple or single survives. Standard life tables give the survival probabilities.

Every time period each couple could generate one of three types of households: the couple could survive, the husband could die leaving a widow, or the wife could die leaving a widower. The probabilities of each of these outcomes can be calculated from life tables, and the probabilities used to weight each of the outcomes, thus producing expected values of the number of households, wealth, consumption and income. An alternative to probability weighting is to use Monte Carlo methods. Each time period a random number is drawn that takes either the value 1 with probability $1 - h_t$ or 0 with probability h_t, where h_t is the probability that at least one of the spouses dies. If the random number is 1 the couple continues, and its income and consumption are accumulated. If the random number is 0, further drawings are made to determine whether the wife or the husband is the survivor. The fraction of the households that continue will on average be the same as the fraction calculated by probability weighting, and the average levels of consumption, income, and wealth will be the same.

New widows and widowers have initial conditions that are related to the wealth and annuities of the couples from which they came. Specifically, the widow or widower inherits the bequeathable wealth of the couple. I assume that nominal annuities are in the husband's name, and that the annuities have no survivorship benefits, so that a widower, but not a widow, inherits them. In almost all of the households in the RHS, human capital, which is the present discounted value of future earnings, belongs to the husband; therefore, I assume it is lost if he dies. I also assume that the widow's Social Security benefit, which is based on the earnings of her deceased husband, is larger than the benefit based on her own earnings, so that the widow receives two-thirds of the couple's benefit.

Following the death of a spouse, new singles join the pool of all singles, and their consumption, income, and wealth are forecast from the consumption model of singles as discussed in the third section. The income and consumption of singles are accumulated as long as the single is alive. Single males and single females are dropped from the sample of singles each period with probabilities μ_t and ϕ_t and any bequeathable wealth becomes a bequest.

Expected Consumption and Bequests

There is no general agreement on whether or not the elderly decumulate housing wealth in the way they seem to decumulate nonhousing bequeathable wealth. Therefore, I have two sets of results. In the first set, housing wealth and other bequeathable wealth are aggregated, which means that housing wealth is treated in exactly the same way as nonhousing bequeathable wealth. In the second set of results, I assume that housing wealth does not change with age: whatever housing wealth a single or couple has is eventually passed on to an heir or to the survivor.

Consumption and Bequests Based on Housing Wealth Decumulation

Table 1 shows average resources available to the couples in the 1979 RHS (2,415 couples) and the uses of those resources. The entries are expected present values in 1979 dollars; they are found by averaging over surviving households and discounting at an interest rate of 3 percent. Because the entries are based on the totals over all households they tend to be dominated by the behavior of the most wealthy households.

In 1979 at the beginning of the simulations couples had $46.7 thousand of nonhousing bequeathable wealth and $40.8 thousand of housing wealth. Annuity-type resources (Social Security, Medicare and Medicaid, and other annuities) totaled $74.6 thousand in expected present value. Human capital, which is the expected present value of future earnings, averaged $3.0 thou-

TABLE 1. Sources and Uses of Resouces: Couples, Housing Decumulation, in Thousands of 1979 Dollars

Resources		Uses of Resources	
Nonhousing bequeathable		Nonhousing bequeathable	
wealth	46.7	wealth to survivor	29.1
Housing wealth	40.8	Housing wealth to survivor	25.1
Human capital	3.0	Human capital to survivor	0.6
Social Security	41.2	Human capital lost	1.4
Medicare and Medicaid	14.6	Nonhousing consumption	96.3
Annuities	18.8	Housing consumption	8.4
		Bequests (53 percent housing)	4.0
		Terminal wealth	0.2
Total	165.1	Total	165.1

Source: Author's calculations from RHS.

sand.[8] Average total resources were $165.1 thousand, so that annuity-type resources were 45 percent of the total.

Couples consumed a total of $104.7 thousand of which $96.3 thousand was nonhousing consumption and $8.4 thousand was consumption of housing services. Housing consumption is the discounted flow of housing services that are measured as the real rate of interest (3 percent) times housing wealth. About 72 percent of total consumption came from annuity flows. Thirteen couples survived to the year 2003, and terminal wealth is the wealth held by those couples in 2003.

At the death of one spouse, the survivor received $29.1 thousand in nonhousing wealth, $25.1 thousand in housing wealth, and $0.6 thousand in human capital. Along with annuity flows, these became the initial conditions for new widows and widowers. Because this model is a discrete-time approximation to a continuous time model, both the husband and wife can die during a two-year interval with positive probability and make a true bequest. There were $4.0 thousand in true bequests. Housing wealth comprised 53 percent of these bequests.

During the 24 years of the simulations, couples lived an average of 8.33 years. Therefore, their annual average consumption was $12.1 thousand in 1979 dollars or $22.5 thousand in 1991 dollars. This seems low, especially because it includes an income and consumption value to Medicare and Medicaid. However, official government income measures such as those from the current population reports are nominal measures: they measure nominal income from capital whereas these calculations measure real income from capital at a rate of 3 percent. When the rate of inflation is high, as it was in 1979, the difference is substantial.

In these simulations I assumed that human capital is lost at the death of the husband, and the results show that lost human capital amounted to $1.4 thousand. However, most of the human capital was probably insured by life insurance: in the 1979 RHS on average couples held $9.4 thousand of life insurance. I have calculated the net premium reserve of this insurance, which is a measure of its cash value, to be $5.9 thousand, implying that the insurance part was $3.5 thousand (Hurd 1991). This is very close to estimated human capital (the stream of future earnings to be insured) of $3.0 thousand. Therefore, an alternative assumption, which is not followed here, would have been that at least part of the human capital lost at the death of the husband was recovered by the widow.

---

8. To calculate human capital, I first assumed that anyone with observed earnings in 1979 would have constant real earnings should he or she continue to work. Second, I calculated the probability that he or she would continue to work from observed labor force participation rates by age and from mortality rates. Then human capital is the discounted expected sum of annual future earnings.

Table 2 has results for singles under the assumption of no bequest motive for saving; that is, in the forecasts of the consumption paths of singles, I put α = 0 (see eq. 3.2). Table 2 has averages over all singles that ever lived: 3,174 singles in the 1979 RHS (original singles) and 2,214 widows or widowers after 1979 (new singles). The singles had average initial nonhousing bequeathable wealth of $24.0 thousand. This was composed of $18.7 thousand per original single and $31.7 thousand per new single. Thus the new singles were considerably better off than original singles. Initial housing wealth averaged $23.0 thousand, $19.9 thousand per original single, and $27.3 thousand per new single. Total resources were $92.5 thousand.

The singles had nonhousing consumption of $75.8 thousand of which $8.4 thousand was Medicare and Medicaid. Bequests were $11.8 thousand, which is about 25.1 percent of the total of bequeathable nonhousing and housing wealth. Forty-seven percent of bequests were housing wealth. Terminal wealth is wealth held by the singles who survived to 2003. There were 728 such singles with an average age of about 93; according to the forecasts the 728 singles held on average about $3.0 thousand, which is just $.4 thousand averaged over the complete sample of singles.

The results in tables 1 and 2 are based on the assumption that no one has a bequest motive for saving. The results in table 3 are based on the assumption that everyone has a bequest motive as measured by $\alpha = 6 \times 10^{-7}$ (see eq. 3.2); said differently, the first results were based on the implicit assumption that no one has a child; the second results are based on the implicit assumption that everyone has a child. Because a bequest motive does not alter the behavior of couples, no additional results need to be given for couples. Table 3 has the results for singles.

To see the effect of the bequest motive as measured here, compare tables 2 and 3. Resources are the same because the bequest motive affects neither

TABLE 2. Sources and Uses of Resources: Singles, Housing Decumulation, No Bequest Motive, in Thousands of 1979 Dollars

Resources		Uses of Resources	
Nonhousing bequeathable wealth	24.0	Human capital lost	0.2
Housing wealth	23.0	Nonhousing consumption	75.8
Human capital	0.8	Housing consumption	4.3
Social Security	25.5	Bequests (47 percent housing)	11.8
Medicare and Medicaid	8.4	Terminal wealth	0.4
Annuities	10.9		
Total	92.5	Total	92.5

Source: Author's calculations from RHS.

TABLE 3. Sources and Uses of Resources: Singles, Housing Decumulation, Bequest Motive, in Thousands of 1979 Dollars

Resources		Uses of Resources	
Nonhousing bequeathable wealth	24.0	Human capital lost	0.2
Housing wealth	23.0	Nonhousing consumption	75.5
Human capital	0.8	Housing consumption	4.4
Social Security	25.5	Bequests (47 percent housing)	12.1
Medicare and Medicaid	8.4	Terminal wealth	0.4
Annuities	10.9		
Total	92.5	Total	92.5

Source: Author's calculations from RHS.

initial conditions nor the behavior of couples. Therefore, resources of both original and new singles will not change if either singles or couples have a bequest motive.

The bequest motive causes slightly more wealth to be held so that housing consumption, which is proportional to housing wealth, increases by $0.1 thousand. Nonhousing consumption, which is partly financed by wealth decumulation, falls by $0.8 thousand. Bequests per single household increase marginally from $11.8 thousand to $12.1 thousand. The effects of the bequest motive are small because α is small.

To get an idea of the sensitivity of the results to α, table 4 has results for a "strong" bequest motive: I use $\alpha^* = \alpha + \hat{\sigma}(\hat{\alpha})$ in the simulations where $\hat{\sigma}(\hat{\alpha})$ is the estimated standard error of $\hat{\alpha}$. $\alpha^* = 6 \times 10^{-7} + 32 \times 10^{-7} = 38 \times 10^{-7}$, which increase the strength of the bequest motive by a factor of 6 and $^1/_3$. Table 4 should be compared with table 2.

TABLE 4. Sources and Uses of Resources: Singles, Housing Decumulation, Strong Bequest Motive, in Thousands of 1979 Dollars

Resources		Uses of Resources	
Nonhousing bequeathable wealth	24.0	Human capital lost	0.2
Housing wealth	23.0	Nonhousing consumption	73.3
Human capital	0.8	Housing consumption	4.6
Social Security	25.5	Bequests (47 percent housing)	13.8
Medicare and Medicaid	8.4	Terminal wealth	0.6
Annuities	10.9		
Total	92.5	Total	92.5

Source: Author's calculations from RHS.

Consumption excluding Medicare and Medicaid decreases from $71.7 thousand to $69.5 thousand, a decrease of about 3 percent. Because more wealth is held, bequests increase by about 17 percent. Even taking this increase in bequests ($2.0 thousand) as a measure of desired bequests, it represents just 4 percent of the sum of initial housing and nonhousing bequeathable wealth.

Consumption and Bequests Based on No Housing Wealth Decumulation

In a second set of results I assume that housing wealth does not change. For couples this simply means that, as before, nonhousing bequeathable wealth declines by 1.85 percent per year; but, now, housing wealth does not change. Nonhousing consumption is the sum of income and the change in total bequeathable wealth, and, therefore, it should be less. Housing consumption is, as before, the imputed income from housing wealth, but because more housing wealth is held it should be greater.

To represent constant housing wealth in the consumption decisions of singles I enter the consumption flow from housing as part of real annuities. This has two effects that I have discussed in prior research (Hurd 1987a): because bequeathable wealth is smaller by the amount of housing wealth, the rate of wealth decumulation will increase; and because real annuities increase, the rate of wealth decumulation will increase further.

Table 5 has the results for couples. The sources of resources are the same as in table 1. The uses change in a predictable way: the surviving spouse receives more housing wealth; the couple has less nonhousing consumption

TABLE 5. Sources and Uses of Resources: Couples, No Housing Decumulation, in Thousands of 1979 Dollars

Resources		Uses of Resources	
Nonhousing bequeathable wealth	46.7	Nonhousing bequeathable	
Housing wealth	40.8	wealth to survivor	29.1
Human capital	3.0	Housing wealth to survivor	29.0
Social Security	41.2	Human capital to survivor	0.6
Medicare and Medicaid	14.6	Human capital lost	1.4
Annuities	18.8	Nonhousing consumption	91.3
		Housing consumption	9.1
		Bequests (57 percent housing)	4.4
		Terminal wealth	0.2
Total	165.1	Total	165.1

Source: Author's calculations from RHS.

because housing wealth is not used to finance nonhousing consumption; the couple has more housing consumption; true bequests rise and a greater percentage of bequests are in housing wealth (57 percent).

The results for singles in table 6 should be compared with those in table 2. The differences are substantial. Singles have more resources because of the increase in housing wealth of new singles, but the largest differences are in uses of resources. Nonhousing consumption is much less: for example, nonhousing consumption excluding Medicare and Medicaid falls from $67.4 thousand to $55.3 thousand, a decline of 18 percent. Housing consumption increases but total consumption excluding Medicare and Medicaid falls by 12 percent. The increase in initial resources and the decline in consumption means that more wealth is held, and therefore, more wealth is bequeathed: bequests almost double. They become 44 percent of the total of initial housing and nonhousing bequeathable wealth and 23 percent of total resources. Because nonhousing bequeathable wealth declines faster than in table 2, the percentage of bequests in the form of housing wealth increases to 74 percent.

Table 7 has results based on a bequest motive. They are little different from the results in table 6. Table 8 has results based on a strong bequest motive ($\alpha = 38 \times 10^{-7}$). Bequests are only $1.1 thousand or 5 percent greater than in table 6 (no bequest motive, no housing decumulation). In the earlier tables based on housing wealth decumulation the effect of a strong bequest motive was greater. The difference is that, when there is no change in housing wealth, less wealth is affected by a bequest motive.

Overall Effects of the Bequest Motive

Tables 1 through 8 count some households twice because the new singles are actually the survivors of couples. An overall assessment of the magnitude of

TABLE 6.   Sources and Uses of Resources: Singles, No Housing Decumulation, No Bequest Motive, in Thousands of 1979 Dollars

Resources		Uses of Resources	
Nonhousing bequeathable wealth	24.0	Human capital lost	0.2
Housing wealth	24.7	Nonhousing consumption	63.7
Human capital	0.8	Housing consumption	6.9
Social Security	25.5	Bequests (74 percent housing)	21.2
Medicare and Medicaid	8.4	Terminal wealth	2.3
Annuities	10.9		
Total	94.3	Total	94.3

Source: Author's calculations from RHS.

TABLE 7. Sources and Uses of Resources: Singles, No Housing Decumulation, Bequest Motive, in Thousands of 1979 Dollars

Resources		Uses of Resources	
Nonhousing bequeathable wealth	24.0	Human capital lost	0.2
Housing wealth	24.7	Nonhousing consumption	63.5
Human capital	0.8	Housing consumption	6.9
Social Security	25.5	Bequests (73 percent housing)	21.3
Medicare and Medicaid	8.4	Terminal wealth	2.3
Annuities	10.9		
Total	94.3	Total	94.3

Source: Author's calculations from RHS.

bequests and the effects of the bequest motive require that the tables be combined. The aim is to find average resources per original 1979 RHS household and average bequests from those resources. A couple, for example, should contemplate a multistage process: consume while both spouses are alive; transfer assets to a surviving spouse; consumption by the surviving spouse; and eventually bequeath to an heir. The effects of a bequest motive can be seen in the ratio of eventual bequests to initial bequeathable wealth including housing wealth.

Table 9 shows average bequests per original household. It includes bequests directly from a couple to an heir, which happens when both spouses die within two years, and those from the surviving spouse to the heir. With housing decumulation and no bequest motive, average bequests per original household are $13.2 thousand; this increases to $15.1 thousand with a strong bequest motive. These are rather substantial fractions of the total of nonhous-

TABLE 8. Sources and Uses of Resources: Singles, No Housing Decumulation, Strong Bequest Motive, in Thousands of 1979 Dollars

Resources		Uses of Resources	
Nonhousing bequeathable wealth	24.0	Human capital lost	0.2
Housing wealth	24.7	Nonhousing consumption	62.4
Human capital	0.8	Housing consumption	6.9
Social Security	25.5	Bequests (70 percent housing)	22.3
Medicare and Medicaid	8.4	Terminal wealth	2.4
Annuities	10.9		
Total	94.3	Total	94.3

Source: Author's calculations from RHS.

ing and housing bequeathable wealth: 22.0 percent and 25.2 percent. If households do not decumulate housing wealth, the level of bequests is considerably greater: $22.4 thousand with no bequest motive rising to $23.5 thousand with a strong bequest motive. Bequest are 37.5 percent and 39.5 percent of total bequeathable wealth.

It is clear from table 9 that, as modeled here, the important determinant of the magnitude of bequests is not the strength of the bequest motive but whether housing wealth is decumulated to finance nonhousing consumption. We need a better understanding of the determinants of housing choice before we can have a more accurate understanding of the determinants and magnitude of bequests by households.

Conclusion

I used the difference in the rates of wealth decumulation by parents and by nonparents to measure desired bequests. Without this or a similar kind of specification, desired bequests cannot be separated from accidental bequests. Because in the RHS there is little difference in the rates of wealth decumulation by parents and by nonparents, the estimate of the marginal utility of bequests in the behavioral model of consumption by singles was small. Therefore, estimates of desired bequests based on forecasts over the population of couples and singles produced small measures of desired bequests. Total bequests are a substantial fraction of initial total bequeathable wealth, but they are almost completely accidental bequests, the result of uncertainty about the date of death.

It should be noted that the simulations in this paper are based on a rather small estimate of the risk aversion parameter ($\gamma = 1.12$) compared to what has

TABLE 9.   **Bequests per Household and the Fraction of Wealth Bequeathed**

	Housing Decumulation		No Housing Decumulation	
	Average Bequests[a]	Fraction[b]	Average Bequests[a]	Fraction[b]
No bequest motive	13.2	.220	22.4	.375
Bequest motive	13.4	.226	22.5	.377
Strong bequest motive	15.1	.252	23.5	.393

Memorandum: Bequeathable wealth per original household
Couples: 87.5   Singles: 38.6   All: 59.7

Source: Author's calculations from RHS.
[a] Thousands of dollars in 1979 dollars.
[b] Fraction of total bequeathable wealth.

been assumed in the literature.[9] As large as bequests are in this model, they would be even larger if I were to use larger values of risk aversion: greater risk aversion would cause the consumption path to flatten which, in turn, would cause more wealth to be held. Hence, bequests would be greater.

The most important determinant of bequests in this paper is whether or not households decumulate housing wealth. Further research is needed on this important question.

REFERENCES

Barro, Robert J. 1974. "Are Government Bonds Net Wealth." *Journal of Political Economy* 82:1095–1117.
Bernheim, Douglas B. 1987. "Dissaving after Retirement: Testing the Pure Life Cycle Hypothesis." In *Issues in Pension Economics,* ed. Zvi Bodie, John B. Shoven, and David A. Wise, 237–74. Chicago: University of Chicago Press.
Blinder, Alan S., Roger H. Gordon, and Donald E. Wise. 1983. "Social Security, Bequests and the Life Cycle Theory of Saving: Cross-Sectional Tests." In *Income Distribution and Economic Inequality,* ed. Zvi Grilliches. New York: Halstead Press.
Danziger, Sheldon, Jacques van der Gaag, Eugene Smolensky, and Michael Taussig. 1982. "The Life Cycle Hypothesis and the Consumption Behavior of the Elderly." *Journal of Post Keynesian Economics* 5 (2): 208–27.
Darby, Michael R. 1979. *Effects of Social Security on Income and the Capital Stock.* Washington, D.C.: American Enterprise Institute.
Davies, James. 1981. "Uncertain Lifetime, Consumption and Dissaving in Retirement." *Journal of Political Economy* 86:561–77.
Friedman, Benjamin M., and Warshawsky, Mark. 1988. "Annuity Prices and Saving Behavior in the United States." In *Pensions in the U.S. Economy,* ed. Zvi Bodie, John B. Shoven, and David A. Wise, 55–77. Chicago: University of Chicago Press.
Hubbard, R. Glen. 1987. "Uncertain Lifetimes, Pensions and Individual Saving." In *Issues in Pension Economics,* ed. Zvi Bodie, John B. Shoven, and David A. Wise, 175–206. Chicago: University of Chicago Press.
Hurd, Michael D. 1987a. "The Marginal Value of Social Security." NBER Working Paper, no. 2411. Cambridge: National Bureau of Economic Research.
———. 1987b. "Savings of the Elderly and Desired Bequests." *American Economic Review* 77, no. 3: 298–312.
———. 1989. "Mortality Risk and Bequests." *Econometrica* 57 (4):779–813.
———. 1990. "Research on the Elderly: Economic Status, Retirement, and Consumption & Saving." *Journal of Economic Literature* 28 (June): 565–637.
———. 1991. "The Income and Savings of the Elderly." Department of Economics, State University of New York, Stony Brook. Typescript.

---

9. See the discussion in the section entitled "Estimation of a Model of Consumption by Singles."

———. 1992. "Wealth Depletion and Life-Cycle Consumption by the Elderly." In *Topics in the Economics of Aging,* ed. David Wise, 135–60. Chicago: University of Chicago Press.

Hurd, Michael D., and John B. Shoven. 1985. "Inflation Vulnerability, Income, and Wealth of the Elderly, 1969–1979." In *Horizontal Equity, Uncertainty, and Economic Well-Being,* ed. Martin David and Timothy Smeeding, 125–72. Chicago: University of Chicago Press.

King, Mervyn, and L. Dicks-Mireaux. 1982. "Asset Holdings and the Life-Cycle." *Economic Journal* 92 (June): 247–67.

Kotlikoff, Laurence J. 1988. "Intergenerational Transfers and Savings." *Journal of Economic Perspectives* 2 (2):41–59.

Kotlikoff, Laurence J., John B. Shoven, and Avia Spivak. 1987. "Annuity Markets, Savings, and the Capital Stock." In *Issues in Pension Economics,* ed. Zvi Bodie, John B. Shoven, and David A. Wise, 211–34. Chicago: University of Chicago Press.

Kotlikoff, Laurence J., and Avia Spivak. 1981. "The Family as an Incomplete Annuities Market." *Journal of Political Economy* 89 (April): 372–91.

Kotlikoff, Laurence J., and Lawrence Summers. 1981. "The Role of Intergenerational Transfers in Aggregate Capital Accumulation." *Journal of Political Economy* 89:706–32.

———. 1988. "The Contribution of Intergenerational Transfers to Total Wealth: A Reply." In *Modelling the Accumulation and Distribution of Wealth,* ed. Denis Kessler and Andre Masson, 53–67. New York: Oxford University Press.

Kurz, Mordecai. 1985. "Heterogeneity in Savings Behavior: A Comment." In *Frontiers of Economics,* ed. K. Arrow and S. Harkapohja, 307–27. Oxford: Basil Blackwell.

Lydall, Harold. 1955. "The Life Cycle, Income, Saving, and Asset Ownership." *Econometrica* 23:985–1012.

Menchik, Paul L., and Martin David. 1983. "Income Distribution, Lifetime Savings, and Bequests." *American Economic Review* 73, no. 4: 672–90.

Mirer, Thad. 1979. "The Wealth-Age Relation Among the Aged." *American Economic Review* 69:435–43.

Modigliani, Franco. 1986. "Life Cycle, Individual Thrift, and the Wealth of Nations." *American Economic Review* 76 (3): 297–313.

———. 1988. "The Role of Intergenerational Transfers and Life Cycle Saving in the Accumulation of Wealth." *Journal of Economic Perspectives* 2 (2):15–40.

Projector, Dorothy, and Gertrude Weiss. 1966. *Survey of Financial Characteristics of Consumers.* Washington, D.C.: Board of Governors, Federal Reserve Board.

White, Betsy Buttrill. 1978. "Empirical Tests of the Life-Cycle Hypothesis." *American Economic Review* 68(4):547–60.

Wilhelm, Mark. 1991. "Bequest Behavior and the Effect of Heirs' Earnings: Testing the Altruistic Model of Bequests." Department of Economics, Pennsylvania State University. Typescript.

Yaari, Menahem E. 1965. "Uncertain Lifetime, Life Insurance and the Theory of the Consumer." *Review of Economic Studies* 32:137–50.

CHAPTER 6

Bequests, Fiscal Policy, and Social Security

Toshihiro Ihori

Bequests appear to be relatively prevalent in Japan. A number of studies have applied the methodology of Kotlikoff and Summers (1981) to the case of Japan in order to estimate the shares of life-cycle and transfer wealth (wealth deriving from intergenerational transfers). As summarized in table 1, the share of transfer wealth in Japan appears to be roughly comparable to the corresponding figures for the United States.

There are several theoretical models of bequeathing behavior that have appeared in the literature. One is the altruistic bequest model, where the offspring's indirect utility function enters the parent's utility function as a separate argument. Another is the bequest-as-consumption model, where the bequest itself enters the parent's utility function as a separate argument. Yet another is the bequest-as-exchange model, where the parent gives a bequest to the offspring in exchange for a desirable action undertaken by the offspring. Finally, there is the accidental bequest model, where a parent may leave an unintended bequest to the offspring because lifetime is uncertain and annuities are not priced in an actuarially fair way.

Barro (1974) and Becker (1974) first studied the altruism model. For the bequest-as-consumption model, see in particular Yaari 1964, Becker 1981, Menchik and David 1982, Seidman 1983, and Gravelle 1991. Bernheim, Shleifer, and Summers (1985) proposed the bequest-as-exchange model. Also, considerable work has been done on the accidental bequest model. The altruistic model implies that households can be represented dynastically, as though they would live infinitely. Other bequest models mean that a household's behavior can be described by the life-cycle framework where overlapping generations are concerned with a finite number of periods.

Several empirical studies (see specifically Dekle 1990 and Ohtake 1991)

Presented at the IPTP International Conference on Savings and Bequests held on March 17 and 18, 1992. I thank Tadashi Yagi, Pierre Pestieau, and the participants at the conference for their useful comments on an earlier version of this paper.

137

also shed light on the nature of the bequest motive in Japan. These findings suggest intended bequests. Hayashi (1986) concluded that bequests are the main cause of Japan's high saving rate and that the altruism model may be appropriate. On the other hand, Horioka (1991) pointed out that the bulk of these bequests appear to be unintended or accidental bequests, all of which are consistent with the life-cycle model. Whether the dynasty model or the life-cycle model has greater applicability to the case of Japan is an unsettled issue.

The organization of this essay is as follows. The next section investigates the normative effects of government spending in the case where altruistic bequests are operative and, hence, debt neutrality holds. When we follow the altruistic model, the financing method operating between current taxation and debt issuance is irrelevant. In such a case, the only meaningful fiscal policy is to change the level of public spending. The intention here is to explore the normative aspects of the size of public spending.

The third section studies the effect of bequest taxes on capital accumulation when intentional bequests exist. This section employs the altruistic bequest model, bequest-as-consumption model, and bequest-as-exchange model, and intends to explore the negative effect of bequest taxes on capital formation. The section delves into the possible trade-off relationship between efficiency and equity with respect to bequest taxes.

In the fourth section the effect of fiscal policy on economic growth when intergenerational transfers are crucial is assessed. This section in particular considers the effect of social security programs on the growth rate. The

TABLE 1. Estimates of the Share of Transfer Wealth

Author(s) of Study	Year	Share of Transfer Wealth
	Japan	
Campell	1974–84	At most 28.1
Dekle	1968–83	3–27
Hayashi	1969–74	At least 9.6
Barthold and Ito		At least 27.7–41.4
Dekle	1983	At most 48.7
	The United States	
Ando and Kennickell	1960–80	15.0–41.2
Kotlikoff and Summers	1974	20–67
Barthold and Ito		At least 25
Menchik and David	1946–64	18.5
Projector and Weiss		15.5
Barlow et al.	1964	14.3–20.0
Morgan et al.		Less than 10

Source: Horioka 1991.

section provides valuable understanding of the possible crowding-out effect of social security.

Finally, a conclusion is offered.

Fiscal Policy and the Optimal Size of Government Spending

Altruistic Bequests and Debt Neutrality

The effects of fiscal policy on private consumption and aggregate demand have stimulated a considerable amount of research since Barro's revival of the "Ricardian neutrality" proposition (1974). It is now well known that if the altruistic bequests are fully operative, to a first approximation, the choice between current taxation and debt issuance to finance a given government expenditure stream is irrelevant to the determination of the level of aggregate demand. Kormendi (1983) obtained empirical results for the U.S. economy favorable to that proposition, while Feldstein (1982) rejected Ricardian neutrality. In place of the conventional consumption function methodology, Aschauer (1985) presented an alternative approach that exploits restrictions placed on the data by the first-order necessary conditions for intertemporal optimization in consumption. His empirical evidence is supportive of the joint hypothesis of rational expectations and Ricardian neutrality for the U.S. economy. Homma et al. (1986) provided evidence that the more recent data are more consistent with Ricardian neutrality for the Japanese economy.

In this section normative implications of fiscal spending are investigated in the case where altruistic bequests are operative and, hence, debt neutrality holds. Note that in such a case, the only meaningful fiscal policy is to change the level of public spending.

Analytical Framework

When the altruistic model is employed, the analytical model may be described by the standard infinite-horizon model where individuals would act as though they would live infinitely. Specifically, the individual's utility function is given by

$$V_t = \sum_{j=0}^{\infty} \left(\frac{1}{1+\rho} \right)^j U(C_{t+j}^*),$$ (1)

where ρ is a constant rate of time preferences; $U(\bullet)$ is a time invariant, concave momentary utility function; and C^* denotes the level of "effective" consumption in period t. Effective consumption is taken to be a function of private consumption expenditure C and government expenditure on consumption goods G. Following Aschauer and Greenwood (1985), it is assumed that a unit of government expenditures yields the same utility as μ/G units of private consumption. μ is assumed to be dependent on G. The greater the level of government expenditures, the smaller utility a unit of government goods and services yields in terms of private consumption:

$$C_t^* = C_t + \mu(G_t), \ \mu' > 0 \ \mu'' < 0. \tag{2}$$

Here, μ' may be regarded as the marginal rate of substitution between private consumption and government consumption.[1]

In the perfect capital market, the representative individual may accumulate or decumulate assets at the assumed constant real rate of interest, r. His budget constraint in period t is given by

$$\frac{W_{t+1}}{1+r} - W_t + C_t = Y_t - T_t, \tag{3}$$

where W_t is the beginning of period holdings of one-period assets (which include government debt), Y_t is labor earnings, and T_t is tax payments (net of transfers). Under the solvency condition, forward substitution in equation 3 yields

$$\sum_{j=0}^{\infty} \left(\frac{1}{1+r}\right)^j C_{t+j} = W_t + \sum_{j=0}^{\infty} \left(\frac{1}{1+r}\right)^j (Y_{t+j} - T_{t+j}), \tag{4}$$

which means that the present discounted value of private consumption is equal to initial asset holdings plus the present discounted value of after-tax earnings.

The government budget constraint in period t is

$$\frac{B_{t+1}}{1+r} - B_t = G_t - T_t, \tag{5}$$

where B_t is the beginning of an outstanding period of government debt of one-period maturity. Under the solvency condition, equation 5 may be utilized to produce

---

1. The recent empirical work of Kormendi (1983) and Aschauer (1985) reported values of μ' in the range of 0.20 to 0.40 by assuming constant μ'. However, in order to elaborate the normative aspect of government spending changes, it is not assumed that μ' is constant and between 0 and 1.

$$\sum_{j=0}^{\infty} \left(\frac{1}{1+r} \right)^j T_{t+j} = B_j + \sum_{j=0}^{\infty} \left(\frac{1}{1+r} \right)^j G_{t+j}, \tag{6}$$

which means that the present discounted value of tax revenues is equal to the initial government debt plus the present discounted value of government purchases.

The representative individual is assumed to be forward looking in regard to the fiscal affairs of the government under the assumption of the altruistic bequests. Therefore, the private and public sectors can be integrated by the substitution of the government budget constraint (eq. 6) into the private budget constraint (eq. 4) to obtain the following effective lifetime budget constraint:

$$\sum_{j=0}^{\infty} \left(\frac{1}{1+r} \right)^j (C_{t+j} + G_{t+j}) = W_t - B_t + \sum_{j=0}^{\infty} \left(\frac{1}{1+r} \right)^j Y_{t+j}. \tag{7}$$

The maximization of the individual's objective function (eq. 1) subject to the effective intertemporal budget constraint (eq. 7) yields the first-order necessary condition

$$\Delta U^{t+j} = \lambda \left(\frac{1+\rho}{1+r} \right)^j \quad (j = 0, 1, 2, \ldots) \tag{8}$$

along with the intertemporal budget constraint (eq. 7). Here, ΔU is the marginal utility of effective consumption and λ is a Lagrangean multiplier attached to equation 7 in the consumer's maximization problem. The consideration of the choice of consumption in the adjacent periods $(t, t+j)$ then leads to the Euler equation:

$$\Delta U^{t+j} = \left(\frac{1+\rho}{1+r} \right)^j \Delta U^t. \tag{9}$$

The optimal size of government spending G^* is derived by the maximization of equation 1 subject to equation 7 with respect to G_{t+j} as well as C_{t+j}. The necessary conditions are

$$\mu'(G_{t+j}) = \mu'(G_t) \quad (j = 1, 2, \ldots) \tag{10}$$

$$1 = \mu'(G_t). \tag{11}$$

Therefore, G^* is given by $1 = \mu'(G^*)$. In the real competitive economy, the actual level of government spending G is not always equal to G^*.

Government Expenditure Policy

For simplicity, let us assume that government expenditures are initially set at the stationary level, $G_{t+j} = \bar{G}$ ($j = 0, 1, 2, \ldots$). Let $[\bar{C}_{t+j}$ ($j = 0, 1, 2, \ldots$)] and $[\bar{C}^*_{t+j}$ ($j = 0, 1, 2, \ldots$)] denote the initially optimal private consumption program and the corresponding optimal effective consumption program, respectively. From equation 9, the program $[\bar{C}^*_{t+j}]$ satisfies

$$\Delta U(\bar{C}^*_{t+j}) = \left(\frac{1 + \rho}{1 + r} \right)^j \Delta U(\bar{C}^*_t) \quad (j = 1, 2, \ldots). \tag{12}$$

If we assume that the government increases the level of government spending in period $t + 1$ only, then $\Delta G_{t+1} > 0$ and $\Delta G_{t+1+j} = 0$ ($j = 1, 2, \ldots$). At the beginning of period t, this policy change may be unknown to the individual.[2]

Unanticipated Case
If the individual does not anticipate ΔG_{t+1} in period t, how will he or she determine the private consumption program $[C_{t+j}$ ($j = 0, 1, 2 \ldots$)] if the individual does not know ΔG_{t+1} until period $t + 1$, $C_t = \bar{C}_t$? In period $t + 1$, the individual knows ΔG_{t+1}. It is useful to note the following result: $C_{t+1} = \bar{C}_{t+1} - \Delta G_{t+1}$ is optimal if and only if $-1 + \mu'(G_{t+1}) = 0$.

We call the private consumption program $(\bar{C}_t, \bar{C}_{t+1} - \Delta G_{t+1}, \bar{C}_{t+2}, \bar{C}_{t+3}, \ldots)$ the benchmark private consumption program, where the burden of $\Delta G > 0$ is entirely levied on the private consumption in the same period. We have the following result: the optimal private consumption program in the unanticipated case $(C^u_{t+1}, C^u_{t+2}, C^u_{t+3}, \ldots)$ satisfies

$$C^u_{t+1} \gtreqless \bar{C}_{t+1} - \Delta G_{t+1}, \, C^u_{t+1+j} \gtreqless \bar{C}_{t+1+j} \, (j = 1, 2, \ldots)$$

if and only if $\bar{G} \gtreqless G^*$.

Anticipated Case
We now consider the case where ΔG_{t+1} is known to the individual in period t. We have: the optimal private consumption program in the anticipated case $(C^a_t, C^a_{t+1}, C^a_{t+2}, \ldots)$ satisfies

$$C^a_t \gtreqless \bar{C}_t, \, C^a_{t+j} \gtreqless C^u_{t+j} \, (j = 1, 2, \ldots) \text{ if and only if } \bar{G} \gtreqless G^*.$$

---

2. The policy implication of a permanent increase in government expenditure is essentially the same as in the government expenditure policy discussed in this section.

Policy Implication
At the optimal level of government spending G^*, a marginal substitution of G and C does not change C^*. A marginal benefit of ΔG is given by μ' and a marginal cost of ΔG is given by -1 $(= -\Delta C)$ in terms of the effective consumption. If $G < G^*$, the marginal benefit of government expenditure is greater than the marginal cost, and G is perceived as too little. On the other hand, if $G > G^*$, the marginal benefit of government expenditure is greater than the marginal cost, and G is perceived as too much.

If G is initially too little, unanticipated government expenditures in period $t + 1$ have a relatively more expansionary effect on private consumption in period $t + 1$ than anticipated government expenditures, and vice versa. Based on the theoretical considerations, the relative effects of anticipated expansion and unanticipated expansion tell us the discrepancy between actual and optimal government expenditures.

An intuitive explanation is as follows. If G is initially too little, an increase in G_{t+1} raises G^*_{t+1} and $U(G^*_{t+1})$ when the burden of $\Delta G_{t+1} > 0$ is entirely levied on the private consumption in the same period $(\Delta G_{t+1} = -\Delta C_{t+1})$. If the individual anticipates this policy change in advance, it is desirable for him or her to transfer private consumption from period $t + 1$ to period t. By doing so, the Euler equation is restored. If he or she does not anticipate this change in advance, it is impossible to transfer private consumption from period $t + 1$ to period t. Therefore, unanticipated government action will raise private consumption at that time more than anticipated government action.

Geometric Exposition

It may be helpful to represent theoretical results in the previous section diagrammatically. In a two-period context, the effective lifetime budget equation is written as

$$C_1^* + \frac{1}{1 + r} C_2^* = Y_1 + \frac{1}{1 + r} Y_2 - \left(G_1 + \frac{1}{1 + r} G_2\right)$$

$$+ \left[\mu(G_1) + \frac{1}{1 + r} \mu(G_2)\right].$$

In figure 1, line AA corresponds to this budget line, and E_0 is the initial equilibrium point.

Suppose $\Delta G > 0$, which corresponds to a permanent increase in government expenditures. If $\bar{G} < G^*$, an increase in G_2 will raise the right-hand side of the preceding equation. Line AA shifts upward. Line A'A' corresponds to the new budget line. At the beginning of period one, this policy change may

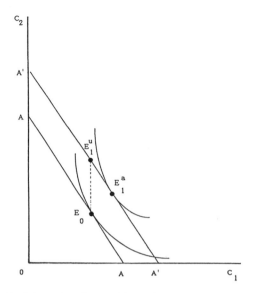

Fig. 1. Anticipated and unanticipated government expenditures

be unknown to the individual. If the individual does not anticipate ΔG_2 in period one, he or she cannot adjust the first-period private consumption. The ex post private consumption program (C_1^u, C_2^u) is given by $(\bar{C}_1, \bar{C}_2 - \Delta G_2)$. The burden of ΔG_2 is levied entirely on C_2. In figure 1, E_1^u corresponds to the consumption program in the unanticipated case.

If ΔG_2 is known in period one, it is possible to change C_1. I_1 is the highest level of utility an individual can attain on $A'A'$, and, in this sense, point E_1^a is optimal. Namely, the consumption program in the anticipated case (C_1^a, C_2^a) is associated with E_1^a.

Comparing E_1^u and E_1^a, it is easy to find $C_1^a > C_1^u$ and $C_2^a < C_2^u$. At point E_1^u, $\Delta U^1 > (1 + r/1 + \rho)\Delta U^2$. In order to restore the Euler equation, C_1 will be increased and C_2 will be reduced. On the other hand, if $\bar{G} > G^*$, line AA will shift downward, and, hence, we have $C_1^a < C_1^u$ and $C_2^a > C_2^u$.

Remarks

There are several remarks to be made concerning the foregoing. First, even if the altruistic bequests are not fully operative and, hence, Ricardian debt neutrality does not perfectly hold, the normative implications will be qualitatively valid. The reason for this is as follows. Suppose some individuals are not forward looking in regard to the government fiscal action. Since they are not concerned with a change in the future government spending, their anticipations about future government action have no impact on future private consumption. So long as there exist other individuals who are forward looking, anticipated and unanticipated changes in government expenditures have different impacts on private consumption in the aggregate economy.[3]

Second, we have assumed that instantaneous utility is dependent only on the effective consumption C*. This is a standard assumption for the recent empirical work of government expenditures (see Kormendi 1983 and Aschauer 1985). In general the utility function would be

$$U = U(C, G). \tag{13}$$

Consequently, the optimal level of G is given by

$$U_C = U_G,$$

where U_i is a partial derivative with respect to i. As the intertemporal transfer of private consumption is determined by the Euler equation 9, the sign of $U_{CC} - U_{GG}$ is crucial.

Namely, if $U_{CG} < U_{CC}$, U_C is increased at $\Delta G = -\Delta C > 0$ and, hence, unanticipated permanent changes in government expenditures in period $t + 1$ have a relatively more expansionary effect on private consumption in period $t + 1$ than anticipated government expenditures and vice versa. Therefore, it is important to investigate the relation between the sign of $U_C - U_G$ (which is relevant to the optimal level of G) and the sign of $U_{CC} - U_{CG}$ (which is relevant to intertemporal transfers). The assumption of effective consumption implies a "one to one" relationship between the signs of $U_C - U_G$ and $U_{CC} - U_{CG}$. On the other hand, if the utility function is additively separable with respect to C and G, we have $U_{CG} = 0$. Hence, we always have $U_{CC} - U_{CG} < 0$ irrespectively of the sign of $U_C - U_G$. In such a case, there would be no difference between the effects of anticipated and unanticipated government expenditures.[4]

Some Empirical Evidence for the Japanese Economy

I provided some evidence of a discrepancy between actual and optimal government spending in two ways for the Japanese economy (Ihori 1987). First, I

---

3. Even if Ricardian neutrality is not perfectly relevant, it is still possible that some individuals engage in intergenerational transfers. The rich individuals may well be forward looking and engage in major intergeneration transfers. Kurz (1984) suggests that 1 percent of the richest households, those who own 20 to 25 percent of the private wealth, must engage in major intergenerational transfers. If so, the normative evaluation of the size of government spending is largely based on the rich individuals' judgment.

4. As for the normative implication of government spending in the general equilibrium growth model, see Ihori 1990.

used a direct approach to estimate a parameter of evaluation μ that exploits restrictions placed on the data by the Euler equation. Second, I used an indirect approach to estimate the relationship between the optimal size and the actual size of government spending. My empirical analysis provided the finding that the level of government spending was regarded as too little in the 1960s, but is regarded as too much in recent years for the Japanese economy.

It is said that public opinion concerning the role of government has changed significantly. The number favoring small government has become predominant among business people. This change is probably caused by the fear that further increases in fiscal burdens would fall on the business community. This concern is a background for the fiscal reconstruction movement in recent years. I suggest that such a concern is shared by the household sector as well (Ihori 1987).

Bequest Taxes and Capital Accumulation

Tax Reform and Bequests

When fiscal policy involves a change in distortionary taxes, such a tax reform will not be neutral even if the altruistic model is applicable. Seidman 1983, Batina 1990a,b, and Batina and Ihori 1991 show that under certain circumstances, imposition of the consumption tax on bequests may reduce the capital intensity of production and may actually reduce welfare as a result.

In this section, the effect of bequest taxation itself on capital accumulation is investigated. It is generally believed that an increase in the bequest tax reduces capital accumulation. However, Seidman (1983) points out the possibility that the bequest tax may stimulate capital formation in the bequest-as-consumption model. An important question is whether or not the conventional conjecture is dependent on one particular type of bequest motive. This section considers the altruistic motive, bequest-as-consumption motive, and bequest-as-exchange motive, and shows that the bequest tax will normally reduce capital formation in all three bequest motives.

Bequest Models

Analytical Framework

Consider a closed economy populated by overlapping generations of two-period living consumers as well as firms and a government. In this subsection the standard life-cycle model is described and extended to include bequests.

There is no growth in population.[5] An agent of generation t supplies one unit of labor inelastically and receives wages w_t out of which the agent consumes c_1^t, and saves s_t in period t. An agent who saves s_t receives bequests $(1 + r_{t+1})b_t$ from his or her parents and receives $(1 + r_{t+1})s_t$ from his or her own savings when old, which the agent then spends entirely on consumption c_2^t, and makes a bequest b_{t+1} to his or her offspring and pays bequest taxes ϕb_{t+1} in period $t + 1$. For simplicity, the government fixes bequest tax rates: $\phi_t = \phi_{t+1} = \phi$.[6]

An agent of generation t's budget constraints are given by

$$w_t - c_1^t - s_t = 0, \tag{14.1}$$

$$(1 + r_{t+1})(s_t + b_t) - c_2^t - (1 + \phi)b_{t+1} = 0. \tag{14.2}$$

Competitive profit maximization and a neoclassical technology require that firms hire labor and demand capital in such a way that

$$w_t = w(r_t), \; w'(r_t) = -k_t, \tag{15}$$

where $w(\bullet)$ is the factor price frontier and k_t is the amount of capital per worker in period t.

The government collects taxes on bequests ϕb_t. The policy experiment considered throughout this section is uncompensated in that the public expenditures financed by the revenues do not affect individual decisions such as savings and bequests. This is the case when the individual's utility function is separable between private actions and public spending or if the revenue is wasted. This assumption is standard in overlapping generations models and enables us to concentrate exclusively on tax effects.

In an equilibrium, agents can save by holding capital. In this economy, equilibrium in the financial market requires

$$s_t + b_t = k_{t+1}. \tag{16}$$

Alternative Bequest Motives

We will assume that the utility function is quasi-concave, twice continuously differentiable, and monotone with indifference curves that are asymptotic to all axes. This will be sufficient to generate an interior solution to the parent's

---

5. Even if population growth is positive, the qualitative results would be the same so long as r is greater than n, the rate of population growth.

6. A number of economists have advocated taxing bequests under the consumption tax policy. See the discussion in Mieskowski 1980, for example.

decision problem. We will consider three motives for bequeathing. In the bequest-as-consumption model, we will assume that the parent cares about the bequest itself. The parent's utility function is given by

$$u_t = u(c_1^t, c_2^t, b_{t+1}), \tag{17.1}$$

where b_{t+1} is the bequest that a member of generation t gives to his or her offspring in period $t + 1$.

In the altruism model, we will assume that the parent cares about the welfare of his or her offspring instead of the bequest itself. The parent's utility function is given by

$$u_t = u(c_1^t, c_2^t, u_{t+1}), \tag{17.2}$$

where $u_{t+1} = u(c_1^{t+1}, c_2^{t+1}, u_{t+2})$, and so on, and where $0 < \partial u_t/\partial u_{t+1} = \lambda < 1$. λ is the parent's marginal benefit of his or her offspring's utility. We will assume that λ is constant.

In the bequest-as-exchange model of strategic bequests, the parent cares about some service or action undertaken by the offspring, and the bequest given to the offspring is the payment for the service or action. Undertaking the action reduces utility. The parent's preferences are represented by a utility function given by

$$u_t = u(c_1^t, c_2^t, -a_t, a_{t+1}) \tag{17.3}$$

where a_t is the action the parent undertakes for his or her parent and a_{t+1} is the action the parent would like his or her offspring to undertake.[7] We will assume that $\partial u_t/\partial a_{t+1} > 0$, $\partial u_t/\partial(-a_t) > 0$, $0 < (\partial u_t/\partial a_{t+1})/[\partial u_t/\partial(-a_t)] = \eta < 1$, and that η is constant. η is the ratio of the parent's marginal benefit of his or her offspring's action to the parent's marginal cost of undertaking action for his or her parent.

Bequest Tax Incidence

Bequest-as-Consumption Model

In the bequest-as-consumption model, the first-order conditions for s_t and b_{t+1} can be written as

$$(1 + r_{t+1})\partial u_t/\partial c_2^t - \partial u_t/\partial c_1^t = 0 \tag{18.1}$$

---

7. a is defined in terms of time. Namely, the endowment of time is divided between labor supply, leisure, and the action.

and

$$\partial u_t / \partial b_{t+1} - (1 + \phi)\partial u_2 / \partial c_2^t = 0. \tag{18.2}$$

Equation 18.1 governs the optimal intertemporal consumption decision of the parent while equation 18.2 governs the optimal bequest decision. In the steady state we have

$$[(\partial u / \partial b)/(\partial u / \partial c_1)](1 + r) = 1 + \phi. \tag{19}$$

If $[(\partial u / \partial b)/(\partial u / \partial c_1)]$ is constant, an increase in ϕ will raise r and reduce capital accumulation. If c_1 and b are perfect substitutes, or if c_1 and b are linearly dependent, such as $u(c_1 + \xi b, c_2)$, then $[(\partial u / \partial b)/(\partial u / \partial c_1)]$ is constant.

In general $[(\partial u / \partial b)/(\partial u / \partial c_1)]$ is not necessarily constant, and, hence, equation 19 does not necessarily imply the negative effect of ϕ on capital accumulation. In such a case it is necessary to investigate the general equilibrium effect. The consumption and bequest functions are respectively given as

$$c_1^t = c_1(w_t, r_{t+1}, b_t, \phi), \tag{20}$$

$$c_2^t = c_2(w_t, r_{t+1}, b_t, \phi), \tag{21}$$

and

$$b_{t+1} = b(w_t, r_{t+1}, b_t, \phi). \tag{22}$$

From the second-period budget constraint for the agent 14.2, we have the following total saving $(s + b)$ function:

$$s_t + b_t = [c_2(w_t, r_{t+1}, b_t, \phi)$$

$$+ (1 + \phi)b(w_t, r_{t+1}, b_t, \phi)]/(1 + r_{t+1}). \tag{23}$$

Thus, the economy may be summarized by the following two equations:

$$c_2[w(r_t), r_{t+1}, b_t, \phi] + (1 + \phi)b[w(r_t), r_{t+1}, b_t, \phi]$$

$$= -w'(r_{t+1})(1 + r_{t+1}) \tag{24}$$

and

$$b_{t+1} = b[w(r_t), r_{t+1}, b_t, \phi]. \tag{25}$$

In the steady state equilibrium, $b_{t+1} = b_t = b$. From equations 20, 21, and 22, we can solve for the steady state reduced form functions[8]

$$c_1 = \hat{c}_1(w, r, \phi), \tag{20)'}$$

$$c_2 = \hat{c}_2(w, r, \phi), \tag{21)'}$$

and

$$b = \hat{b}(w, r, \phi). \tag{22)'}$$

If own consumption and the bequest are normal goods, then the second-period consumption and the bequest will be increasing with w and r. Also, bequests will be decreasing with ϕ. Furthermore, if the substitution effect outweighs the income effect, then the second-period consumption will be decreasing with ϕ. For example, if the utility function is separable, then these results follow. Thus, under plausible assumptions we have in a steady state

$$\hat{c}_2' = \partial \hat{c}_2 / \partial \phi < 0, \; \hat{b}' = \partial \hat{b} / \partial \phi < 0, \; \hat{c}_{2r} = \partial \hat{c}_2 / \partial r > 0,$$

$$\hat{b}_r = \partial \hat{b} / \partial r > 0.$$

The intuition is that when the parent makes the bequest he or she will take into account the tax on the bequest. An increase in ϕ causes an increase in the price of bequests, inducing negative income and substitution effects on bequests.

We have

$$dr/d\phi = -\frac{1}{\Delta} (\hat{c}_2' + (1 + \phi)\hat{b}' + \hat{b}), \tag{26}$$

where $\Delta = w'\hat{c}_{2w} + \hat{c}_{2r} + w''(1 + r) + w' + \hat{b}_w w' + \hat{b}_r$. If $\Delta > 0$, then the initial equilibrium will be stable. If the term $\hat{c}_2' + (1 + \phi)\hat{b}' + \hat{b}$ is negative, $dr/d\phi > 0$. In other words, if the negative income and substitution effects of the imposition of the bequest taxation are large enough, the bequest tax will normally reduce the total supply of savings ($s + b$) in the economy and, hence, reduce capital accumulation. As pointed out by Seidman (1983), al-

---

8. These are reduced form functions in the following sense. Here, the interest is in the steady state response to the tax policy. In a steady state, the inheritance that the agent receives is equal to the bequest he or she gives. Both the inheritance and the bequest will respond to the tax policy in a steady state. The reduced form functions 20', 21', and 22' capture both of these effects.

though we cannot rule out the possibility that the bequest tax may stimulate capital formation, it is likely that the bequest tax will reduce capital formation.

Altruistic Model

In the altruistic model, the first-order conditions are given by equation 18, and for the bequest

$$(\partial u_{t+1}/\partial u_{t+2})(1 + r_{t+2})(\partial u_{t+1}/\partial c_2^{t+1}) - (1 + \phi)\partial u_t/\partial c_2^t = 0. \tag{27}$$

In the steady state, this condition becomes

$$\lambda(1 + r) = 1 + \phi \tag{28}$$

The (LHD) of equation 28 means the marginal benefit of bequests and the (RHD) of equation 28 implies the marginal cost of the bequest. Since an increase in the bequest tax raises the marginal cost of bequeathing and λ is constant, an increase in ϕ raises r. In other words, an increase in the bequest tax reduces capital accumulation in the long run.

Bequest-as-Exchange Model

In the bequest-as-exchange model, the parent chooses the bequest subject to his or her budget constraint and, in addition, a self-selection constraint. Namely, the offspring will undertake the action if

$$u_{t+1}^0[w_{t+1} - s_{t+1}, (1 + r_{t+2})(s_{t+1} + b_{t+1}) - (1 + \phi)b_{t+2},$$

$$-a_{t+1}, a_{t+2}] \geq u_{t+1}^0[w_{t+1} - s_{t+1}, (1 + r_{t+2})s_{t+1}$$

$$- (1 + \phi)b_{t+2}, 0, a_{t+2}], \tag{29}$$

where $u^0(\bullet)$ is the offspring's utility function. The utility on the right-hand side of the inequality equation 29 is the amount of utility the offspring receives if he or she refuses to undertake the action and the parent disinherits him or her.

Solving the budget constraints (eqs. 14.1 and 14.2) for c_1^t and c_2^t and substituting the parent's utility function (eq. 17.3), we have

$$L = u[w_t - s_t, (1 + r_{t+1})(s_t + b_t) - (1 + \phi)b_{t+1}, -a_t, a_{t+1}]$$

$$- \alpha_{t+1}\{u_{t+1}^0[w_{t+1} - s_{t+1}, (1 + r_{t+2})(s_{t+1} + b_{t+1})$$

$$- (1 + \phi)b_{t+2}, -a_{t+1}, a_{t+2}]$$

$$- u_{t+1}^0 [w_{t+1} - s_{t+1}, (1 + r_{t+2})s_{t+1}$$

$$- (1 + \phi)b_{t+2}, 0, a_{t+2}]\},$$

where α_{t+1} is the Lagrangean multiplier for the self-selection constraint at time $t + 1$. The parent chooses (s_t, b_{t+1}, a_{t+1}) subject to the self-selection constraint. Hence, the first-order conditions for the parent's problem are as follows:

$$\partial L/\partial s_t = (1 + r_{t+1})\partial u_t/\partial c_2^t - \partial u_t/\partial c_1^t = 0,$$

$$\partial L/\partial b_{t+1} = \alpha_{t+1}(1 + r_{t+2})\partial u_{t+1}^0/\partial c_2^{t+1} - (1 + \phi)\partial u_t/\partial c_2^t = 0,$$

and

$$\partial L/\partial a_{t+1} = \partial u_t/\partial a_{t+1} - \alpha_{t+1}\partial u_{t+1}^0/\partial(-a_{t+1}) = 0.$$

Assuming the constraint is binding, $\alpha_{t+1} = (\partial u_t/\partial a_{t+1})/[\partial u_{t+1}^0/\partial(-a_{t+1})]$. Therefore, in the steady state we have

$$(1 + r)(\partial u/\partial a)/[\partial u/\partial(-a)] = (1 + r)\eta = 1 + \phi. \tag{30}$$

This condition is similar to equation 19 in the bequest-as-consumption model and equation 28 in the altruistic model. The LHD of equation 30 is the marginal benefit of bequests, and the RHD of equation 30 is the marginal cost of bequests. An increase in bequests raises the parent's marginal cost by $1 + \phi$, while it raises the offspring's utility, inducing the offspring's action. This will raise the parent's marginal benefit by $(1 + r)\eta$. Since η is constant, an increase in ϕ reduces capital accumulation in the long run. If $-a_t$ and a_{t+1} are perfect substitutes, or both are linearly dependent such as $u(c_1, c_2, -a_t + \eta a_{t+1})$, η is constant. Note that in this formulation the bequest-as-exchange motive works even if the parent has a single child.

The parent in the bequest-as-exchange model will take the economic circumstances of his offspring into account in choosing the bequest in a manner that is similar to the altruism model. If bequests are taxed when given in exchange for the action, the bequest decision will be distorted as in the altruism model. Under our policy experiment, the parent will reduce his saving for a bequest and the offspring will reduce the amount of the action he undertakes.[9]

9. If λ and μ are not constant, we have equations 20 through 26 as in the bequest-as-consumption model. Since an increase in ϕ causes an increase in the price of bequests, we

Remarks

We have shown that an increase in the bequest tax will normally reduce capital accumulation in all of the three intentional bequest motives. Thus, the bequest tax will reduce the long-term welfare in terms of dynamic efficiency. On the other hand, an increase in bequest taxation may be justified in terms of intragenerational equity. If so, our analysis explores a possible trade-off between efficiency and equity with respect to the bequest taxation.

The choice between human capital investment and material bequests has not been incorporated as a form of wealth transfer to the offspring. As shown in Yagi 1991, an increase in the bequest tax may stimulate human capital investment, inducing a rise in labor productivity and, hence, an increase in capital accumulation.

Bequests, Social Security, and Economic Growth

Endogenous Growth Model

When the altruistic bequest model is not fully applicable, it seems possible to argue that the class of infinitely lived models developed in the second section is too narrow to accommodate some forms of heterogeneity. In particular, it is impossible to understand the effect of intergenerational income redistribution on growth. It also seems impossible to understand the effect of the growth rate in the standard overlapping generations model developed in the preceding section where the growth rate is exogenously given.

Recent models of endogenous economic growth can generate long-run growth without relying on exogenous changes in technology or population. A general feature of these models is the presence of constant or increasing returns in the factors that can be accumulated. In this section, I incorporate a public sector into a simple, constant returns model of economic growth developed in Barro 1990 and Jones and Manuelli 1990. Here, there are interesting choices about the relationships among the size of government, productivity of the public sector, saving behavior, and rate of economic growth.

Jones and Manuelli (1990) investigated a growth effect of redistribution using the standard two-period overlapping generations model. They showed that an income tax–financed redistributive policy can be used to induce equilibrium growth. By incorporating bequests and public capital into the model, their analysis is extended in the following sense. First, it is shown that the competitive equilibrium can grow when voluntary intergenerational transfers

---

normally expect that the bequest tax will reduce the total supply of savings and, hence, capital accumulation.

are operative. Second, the negative effect of social security programs on the growth rate is explored.

Analytical Framework

In this section, the long-run properties of a model in which individuals live for a finite number of periods is explored. To make the point clear, consider a two-period overlapping generations model similar to Samuelson 1958 and Diamond 1965 with private capital. The standard overlapping generations model is extended to allow for public capital as well as bequests.

Production Sector
Each household has access to the production function

$$y = f(K) = AK, \tag{31}$$

where y is output per worker and K is capital per worker. Following Rebelo 1991, I assume constant returns to a broad concept of capital that includes human capital as well as physical capital. Each person works a given amount of time using human capital; there is no labor-leisure choice.

We now incorporate a public sector of production. Let g be the quantity of public capital owned by the government. We assume that the services of public capital are provided to the private sector without user charges and are not subject to congestion effects.

We only consider the role of public stock as an input to production. Production exhibits constant returns to scale in private capital k and public capital g together, but diminishing returns in k and g separately. Namely, even with a broad concept of private capital k, which includes nonhuman capital and human capital, production involves decreasing returns to provide outputs if the complementary government capital g does not expand in a parallel manner.

Given constant returns to scale, we have

$$K = k^{1-\alpha}g^{\alpha}.$$

Or the production function can be written as

$$y/k = A(g/k)^{\alpha}, \tag{32}$$

where $0 < \alpha < 1$, and it is assumed that the production function is that of Cobb-Douglas.[10]

---

10. A number of questions arise concerning the specification of public services as input to production. First, Barro (1990) considered the case of the government doing no production and

Thus, we have

$$q_k = \partial y / \partial k = A \beta^\alpha (1 - \alpha) \qquad (33.1)$$

and

$$q_g = \partial y / \partial g = A \beta^{\alpha-1} \alpha, \qquad (33.2)$$

where q_k and q_g are the marginal productivity of private capital and public capital, respectively. β is the ratio of public to private capital (g/k). Both private and public capital depreciate at a rate of δ. Hence, the rate of return on private capital r, which is equal to the market rate of interest, is given by

$$r = q_k - \delta. \qquad (34)$$

The long-run optimality condition of the allocation of capital between the private and public sectors is given as the arbitrage condition:

$$q_k = q_g, \text{ or } \beta = \alpha / (1 - \alpha). \qquad (35)$$

Intergenerational Transfer
In this section, the bequest-as-consumption model is adopted. Physical capital and human capital are perfect substitutes in our model. When the young individual works a given amount of time using human capital that is left by the parent, it is assumed that the inheritance from the parent determines the lifetime income.

A representative individual born at time t solves

$$\text{Max } u^t = u(c_1^t, c_2^t, b_{t+1}) \qquad (36)$$

subject to

$$c_1^t + s_t + b_{t+1} = (1 + r_t) b_t \qquad (37)$$

and

$$c_2^t = (1 + r_{t+1}) s_t, \qquad (38)$$

owning no capital. The government there just buys a flow of output from the private sector. A second issue arises if public services are nontrivial for the users. Barro and Martin (1990) considered three versions of public services: 1) publicly provided private goods that are rival and excludable; 2) publicly provided public goods that are nonrival and nonexcludable; and 3) publicly provided goods that are subject to congestion. The present model can be modified to include this aspect of public services without altering the general nature of the results.

where c_i is consumption in the ith period of each individual's life, b_t is the inheritance received when young, b_{t+1} is the bequest that is determined when young, and s_t is the savings. Although the inheritance could be assumed to be entirely financial or physical, I follow the interpretation suggested by Becker and Tomes (1979) under which b includes transfers in support of human capital accumulation as well.

It is useful to compare this model with the model presented in the preceding section. Contrary to the second section, the inheritance is now determined when young and is saved for the parent's child. Here, the labor income of the younger generation includes wage income w and equals rk because k includes human capital. Private capital is held by the older generation in the form of their savings and by the younger generation in the form of their inheritance received. It is assumed for simplicity that the return on public capital, $q_g g$, is not distributed to the private sector.

Capital Accumulation
Capital accumulation is given as

$$s_t + b_{t+1} = k_{t+1}.^{11} \tag{39}$$

Suppose for simplicity that the utility function is given by the Cobb-Douglas production function. The consumption and bequest functions are then respectively given as

$$c_1^t = \epsilon_1(1 + r_t)b_t, \tag{40.1}$$

$$c_2^t = \epsilon_2(1 + r_t)(1 + r_{t+1})b_t, \tag{40.2}$$

and

$$b_{t+1} = \epsilon_3(1 + r_t)b_t \tag{40.3}$$

where $\epsilon_1 + \epsilon_2 + \epsilon_3 = 1$. In this case, from equations 40.2 and 40.3, equation 39 may be rewritten as

$$b_{t+1} = \epsilon k_{t+1}, \tag{39'}$$

where $0 < \epsilon = \epsilon_3/(\epsilon_2 + \epsilon_3) < 1$.

In the long-run equilibrium, all of the variables grow at a rate γ. Since

---

11. Since b_{t+1} is now determined when young, we have b_{t+1} in equation 39 instead of b_t in equation 16.

we have $b_t = \gamma b_{t-1}$, from equation 40.3 the economic growth rate γ is given as

$$\gamma = \epsilon_3(1 + r), \tag{41}$$

which can be greater than 1 if ϵ_3 and r are high. In this economy considering equations 33.1 and 34, equation 41 is rewritten as

$$\gamma = \epsilon_3[A\beta^\alpha(1 - \alpha) + 1 - \delta]. \tag{42}$$

Equation 42 means that it is possible to have positive economic growth even in the finite horizon lifetime model when we allow for intergenerational transfers.

Social Security and Economic Growth

Fully Funded Program
Let us now consider the case where the government employs social security programs when private intergenerational transfers in the form of b are present. When the government employs a fully funded social security program, the private budget constraints are given as

$$c_1^t + s_t + b_{t+1} + e_t = (1 + r_t)b_t \tag{43}$$

and

$$c_2^t = (1 + r_{t+1})s_t + (1 + h_{t+1})e_t, \tag{44}$$

where e_t is a contribution of generation t and h_{t+1} is the rate of return on the social security program in period $t + 1$. For simplicity, we assume that contributions are a linear function of income in the younger period $(1 + r_t)b_t$:

$$e_t = \theta(1 + r_t)b_t, \tag{45}$$

where θ is the contribution rate $0 < \theta < 1$.
It is plausible to assume that contributions are invested in public capital:

$$e_t = g_{t+1}. \tag{46}$$

And, hence, the rate of return on the contribution is given by the net rate of return on public capital:

$$h_t = q_{gt} - \delta. \tag{47}$$

From the budget constraint, we now have

$$c_1^t = \epsilon_1 E_t(1 + r_t)b_t, \tag{48.1}$$

$$c_2^t = \epsilon_2 E_t(1 + r_t)(1 + r_{t+1})b_t, \tag{48.2}$$

and

$$b_{t+1} = \epsilon_3 E_t(1 + r_t)b_t, \tag{48.3}$$

where $E_t(1 + r_t)b_t$ is lifetime income and $E_t = 1 - (r_{t+1} - h_{t+1})/(1 + r_{t+1})\theta$. E increases with h. If $r > h$, then $0 < E < 1$. If $r = h$, then $E = 1$. If $r < h$, then $E > 1$. Hence, the private saving function is given as

$$s_t = \epsilon_2(1 + r_t)E_t b_t - \frac{1 + h_{t+1}}{1 + r_{t+1}} e_t. \tag{49}$$

Thus,

$$b_{t+1} + s_t = b_t(1 + r_t)\left[E_t(\epsilon_3 + \epsilon_2) - \frac{1 + h_{t+1}}{1 + r_{t+1}} \theta \right] = k_{t+1}. \tag{39''}$$

If the contribution rate θ is exogenously given, r is not necessarily equal to h. Substituting $q_k = A\beta^\alpha(1 - \alpha)$ and $q_g = A\beta^{\alpha-1}\alpha$ into equation 48.3, we have

$$\gamma = \epsilon_3\{A\beta^\alpha(1 - \alpha) + 1 - \delta - \theta A[\beta^\alpha(1 - \alpha) - \beta^{\alpha-1}\alpha]\}. \tag{50}$$

And given the contribution rate in equations 45, 46, and 39'', β is determined by

$$\beta = \frac{g}{k} = \theta / \left\{ E(\epsilon_3 + \epsilon_2) - \frac{1 + h}{1 + r} \theta \right\}. \tag{51}$$

Since β is dependent on ϵ_2 as well as on ϵ_3, γ is likewise dependent on ϵ_2 as well as on ϵ_3. Equation 51 gives β as a function of θ, ϵ_2, and ϵ_3 because E is a function of β and θ. We know $\partial E/\partial \theta < 0$, but the sign of $\partial E/\partial \beta$ is ambiguous. $-(1 + h)/(1 + r)$ is increasing with β. Thus, from equation 51, an increase in θ will normally raise β. β also decreases with ϵ_2 and ϵ_3.

In figure 2, the vertical line BB corresponds to equation 51, which

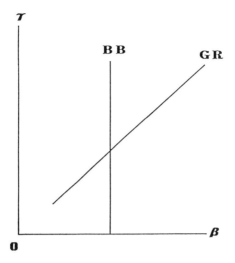

Fig. 2. Social security and growth: fully funded program

determines the long-run public-to-private capital ratio. The upward-sloping curve GR corresponds to equation 50, which determines the long-run growth rate. An increase in θ will shift curve BB to the right and β will be raised. If $r > (<) h$ and $\theta < (>) \beta/1 + \beta$, an increase in θ will shift curve GR downward (upward). Hence, if $r \leq h$ and θ is low, an increase in θ will raise γ, and if $r > h$, an increase in θ may lower γ. In other words, if public capital is optimal or underaccumulated, an increase in the fully funded social security program will stimulate the growth rate, and if public capital is overaccumulated, such an increase in θ may reduce the growth rate. When θ is very low, it is likely that public capital is underaccumulated.[12] In this sense, a low level of θ will be associated with the positive effect of θ on γ, and vice versa.[13]

---

12. Nemoto, Kamada, and Kawamura (1990) assessed the optimality of Japanese public capital using the social discount rates for public investment. They found that actual levels of public capital stocks during the 1960–82 period had been persistently less than optimal levels based on a variant of Burgress's (1988) social discount rate. Their result implies the deficiency of public capital, which happens to be consistent with intuitive claims prevailing in Japan. They also found that public capital had been accumulated at a higher rate than the optimal level had grown and, hence, that the gap between actual and optimal levels of public capital had continuously diminished. If so, equation 51 in the second case suggests that higher growth of public capital has stimulated the Japanese growth rate. Furthermore, an increase in the contribution rate in the Japanese social security system thus far has probably stimulated the growth rate as well.

13. In the conventional overlapping generations model, it is well known that the fully funded program has no effect on capital accumulation. In the present framework, if $r = h$, $E = 1$ and the income effect of the fully funded program is zero as in the conventional model. However,

If θ is low, an increase in ϵ_2 will shift curve BB to the left, and γ will be reduced. When ϵ_2 is raised, private capital accumulation is stimulated and the ratio of public-to-private capital β is reduced. As shown in equation 51, this will reduce the rate of interest and, hence, the growth rate. On the other hand, an increase in ϵ_3 will shift curve BB to the left and curve GR upward, and, hence, γ may be raised.

Pay-as-You-Go Program

When the social security system is a pay-as-you-go program, $h = 0$ and e_t is changed into e_{t+1} in equation 44 in the preceding formulation. Note that the population growth is assumed away. Thus, $E = 1 - \theta$. In this system, we need a fund for financing public capital. Since the return on public capital is not distributed to the private sector, we consider the following two cases.

Case (i): Public Investment Financed by Lump Sum Taxes

Let us first introduce a lump sum tax policy to attain the arbitrage condition (eq. 35). Let T_t be a lump sum transfer to the younger generation at time t. The government budget constraint is now

$$(1 + q_{gt} - \delta)g_t - T_t = g_{t+1}. \tag{52}$$

The bequest function is now

$$b_{t+1} = \epsilon_3[(1 + r_t)(1 - \theta)b_t + T_t]/(1 - \theta\epsilon_3). \tag{53}$$

Thus, we have

$$\epsilon\gamma = \epsilon_3[(1 + r)(1 - \theta)\epsilon - \gamma\beta + (1 + q_g - \delta)\beta]/(1 - \theta\epsilon_3). \tag{54}$$

Considering the arbitrage condition (eq. 35), we finally get

$$\gamma = [A\alpha^\alpha(1 - \alpha)^{1-\alpha}(1 - \theta) + 1 - \delta]\{(1 - \theta)\epsilon_3$$
$$+ [\epsilon_2 + (1 - \theta)\epsilon_3]\beta\}/\{1 - \theta\epsilon_3 + [\epsilon_2 + (1 - \theta)\epsilon_3]\beta\}, \tag{55}$$

where $\beta = \alpha/(1 - \alpha)$. In this economy, an increase in θ will reduce γ. The higher is the contribution rate of the pay-as-you-go system, the lower is

---

in the model presented, an increase in the ratio of public-to-private capital β will always raise the marginal productivity of the private capital and, hence, the rate of economic growth. Since this substitution effect always works, the increase in the contribution rate will raise the growth rate even if $r = h$ initially. This is a new result that can only be obtained in the finite horizon endogenous growth model.

the growth rate. Note also that a higher ϵ_2 or ϵ_3 means a higher growth rate. The stronger the motive for the life cycle behavior and/or the intergenerational transfer is, the higher the rate of growth. Note that the result is the same if we transfer the return on public capital to the private sector.

Case (ii): Public Investment Financed by Capital Income Tax

Suppose that the government finances public investment by imposing capital income taxes: τ. The government budget constraint is now

$$(1 + q_{gt} - \delta)g_t + \tau q_{kt}k_t = g_{t+1}. \tag{56}$$

The bequest function is now

$$b_{t+1} = \epsilon_3[1 - \theta + r_t(1 - \tau)(1 - \theta)]/(1 - \theta\epsilon_3)b_t. \tag{57}$$

Thus, we have

$$\gamma = (1 + A\alpha\beta^{\alpha-1} - \delta) + \tau A\beta^{\alpha-1}(1 - \alpha) \tag{58}$$

and

$$\gamma = \epsilon_3[1 - \theta + (1 - \tau)(1 - \theta)A(1 - \alpha)\beta^\alpha - (1 - \tau)$$

$$\times (1 - \theta)\delta]/(1 - \theta\epsilon_3). \tag{59}$$

We can draw a diagram of the long-run equilibrium in figure 3. Line GB corresponds to equation 58, which is downward sloping. Curve GR corresponds to equation 59, which is upward sloping. An increase in τ will shift curve GB to the right and shift curve GR downward. Hence, β is increased, but the effect on γ is ambiguous. From the comparative static analysis, we know that the sign of $d\gamma/d\tau$ corresponds to the sign of $-1 + (1 - \tau)A\alpha$ $(1 - \alpha)\beta^{\alpha-1}$. Thus, if τ is very low (high), it is likely that $d\gamma/d\tau$ is positive (negative).

An increase in θ will shift curve GR downward and, hence, β is increased and γ is reduced. In other words, an increase in the pay-as-you-go social security contribution will reduce the growth rate. In the pay-as-you-go program, the contribution reduces the lifetime income. In this sense, an increase in θ has the same effect as an increase in the capital income tax. Since an increase in θ reduces the net rate of interest on private capital, it will reduce the growth rate.

An increase in ϵ_3 will stimulate the growth rate as in the fully funded program. Note that ϵ_2 is irrelevant to the growth rate.

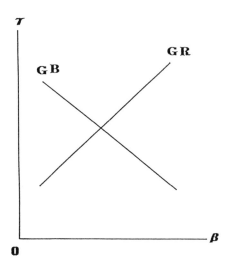

Fig. 3. Social security and growth: pay-as-you-go program

Policy Implications

This analysis has shown how the long-run growth rate is related to the preference, technology, and social security programs. As in the standard infinite
horizon model, the finite horizon model with intergenerational transfers can
produce the positive growth rate. A higher level of marginal productivity
(high q_k and q_g), a higher level of productivity (high A), and a lower deprecia-
tion rate (low δ) result in higher growth. It has also been shown that the
stronger the motive is for the intergenerational transfer, the higher the rate of
growth. When the government does not employ the optimal investment policy, an increase in the ratio of public-to-private capital (β) raises the growth
rate. Furthermore, the more the transfer from the older generation to the
younger generation is conducted by the government, the higher the rate of
growth.

    As summarized in table 2, this analysis has shown that the bequest
motive (ϵ_3) is a crucial factor for growth. The saving motive for bequests ϵ_3
stimulates the growth rate for all the cases, while the saving motive for old age
ϵ_2 may not necessarily stimulate the growth rate. In this sense, the bequest
motive is more important than the preparation motive for old age to attain high
growth. Whether the dynasty model or the life-cycle model has greater applicability in the case of Japan is an unsettled issue. However, it seems fair to say
that intergenerational transfers are important in Japan, which suggests ϵ_3 is
high. Thus, our analysis means that the high level of intergenerational trans-

fers can be valuable in promoting the high economic growth of the Japanese economy.

As for the effect of social security programs on the growth rate, if the social security program is fully funded, an increase in the contribution rate will stimulate the growth rate when the contribution rate is low and depress the growth rate when the contribution rate is high. If the program is pay-as-you-go, an increase in the contribution rate will normally reduce the growth rate. If the future reform of Japanese social security programs implies a higher degree of transfers from the young to the old, then our analysis suggests that such a reform may lead to a reduction in the growth rate.

Concluding Remarks

My investigation of several macroeconomic implications of fiscal policy and social security programs when intentional bequests are operative was presented herein. It seems that there are three important problems with the Japanese fiscal system to be sorted out in the near future: (1) how to control public spending, (2) how to impose taxes on intergenerational transfers, and (3) how to reform the social security programs. In this paper I provided some useful analytical tools for exploring these problems.

First, I examined the normative effects of government spending in the case where altruistic bequests are operative and, hence, debt neutrality holds. I explored the normative aspects of the size of public spending, and the relative effects of anticipated expansion and unanticipated expansion indicated the discrepancy between actual and optimal government expenditures. I observed that public opinion concerning the role of government has changed significantly. The number favoring a small government has become predominant among business people. This change is probably caused by the fear that further increases in fiscal burdens would fall on the business community. This concern has served as the background for the fiscal reconstruction movement under way in recent years.

Next I investigated the effect of bequest taxes on capital accumulation

TABLE 2. Social Security and Economic Growth

	θ	ϵ_2	ϵ_3
Fully funded	+ if θ is low	−	+?
	− if θ is high	+	+
Pay-as-you-go			
case (i)	−	+	+
case (ii)	−	0	+

when intentional bequests are operative. I employed the altruistic bequest model, bequest-as-consumption model, and bequest-as-exchange model, with the intention of exploring the negative effect of bequest taxes on capital formation. I showed that an increase in the bequest tax normally reduces capital accumulation in all three intentional bequest motives. Thus, I confirmed that the bequest tax was to reduce the long-run welfare in terms of dynamic efficiency. On the other hand, the results showed that an increase in bequest taxation may be justified in terms of intragenerational equity. If so, the analysis presented explored the possible trade-off between efficiency and equity with respect to the bequest taxation.

Finally, I made an investigation into the effect of fiscal policy on economic growth when intergenerational transfers are crucial. I concluded that the analysis presented in this paper provides valuable understanding of the possible crowding-out effect of social security on economic growth. If the future reform of Japanese social security programs implies a higher degree of transfers from the young to the old, then my analysis suggests that such a reform may lead to a reduction in the growth rate.

REFERENCES

Aschauer, D. A. 1985. "Fiscal policy and aggregate demand." *American Economic Review*, 117–27.
Aschauer, D. A., and J. Greenwood. 1985. "Macroeconomic effects of fiscal policy." *Carnegie-Rochester Conference Series on Public Policy* 23:91–138.
Barro, R. J. 1974. "Are government bonds net wealth?" *Journal of Political Economy* 82:1095–1117.
————. 1990. "Government spending in a simple model of endogenous growth." *Journal of Political Economy* 98:s103–25.
Barro, R. J., and X. Sala-i Martin. 1990. "Public finance in models of economic growth." NBER Working Paper, no. 3362.
Batina, R. G. 1990a. "On the consumption tax and the tax treatment of bequests in different models of bequeathing." Department of Economics, Washington State University. Manuscript.
————. 1990b. "The international transmission effects of non-neutral consumption taxation." Department of Economics, Washington State University. Manuscript.
Batina, R. G., and T. Ihori. 1991. "International spillover effects of consumption taxation." *Journal of Japanese and International Economies* 15:404–20.
Becker, G. S. 1974. "A theory of social interactions." *Journal of Political Economy* 82:1063–91.
————. 1981. *A Treatise on the Family.* Cambridge, MA: Harvard University Press.
Becker, G. S., and N. Tomes. 1979. "An equilibrium theory of the distribution of income and intergenerational mobility." *Journal of Political Economy* 87:1153–89.

Bernheim, D., A. Shleifer, and L. Summers. 1985. "The strategic bequest motive." *Journal of Political Economy* 93:1045–76.

Burgress, D. F. 1988. "Complementarity and the discount rate for public investment." *Quarterly Journal of Economics* 102:527–41.

Dekle, R. 1990. "Do the Japanese elderly reduce their total wealth? A new look with different data." *Journal of the Japanese and International Economies* 4:309–17.

Diamond, P. A. 1965. "National debt in a neoclassical growth model." *American Economic Review* 55:1126–50.

Feldstein, M. 1982. "Government deficits and aggregate demand." *Journal of Monetary Economics,* 1–20.

Gravelle, J.G. 1991. "Income, consumption, and wage taxation in a life-cycle model: Separating efficiency from redistribution." *American Economic Review* 81:985–95.

Hayashi, F. 1986. "Is Japan's saving rate so apparently high?" In *NBER Macroeconomics Annual 1986,* ed. Stanley Fischer, 147–210.

Homma, M., N. Abe, N. Atoda, T. Ihori, M. Kandori, and T. Mutoh. 1986. *The Debt Neutrality Hypothesis* (in Japanese). Tokyo, Japan: Economic Planning Agency.

Horioka, C. Y. 1991. "Savings in Japan." Osaka University Discussion Paper, no. 248. Osaka, Japan.

Ihori, T. 1987. "The size of government spending and the private sector's evaluation." *Journal of Japanese and International Economies* 2:82–96.

———. 1990. "Government spending and private consumption." *Canadian Journal of Economics* 23:60–69.

Jones, L. E., and R. E. Manuelli. 1990. "Finite lifetimes and growth." NBER Working Paper, no. 3469.

Kormendi, R. C. 1983. "Government debt, government spending, and private sector behavior." *American Economic Review* 73:994–1010.

Kotlikoff, L. J., and L. H. Summers. 1981. "The role of intergenerational transfers in aggregate capital accumulation." *Journal of Political Economy* 89:706–32.

Kurz, M. 1984. "Capital accumulation and the characteristics of private intergenerational transfers." *Economica* 51:1–22.

Menchik, P., and M. David. 1982. "The incidence of a lifetime consumption tax." *National Tax Journal* 35:189–204.

Mieskowski, P. 1980. *The Advisability and Feasibility of an Expenditure Tax System.* In *The Economics of Taxation,* ed. H. Aaron and M. Boskin, 179–201. Washington, D.C.: The Brookings Institution.

Nemoto, J., K. Kamada, and M. Kawamura. 1990. "Measuring social discount rates and optimal public capital stocks in Japan, 1960–1982." Nagoya University, International Economic Conflict Discussion Paper, no. 48. Nagoya, Japan.

Ohtake, F. 1991. "The bequest motive and the saving/labor supply of the aged" (in Japanese). *Keizai Kenkyu* 42:21–30.

Rebelo, S. 1991. "Long run policy analysis and long run growth." *Journal of Political Economy* 99:500–521.

Samuelson, P. 1958. "An exact consumption loan model of interest with or without the social contrivance of money." *Journal of Political Economy* 66:467–82.

Seidman, L. S. 1983. "Taxes in a life cycle growth model with bequests and inheritances." *American Economic Review* 73:437–41.

Yaari, M. 1964. "On the consumer's lifetime allocation process." *International Economic Review* 5:304–17.

Yagi, T. 1991. "Macroeconomic impact of inheritance tax." Nagoya University. Manuscript. Nagoya, Japan.

CHAPTER 7

Intergenerational Altruism and the Effectiveness of Fiscal Policy—New Tests Based on Cohort Data

Andrew B. Abel and Laurence J. Kotlikoff

In recent years Barro's (1974) ingenious model of intergenerational altruism has taken its place among the major theories of consumption and saving. The model, which starts with the simple assumption that parents care about the welfare of their children, yields the remarkably strong conclusion that, apart from distorting marginal incentives, deficits and all other government redistributions between generations have no effect on the economy. The possibility that deficits, unfunded social security, and similar policies do not matter has received considerable attention.

Despite its policy importance, there have been few direct tests of the intergenerational altruism model. The main difficulty in directly testing the model at the microlevel is the relative lack of data detailing both the consumption and resources of altruistically linked households. In addition, it is difficult to determine from the data which households are altruistically linked to each other. Direct tests of the model with macrodata are also problematic because they require the aggregation of different clans (sets of altruistically linked households) each of which may have a different utility function.

In this essay we present a new direct test of the altruism model. The test

The earlier version of this paper (entitled "Does the Consumption of Different Age Groups Move Together? A New Nonparametric Test of Intergenerational Altruism," NBER Working Paper, no. 2490, 1988) appears to have been the first in a series of papers by economists, including Townsend (1989), Altonji, Hayashi and Kotlikoff (1992), Cochran (1991), and Mace (1991) to test the equality in Euler errors implied by risk sharing, whether the risk sharing is altruistically motivated or not. We thank Joseph Altonji, Robert Barsky, Gary Becker, Jinyong Cai, Gary Chamberlain, Jagadeesh Gokhale, Fumio Hayashi, Robert Lucas, Kevin Murphy, Sherwin Rosen, Robert Townsend, Lawrence Weiss, and seminar participants at Brown University, the University of Chicago, and at the National Bureau of Economic Research's summer workshop on financial markets for very helpful comments. Jinyong Cai and Jagadeesh Gokhale provided outstanding research assistance. This research was funded by the National Science Foundation. Our data are from the 1980 through 1985 Consumer Expenditure Surveys, which are publicly available through the Bureau of Labor Statistics.

is based on a property of the model that, as of the first draft of this essay, had not previously been exploited. This property is that the Euler errors (i.e., disturbances in the Euler equations) of altruistically linked members of clans are identical. Assuming utility is homothetic and time separable, this equality of Euler errors means that, controlling for clan preferences about the age distribution of consumption, the percentage changes over time in consumption of all clan members are equal. Intuitively, since consumption of each clan member is based on overall clan resources, and not on the distribution of resources over clan members, any shocks to the resources of specific clan members will be spread across all clan members. Under the homotheticity and time separability assumptions, spreading shocks over all clan members means changing the consumption of all members by the same percentage.

Ideally, one would test this proposition by simply comparing changes in the consumption of different clan members. Unfortunately, the requisite clan-specific data is not generally available (see Altonji, Hayashi, and Kotlikoff 1992 for an exception); indeed, it may be very difficult to determine who is and who is not a member of a particular altruistically linked clan. As indicated by Kotlikoff (1989) and Bernheim and Bagwell (1988), clans may be quite large because of current as well as potential intermarriage.

How can we use our Consumer Expenditure Survey data on household consumption to test intergenerational altruism when we cannot identify which households should be grouped together in clans? Our test is based on the implication of the altruism model that, after controlling for demographics, all clan members should change their consumption by the same percentage in any given period. If clans are large, and all clans have the same age structure, then the average Euler error in each age group of households in our sample should be the same, under intergenerational altruism. However, the assumption of identical age structures within each clan seems too strong. A weaker assumption is that the age structure of clans is independent of their Euler errors; that is, the fact that a clan accounts for a larger than average fraction of households in an age group does not help predict how its Euler error will differ, on average, from the average Euler error across clans. Even with this weaker assumption we can test the intergenerational altruism hypothesis by comparing the average Euler errors of different age groups.

Testing the altruism model by comparing average cohort percentage changes in consumption is particularly advantageous because it is non-parametric; in determining whether the average consumption of different age cohorts moves together we place no restrictions on preferences beyond the assumptions of homotheticity and time separability. In particular, each clan can have quite different preferences.

The new quarterly Consumer Expenditure Survey (CES), which, as of the time of this study, is available from the middle of 1980 through the middle of 1985, provides an excellent data set for determining whether the consumption of different age groups moves together. The CES records the consumption of each sample household for up to four quarters, and thus can be used to determine the average quarterly percentage change in consumption of households in a given age group.

The null hypothesis of our test is that, after controlling for demographics, cohort differences in the average percentage change in consumption (average Euler errors) are due simply to sampling and measurement error. Alternative hypotheses, suggested by the life-cycle model, are that, after controlling for demographics, (1) the percentage changes in the average consumption of any two cohorts are more highly correlated the closer in age are the two cohorts, (2) the variance in the percentage change in consumption is a monotone function of the age of the cohort, and (3) cohort differences in consumption changes depend on cohort differences in resource shocks, which may be proxied by cohort differences in income changes. While the data do not reject the altruism model against alternatives (1) and (2), they do reject the altruism model against alternative (3); that is, we find no age structure to the variance-covariance matrix of cohort Euler errors, but we do find that cohort differences in Euler errors are significantly correlated with cohort differences in income changes.

This essay proceeds in the next section by reviewing briefly the empirical literature bearing on the intergenerational altruism hypothesis. The third section presents the model of altruistically linked households and develops the proposition that Euler errors are equal for all clan members. The fourth section derives a statistical model to test this proposition. The fifth section discusses the statistical implications of the selfish life-cycle model, which represents at least one important alternative to the altruism model. The sixth section describes the data. The seventh section contains the empirical results. The last section summarizes the findings and concludes with a discussion of the implications of the findings for the effectiveness of fiscal policy.

Empirical Research Bearing on the Altruism Hypothesis

The largest body of empirical literature bearing on the altruism hypothesis relates the time series of aggregate consumption to the time series of social security wealth. Chief among these studies are those of Feldstein (1974), Darby (1979), and Leimer and Lesnoy (1980). Studies relating the consumption time series to other aspects of fiscal policy include Kormendi (1983), and Aschauer (1985). The results of this body of research can be summarized with one word: ambiguous. Even were the results all in agreement, it would be difficult to know precisely what had been learned; as pointed out by Auerbach and Kotlikoff (1983) and Williamson and Jones (1983), if the life-cycle model is taken as the null hypothesis in these studies, the models are misspecified because of the inability to aggregate the behavior of different age groups. Auerbach and Kotlikoff (1983) show that the regression procedures would reject the life-cycle model even using data taken from a pure life-cycle economy. An alternative view of these regressions is that the Barro model is the null hypothesis. But in this case many of the regressions also seem to be misspecified both because of aggregation and because they ignore the government's intertemporal budget constraint.

Recent papers by Boskin and Kotlikoff (1986) and Boskin and Lau (1988) directly test the implication of the intergenerational altruism model that the age distribution of resources does not affect the age distribution of consumption. Both reject the proposition that aggregate consumption is invariant to the age distribution of resources. The findings of these two papers accord with the findings reported here that link cohort differences in Euler errors to cohort differences in income changes. Mace (1991) uses the same CES data that we use to test risk sharing. Her findings in support of risk sharing are strongly contradicted by the results reported here as well as by the findings in Altonji, Hayashi, and Kotlikoff 1989.

A different body of literature that is relevant to the altruism model as well as other neoclassical models is the Euler equation studies of Hall (1978), Flavin (1981), Hall and Mishkin (1982), Mankiw, Rothenberg, and Summers (1982), Lawrence (1983), Shapiro (1984), Altonji and Siow (1987), Zeldes (1989), and others. These studies test intertemporal expected utility maximization, specifically its implication that the Euler error is uncorrelated with previous information. A rejection of this null hypothesis would rule out the altruism model as well as other neoclassical consumption models. The time series tests of the Euler equation provide mixed results. In contrast, most microlevel studies appear to accept the Euler equation restriction for the majority of households. For example, both Zeldes (1989) and Lawrence (1983) use the limited consumption data in the Panel Study of Income Dynamics and reach the conclusion that the Euler equation holds for the great majority of households.

The microlevel studies that are closest to our own are Altonji, Hayashi, and Kotlikoff 1992, Townsend 1989, and Cochrane 1991. Altonji, Hayashi, and Kotlikoff use matched consumption and income data on the households of parents and their adult children; their findings strongly reject the altruism model's prediction that the distribution of consumption between parents and children is independent of the distribution of resources between the parent and children. In contrast, Townsend (1989) and Rosenzweig (1988) study the consumption and transfer behavior of households within Indian villages. Townsend reports that the consumption changes of households within each village are highly correlated and Rosenzweig reports substantial income-smoothing transfers; these findings are consistent either with altruism or risk sharing among villagers. Cochran tests for perfect insurance markets with microdata on consumption and certain types of income changes. Not surprisingly, he rejects the proposition that insurance markets are perfect, although he does report that certain income shocks are reasonably well insured.

Finally, there is a microliterature on transfers (see Cox 1987 and Kotlikoff 1988 for summaries) that appears, on balance, to reject the altruism model. Cox (1987), for example, finds that transfers rise with the level of recipients' incomes, and Menchik (1984) reports that, far from being equalizing, most bequests are divided perfectly evenly between children.

The Equal Euler Error Proposition

In this section we model the consumption decisions of households and show that all households within an altruistically linked clan will have the same Euler errors in every period. To model the consumption decisions we must introduce the utility function of the clan. The clan utility function depends on the consumption of present and future households within the clan. We begin by discussing the utility function of a household within a clan at a point in time. After discussing this intratemporal utility function, we combine the intratemporal utility functions of all households in the clan at all points of time.

The Intratemporal Household Utility Function

Let U_{ikt} denote the utility in period t of household k in clan i. The assumptions that the intertemporal utility function is homothetic and time-separable implies that the intratemporal household utility function is isoelastic; that is,

$$U_{i,k,t} = \sum_{a=0}^{D} P_{i,k,t,a}\, \theta_{i,k,t,a} \frac{c_{i,k,t,a}^{1-\gamma_i}}{(1-\gamma_i)}, \tag{1}$$

where $P_{i,k,t,a}$ is the number of members age a in household k, clan i at time t; D is the maximum age of life; $\theta_{i,k,t,a}$ is the weight household k in clan i places on the utility of members age a at time t; and $c_{i,k,t,a}$ is the consumption of the members of clan i who are in household k and are age a at time t. The utility function in equation 1 is written as a function of the consumption of each of the members of the household. For the isoelastic utility function we can express household utility simply as a function of total household consumption at time t. Let $C_{i,k,t}$ denote household k's total consumption at time t, then:

$$C_{i,k,t} = \sum_{a=0}^{D} P_{i,k,t,a} c_{i,k,t,a}. \qquad (2)$$

The optimal allocation of consumption across the individual members of the household is determined by maximizing the intratemporal utility function in equation 1 subject to equation 2. Performing this optimization and substituting the optimal values of $c_{i,k,t,a}$ into equation 1 yields

$$U_{i,k,t} = \phi_{i,k,t_i} \frac{C_{i,k,t}^{1-\gamma_i}}{(1 - \gamma_i)} \qquad (3a)$$

where

$$\phi_{i,k,t} = \left(\sum_{a=0}^{D} P_{i,k,t,a} \theta_{i,k,t,a}^{1/\gamma_i} \right)^{\gamma_i}. \qquad (3b)$$

Equation 3a expresses the utility of the household as a function of total household consumption.

The Clan's Intertemporal Utility Function

The intertemporal utility function of a clan of altruistically linked households is obtained by summing the intratemporal household utility functions across all households in the clan and across the present and all future periods of time, taking account of time preference. Let α_i denote the time preference discount factor for all households in clan i, and let N_{is} denote the number of households in clan i at time s. At time t, the objective function of the clan is

$$V_{i,t} = E_t \sum_{s=t}^{\infty} \alpha_i^{s-t} \sum_{h=1}^{N_{i,s}} \phi_{i,h,s} \frac{C_{i,h,s}^{1-\gamma_i}}{1 - \gamma_i}. \qquad (4)$$

The clan maximizes equation 4 subject to:

$$W_{i,t+1} = (W_{i,t} + e_{i,t} - C_{i,t} - G_t)(1 + r_{i,t}), \qquad (5)$$

where,

$$C_{i,t} = \sum_{h=1}^{N_{i,t}} C_{i,h,t},$$

is total clan i consumption at time t. The term $e_{i,t}$ stands for the possibly uncertain labor earnings of the clan at time t; $r_{i,t}$ is the possibly uncertain rate of return earned by clan i at time t on its portfolio of nonhuman wealth, and $W_{i,t}$ is clan i's net nonhuman wealth at time t. In addition to $e_{i,t}$ and $r_{i,t}$, $\phi_{i,h,s}$ for $s > t$ in equation 4 may be uncertain at time t due to life span uncertainty and uncertainty about clan fertility.

The term G_t in equation 5 stands for government consumption at time t. This is the only way in which fiscal policy enters the clan's budget constraint. Government consumption spending produces an income effect on private consumption spending, because the clan must finance this spending out of its (the economy's) collective output. But regardless of the size of government spending, the budget constraint is invariant to the choice by the government of which clan members will "pay" (mail the government its tax payments) for its spending. The reason is that the clan does its own redistribution across its members, so any redistribution by the government is automatically offset by clan redistribution. The fact that equation 5 does not include any information about the identity of taxpayers automatically implies that government redistribution in this model is ineffective.

The First-Order Conditions

Maximization of equation 4 subject to equation 5 implies the static first-order conditions

$$\phi_{i,k,t} \, C_{i,k,t}^{-\gamma_i} = \phi_{i,h,t} \, C_{i,h,t}^{-\gamma_i}, \tag{6}$$

and the intertemporal first-order conditions

$$E_t[\alpha_i \phi_{i,k,t+1} \, C_{i,k,t+1}^{-\gamma_i} (1 + r_{i,t+1})] = \phi_{i,k,t} \, C_{i,k,t}^{-\gamma_i}. \tag{7}$$

The static first-order conditions in equation 6 characterize the optimal allocation of consumption between households h and k within clan i. The intertemporal first-order condition in equation 7 holds for each household within clan i. Let $\epsilon_{i,k,t+1}$ denote the Euler error at time $t + 1$ for household k in clan i. The Euler error is defined by

$$\alpha_i \phi_{i,k,t+1} \, C_{i,k,t+1}^{-\gamma_i} (1 + r_{i,t+1}) = E_t[\alpha_i \phi_{i,k,t+1} \, C_{i,k,t+1}^{-\gamma_i} (1 + r_{i,t+1})] \epsilon_{i,k,t+1},$$

$$\tag{8}$$

where $E_t \epsilon_{i,k,t+1} = 1$. Using the definition of the Euler error in equation 8 we can rewrite equation 7 as

$$\alpha_i \phi_{i,k,t+1} \, C_{i,k,t+1}^{-\gamma_i} \, (1 + r_{i,t+1}) = \phi_{i,k,t} \, C_{i,k,t}^{-\gamma_i} \, \epsilon_{i,k,t+1}. \tag{7$'$}$$

Equations 6 and 7$'$ together imply that the Euler errors of all households in clan i are identical. That is,

$$\epsilon_{i,k,t+1} = \epsilon_{i,h,t+1} \equiv \epsilon_{i,t+1}. \tag{9}$$

Note that in deriving this result we did not need to restrict different households in a given clan to have identical age compositions or to receive identical weights in the clan utility function.

Are Euler Errors Equalized under the Life-Cycle Model with Perfect Risk Sharing?

An alternative nonaltruistic model with the implication of equal Euler errors across households is the selfish life-cycle model under the assumption of perfect risk sharing and identical isoelastic preferences and identical time preference rates. To see this, note that the equilibrium of such a life-cycle economy with perfect risk sharing may be represented as the solution to a planning problem in which the planner maximizes a weighted sum of individual household expected intertemporal utilities subject to a collective budget constraint (see Townsend 1989). The division of total consumption at each point in time will depend on the household's weight; that is, equation 6 will hold. In addition, since there is a single budget constraint in this problem, the weighted marginal utility of each household's consumption will be equated to the shadow value of this budget constraint at each point in time. Hence, changes (over time) in the weighted value of each household marginal utility will equal the changes (over time) in these shadow prices; i.e., equation 7$'$ will hold. Since the shadow prices and their changes are not household specific, the weighted ratio of changes in marginal utilities of consumption will be the same for each household. Hence, equation 9, the equal Euler error proposition, will hold.

A Test of the Equal Euler Error Proposition Based on Cohort Data

In this section we develop a method of testing the equal Euler error proposition using cohort data. We start by taking logarithms of equation 7$'$, yielding

$$\log(C_{i,k,t+1}/C_{i,k,t}) = (1/\gamma_i)\log(\alpha_i \phi_{i,k,t+1}/\phi_{i,k,t})$$

$$- \log[\epsilon_{i,t+1}/(1 + r_{i,t+1})] \tag{10}$$

Consider all households in clan i whose heads are age a. Take the average of equation 10 over all such households. The resulting average of equation 10 is given by equation 11 where we define the averages of the left hand side and the two terms on the right hand side of equation 10 respectively by

$$Y^a_{i,t+1} = \psi^a_{i,t+1} + \mu_{i,t+1}. \tag{11}$$

Note that the term $\mu_{i,t+1}$ is not indexed by age since the Euler errors of each household in clan i are identical. Next average equation 11 over all clans. This produces equation 12 where $s^a_{i,t}$ is the fraction of age a households that belong to clan i at time t, and M is the total number of clans.

$$\sum_{i=1}^{M} s^a_{i,t} Y^a_{i,t} = \sum_{i=1}^{M} s^a_{i,t} \psi^a_{i,t} + \sum_{i=1}^{M} \mu_{i,t}/M$$

$$+ \sum_{i=1}^{M} s^a_{i,t}(\mu_{i,t} - \sum_{j=1}^{M} \mu_{j,t}/M) \tag{12}$$

In equation 12 the cohort average value of $\mu_{i,t}$ is written as the simple unweighted average of the Euler errors across all clans (the second term on the right hand side of the equation) plus the cohort average value (weighted by each clan's fraction of all cohort households) of the deviation of the clan's Euler error from the unweighted average Euler error over all clans. We assume that this third term on the right hand side, which is the population covariance between a clan's Euler error and its share of the population in the age group, is zero.

We can rewrite the remaining terms in equation 12 more compactly by letting $\bar{Y}^a_t$ denote the left hand side of equation 12, $\bar{\psi}^a_t$ denote the first term on the right hand side of equation 12, and $\bar{\mu}_t$ denote the second term on the right hand side of equation 12.

$$\bar{Y}^a_t = \bar{\psi}^a_t + \bar{\mu}_t \tag{12'}$$

Equation 12' states that the cohort average value of the percentage change in consumption (more precisely, the log of the ratio of consumption at $t + 1$ to consumption at time t) equals a term, $\bar{\psi}^a_t$, which depends on age and time, plus a term $\bar{\mu}_t$, which is independent of age.

Because of sampling and measurement error, the true population mean, $\bar{Y}^a_t$, is not observable. Hence, in equation 13, we set the observed population-weighted sample mean of the logarithm of the ratio of consumption at time $t + 1$ to consumption at time t, $\hat{Y}_t^a$, equal to the true population mean, $\bar{Y}_t^a$, plus a term, η_t^a, that reflects sampling and measurement error. Our null hypothesis is that $\eta_t^a = \omega_t^a / h_t^a$, where ω_t^a is an independently and normally distributed random variable with mean zero and variance σ^2, and h_t^a adjusts for the sampling error in our weighted estimate of $\bar{Y}_t^a$. Specifically, h_t^a equals $\Sigma_k w_{tk}^a{}^2 / (\Sigma_k w_{tk}^a)^2$, where w_{tk}^a is the CES population weight at time t for household k in cohort a. In equation 12' the term $\bar{\psi}^a{}_t$ reflects the average growth in consumption due to demographic changes in household composition. Since we are dealing with data over only a five year interval, in equation 13 we drop the time subscript and treat $\bar{\psi}_t^a$ as a time-invariant, but age-specific constant.

$$\hat{Y}_t^a = \bar{\psi}^a + \bar{\mu}_t + \eta_t^a \tag{13}$$

Equation 13 forms the basis for our statistical test of the equality of average cohort percentage changes in consumption. Under the null hypothesis of equal Euler errors, ω_{at} is i.i.d. across ages a and time periods t with variance equal to σ^2.

If the null hypothesis fails to hold and the weighted average Euler errors differ across age cohorts, the error term η_t^a will capture not only measurement and sampling noise, but also each cohort's time t average Euler error after controlling for age and time effects. Our alternative hypothesis is, therefore, that the ω_{at}s are not simply i.i.d., but depend on age as specified below.

$$E(\omega_{it}\omega_{js}) = 0 \text{ if } s \neq t$$

$$E(\omega_{it}\omega_{jt}) = \rho^{|i-j|}\sigma^2\nu^{i+j} \tag{14}$$

According to equation 14 the variance of ω_{it} increases or decreases with age depending on whether ν exceeds or falls short of unity, and the correlation of ω_{it} and ω_{jt} for $i \neq j$ depends on the size of the age gap, $|j - i|$. For example, if ρ exceeds zero, equation 14 says that the correlation of ω_{it} and ω_{jt} for age groups i and j is larger the closer in age are the age groups i and j. The case in which $\rho = 0$ and $\nu = 1$ corresponds to the null hypothesis. Values of ρ and ν as well as the age and time effects in equation 13 are estimated by maximum likelihood. The Appendix presents the likelihood function and derives the estimators.

Another testable implication of equation 13 is that η_t^a is uncorrelated with changes in cohort a's resources, which may be proxied by changes in its income. To see this note that in equation 13 the term $\bar{\mu}_t$, which equals the common (across cohorts) average Euler error, fully controls for resource changes under the altruism model. Hence, if one adds cohort a's income change to the implicit regression model in equation 13, the coefficient on the cohort's income change should be zero. Another way of saying this is that differences across cohorts with respect to consumption changes should depend only on differences in their demographics (the $\bar{\psi}^a$ terms) and not on the distribution across cohorts of income changes. In addition to testing whether there is a significant age pattern to the variance-covariance matrix of the η_t^as, we add the cohort's income change to equation 13 and estimate the model by ordinary least squares. This procedure is, in differences, the fixed effects test of altruism developed in Altonji, Hayashi, and Kotlikoff 1989.

Consumption Behavior of Selfish Life-Cycle Households: An Alternative Hypothesis

This section motivates the assumption of an age-dependent variance-covariance matrix of the η_t^as under the alternative life-cycle model. The null hypothesis of operative altruistic linkages is that the Euler error is identical across households within a clan; hence, within a clan the Euler error is independent of the age of the household head. In contrast, under the life-cycle model Euler errors of different households within a clan bear no special relation to one another, but we would expect that the variance-covariance matrix of Euler errors across unrelated as well as related households would depend on the households' ages. This section illustrates, with two different preference structures and types of uncertainty, why ρ is likely to differ from zero and ν is likely to differ from unity if the life-cycle model holds.

Example 1: Logarithmic Utility

The first example is based on Samuelson 1969 and assumes only uncertainty with respect to the rate of return. Let $c_{t,a}$ be the consumption at time t of a household whose head is age a; $w_{t,a}$ is the wealth at time t of a household whose head is age a. The decision problem at time t, when the household is age a, is to maximize

$$E_t \left[\sum_{j=0}^{D-a} \beta^j u(c_{t+j,a+j}) \right], \tag{15}$$

and

$$w_{t+1,a+1} = (w_{t,a} - c_{a,t})R_{t+1,a+1}, \tag{16}$$

where D is the age at which the household head dies and $R_{t+1,a+1}$ is the gross rate of return on the portfolio from period t to period $t + 1$. Now suppose that the utility function is logarithmic, $u(c) = \log c$. This optimization problem can be solved by stochastic dynamic programming (Samuelson 1969) to obtain

$$c_{t,D-j} = g_j w_{t,D-j}, \tag{17a}$$

where

$$g_j = \left(\sum_{k=0}^{j} \beta^k \right)^{-1}. \tag{17b}$$

This solution holds regardless of the temporal dependence of the process generating returns $R_{t+1,a+1}$.

Now consider the growth rate in consumption from period t to period $t + 1$. It follows directly from equation 17a that

$$c_{t+1,a+1}/c_{t,a} = (g_{j-1}/g_j)(w_{t+1,a+1}/w_{t,a}). \tag{18}$$

The ratio of wealth in successive periods can be rewritten using equations 16 and 17a as

$$w_{t+1,a+1}/w_{t,a} = (1 - g_j)R_{t+1,a+1}. \tag{19}$$

Substituting equation 19 into equation 18 yields

$$c_{t+1,a+1}/c_{t,a} = (g_{j-1}/g_j)(1 - g_j)R_{t+1,a+1}. \tag{20}$$

Finally, we can use the expression for g_j in equation 17b to simplify the expression for the growth rate of consumption in equation 20 to obtain

$$c_{t+1,a+1}/c_{t,a} = \beta R_{t+1,a+1}. \tag{21}$$

The growth rate of consumption is proportional to the realized gross rate of return from period t to period $t + 1$. If the gross rate of return on a household's portfolio is independent of the age of the household head then $R_{t+1,a+1} = R_{t+1}$ for all a. In this case, all households will have the same Euler error regardless of the age of the household head.

Taken at face value, this example suggests that the Euler error is independent of the age of the household head. However, this conclusion depends on the assumption that $R_{t+1,a+1} = R_{t+1}$ for all a. This assumption would be warranted if all households held the same portfolios (up to a scale factor) regardless of age. However, as documented in King and Leape 1984 the composition of actual U.S. household portfolios is significantly different depending on the age of the household head. Young and middle-age households tend to hold a large portion of their wealth in the form of negative holdings of fixed income securities (mortgages), significant holdings of housing, and small holdings of stocks and bonds. Older households, in contrast, hold much more of their wealth in the form of home equity (i.e., their outstanding mortgages are much smaller) and in stocks and bonds.

Because the allocation of portfolios varies systematically with age, and because the rates of return on different assets reflect different stochastic processes, we might expect the conditional variances of the portfolio rates of return, $R_{t+1,a+1}$, to vary systematically with age. Furthermore, because the composition of portfolios is more similar for similar aged households than for households of very different ages, we might expect the Euler errors to be more highly correlated for households of similar age than for households of very different ages.

Example 2: Quadratic Utility

In order to focus on the role of human wealth, as distinct from nonhuman wealth, we change the framework slightly. Now we suppose that utility is quadratic and that the rate of return on nonhuman wealth is constant. In addition, assume that the gross rate of return on nonhuman wealth, R, is equal to β^{-1} (the reciprocal of the time preference discount factor). The only uncertainty that the household faces is in labor income $y_{t,a}$. In this case, it is straightforward to apply the certainty equivalence principle to obtain:

$$E_t(c_{t+j,a+j}) = c_{t,a} \text{ for } j = 0, 1, 2, \ldots, D - a. \tag{22}$$

The lifetime budget constraint of the household implies that the present value of revisions in future labor income, $E_{t+1}(y_{t+1+j,a+1+j}) - E_t(y_{t+1+j,a+1+j})$, is equal to the present value of revisions in future consumption, $E_{t+1}(c_{t+1+j,a+1+j}) - E_t(c_{t+1+j,a+1+j})$. Such that

$$\sum_{j=0}^{D-a-1} R^{-j}[E_{t+1}(y_{t+1+j,a+1+j}) - E_t(y_{t+1+j,a+1+j})]$$

$$= \sum_{j=0}^{D-a-1} R^{-j}[E_{t+1}(c_{t+1+j,a+1+j}) - E_t(c_{t+1+j,a+1+j})]. \tag{23}$$

Equation 22 implies that the revisions in expectations of future consumption are equal to the change in consumption between period t and period $t + 1$, hence:

$$E_{t+1}(c_{t+1+j,a+1+j}) - E_t(c_{t+1+j,a+1+j})$$

$$= c_{t+1,a+1} - c_{t,a} \equiv \Delta c_{t+1,a+1}. \tag{24}$$

To calculate the revision in expectations of future labor income, we first specify the moving average representation of the process for labor income as

$$y_{t,a} = \sum_{k=0}^{a} \xi_k e_{t-k,a-k} + \bar{y}_{t,a}, \tag{25}$$

where $E_{t-1}\{e_{t,a}\} = 0$. With this time series process for labor income, the revisions in expected future (between time t and time $t + 1$) labor income at time $t + 1$ are

$$E_{t+1}(y_{t+1+j,a+1+j}) - E_t(y_{t+1+j,a+1+j}) = \xi_j e_{t+1,a+1}. \tag{26}$$

Substituting the revisions in future consumption equation 24 and the revisions in future labor income equation 26 into equation 23 we obtain

$$\Delta c_{t+1,a+1} = \Gamma_a e_{t+1,a+1}, \tag{27a}$$

where

$$\Gamma_a \equiv \left(\sum_{j=0}^{D-a-1} R^{-j} \xi_j \right) \Big/ \left(\sum_{j=0}^{D-a-1} R^{-j} \right). \tag{27b}$$

The variance of the unforecastable change in consumption, which in this example is equal to the variance of the actual change in consumption, is

$$\text{var}(\Delta c_{t+1,a+1}) = \Gamma_a^2 \, \text{var}(e_{t+1,a+1}). \tag{28}$$

Note that even if the variance of the innovation to the labor income process, $\text{var}(e_{t+1,a+1})$, is independent of age, the variance of the unforecastable change in consumption is age-dependent because Γ_a is, in general, age-dependent. For instance, if the labor income process is i.i.d., then $\xi_0 = 1$ and $\xi_j = 0$ for all nonzero j. In this case,

$$\Gamma_a = \left(\sum_{j=0}^{D-a-1} R^{-j} \right)^{-1},$$

which is an increasing function of age. Alternatively, if the labor income process is a first-order auto-regressive progress with AR coefficient ρ, then $\xi_j = \rho^j$. In this case, $\Gamma_a = [(1 - R^{-1})/(1 - \rho/R)][1 - (\rho/R)^{D-a})/(1 - (1/R)^{D-a})]$. If the process is stationary and ρ is nonnegative, then Γ_a is increasing with age. For a random walk, $\rho = 1$ and $\Gamma_a = 1$ independent of age. If ρ is greater than 1, then Γ_a is decreasing with age.

Equation 28 gives the variance of the Euler error expressed in terms of the change in the level of consumption rather than the change in the logarithm of consumption. In this model, the age-consumption profile will, on average, be flat. Hence, on average, the variance of the percentage change in consumption will vary with age if the variance of the absolute change in consumption varies by age.

The Data

The ongoing Consumer Expenditure Survey (CES), which began in the first quarter of 1980, interviews approximately 4,500 households in each quarter. Most households are interviewed four times in the CES. The four interviews always ask a common set of questions about consumption, but some questions are asked only in the first and fourth interviews, and others are asked only in the fourth interview. Some households are interviewed fewer than four times because they drop out of the sample. Others are interviewed fewer than four times because of the sample design; in an effort to maintain in each quarter the same fraction of households responding to a first, second, third, and fourth interview, the CES administers the second, third, or fourth interviews to some households as their initial interview. If the household's initial interview is a second interview, the household will be interviewed two more times. If a household's initial interview is a third interview, the household will be interviewed once more. And if the household's initial interview is a fourth interview, the household will not be reinterviewed.

The approximately 4,500 interviews in each quarter are spread over each month of the quarter. In the interviews households are asked about their consumption expenditures in the previous three months. Hence, a household interviewed in January 1981 reports consumption expenditures for October, November, and December 1980, while a household interviewed in March 1981 reports consumption expenditures for December 1980 and January and February 1981. Unfortunately, for most expenditure items, households only report total expenditures in the previous three full months and do not provide a month-to-month breakdown of those expenditures. As a consequence, the data for a household interviewed, say, in January cannot readily be combined with data from a household interviewed in February since the two quarterly observations cover overlapping, rather than identical quarters. In effect, each wave of the Consumer Expenditure Survey provides three overlapping sets of observations on quarterly consumption. In our analysis we treat each of the three quarterly data sets separately and refer to them as "quarterly sample" 1, 2, and 3.[1] For purposes of analyzing the quarterly data we considered fifty-eight age cohorts corresponding to ages 23 through 80.

Given the lumpiness of some nondurable consumption expenditures, such as vacation trips, it is useful to test the equal Euler error proposition with semiannual as well as quarterly data. For those households who were interviewed four times, the four quarterly observations can be combined to form observations on semiannual consumption. There are six possible semiannual data sets. For example, households interviewed in January, April, July, and October in year t provide an observation on the ratio of consumption over the period April–September in year t to consumption over the period October in year $t - 1$–March in year t. Households interviewed in July and October of year t and January and April of year $t + 1$ provide an observation on the ratio of consumption over the period October in year t–March in year $t + 1$ to consumption over the period April–September in year t. These types of observations produce a single data set of semiannual changes in consumption. One can also form a data set using households interviewed for the first of four times in April and other households interviewed for the first of four times in October. Hence, the April-July-October-January sequence provides two semiannual data sets. The May-August-November-February sequence provides another two semiannual data sets; and the June-September-December-March sequence provides the final two semiannual data sets.

Because of the smaller number of households who completed all four surveys, we constructed three-year age cohorts; i.e., we combined ages 23, 24, and 25 into one age group, ages 26, 27, and 28 into another age group, etc., up to the age group covering ages 77, 78, and 79. This difference in the definition of an age cohort should be kept in mind when comparing the quarterly and semiannual results presented in the next section; because of the difference in definitions, one would expect the estimated values of ρ and ν based on the semiannual data to be roughly the cube of their respective values based on the quarterly data.

---

1. Quarterly sample 1 corresponds to households interviewed in April, July, October, and January. Quarterly sample 2 corresponds to households interviewed in May, August, November, and February. Quarterly sample 3 corresponds to households interviewed in June, September, December, and March. In constructing the data for quarterly sample 1, as an example, we form ratios of (a) the July reported quarterly consumption to the April reported quarterly consumption, (b) the October reported quarterly consumption to the July reported quarterly consumption, (c) the January reported quarterly consumption to the October reported quarterly consumption, and (d) the April reported quarterly consumption to the January reported quarterly consumption. In forming the average logarithm of the ratio of consumption say in January 1983 to consumption in October 1982, all households who were surveyed in both October 1982 and January 1983 were included.

The definition of aggregate consumption used in this study is total consumption expenditures excluding expenditures on housing, insurance, and consumer durables. We exclude housing both because adjustments to housing consumption are infrequent and because it is very difficult to impute quarterly or semiannual rent accurately for homeowners. Insurance expenditures were excluded because such expenditures represent risk pooling as opposed to consumption per se. In addition, the data records both negative and positive amounts of insurance expenditures, where a negative amount corresponds to a claim payment. Expenditures on durables should clearly be excluded from the definition of consumption. In contrast, imputed rent should be included; unfortunately, data on the stocks of durables are not sufficient for that purpose.

The CES provides population weights in each quarter for each household interviewed. These weights depend on the age of the household head as well as other economic and demographic characteristics. We use the time $t + 1$ sample weights in determining the cohort-specific weighted average value of the logarithm of the ratio of consumption at time $t + 1$ to consumption at time t; that is, we construct a weighted value of $\bar{Y}_{at}$.

Households that reported less than $150 of quarterly expenditure on food were excluded from the sample. This is the only form of sample selection in our analysis. Some preliminary analysis indicated that including households with very small quarterly food expenditure would not materially alter the results.

Empirical Findings

Changes in the Age-Consumption Profile over the Sample Period

As a prelude to examining estimates of ρ and ν, figure 1 illustrates how the age-consumption profile changed over the period 1980 through 1984. Ignoring demographic change, the proposition that each cohort's consumption should change, on average, by the same percentage, implies a time-invariant age-consumption profile. In forming figure 1 we calculated the annual weighted average of quarterly consumption (measured in 1985 dollars) at each individual age for households interviewed in April, August, and December of each of the five years. We combined these weighted averages within each calendar year to produce annual values of average consumption by age of the household. Next we divided annual consumption in year t at each age by the average consumption of 45-year-old households in year t. Finally, we smoothed these relative consumption values for each year by regressing them against an intercept and a fourth order polynomial in age. In these regressions the R^2 values each exceed 0.9. Figure 1 plots the resulting five smoothed polynomials of consumption at a particular age relative to consumption at age 45.

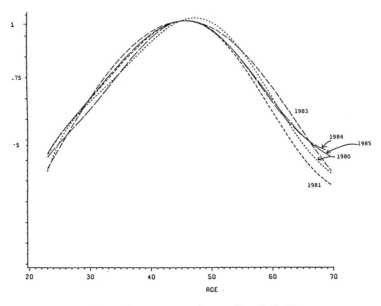

Fig. 1. Age consumption profile, 1980–85

The curve with the most dashes corresponds to 1980, the curve with the second most dashes corresponds to 1981, etc. The curves in the figure suggest that the age-consumption profile flattened out in 1982 and 1984. Compared with 1981, for example, the 1984 relative consumption of 60 year olds is over 10 percent larger. The $F(20, 264)$ value for the test that the five polynomials are the same is 17.94, greatly in excess of the 5 percent critical value of 1.66. To the extent that the changes in the shape of the relative age-consumption profile do not appear to be due to changes in demographics, it provides some evidence against the intergenerational altruism model; however, unlike the next set of findings, these profiles consider levels, not changes in consumption, and, as such, do not control as well for the composition of the sample; that is, the levels of consumption of the elderly in 1983 and 1984 may reflect samples whose older households happened to belong to clans with greater total resources.

Testing for Age-Dependence in Cohort Euler Errors

Table 1 also provides some preliminary data anlysis of the null hypothesis. This table compares quarterly changes in consumption of different age groups for quarterly sample 1. The corresponding tables for quarterly samples 2 and 3 are quite similar. For purposes of table 1 we consider five broad age catego-

TABLE 1. Quarterly Estimates of Average Adjusted Euler Errors
Quarterly Sample I

Age Group	1980.3	1980.4	1981.1	1981.2
23–29	−.033 (0.204)	.055 (.178)	.074 (.178)	−.105 (.181)
30–39	−.101 (0.210)	.057 (.181)	.052 (.178)	−.087 (.174)
40–49	−.084 (0.198)	.100 (.182)	−.004 (.175)	−.082 (.192)
50–59	−.154 (0.179)	.041 (.175)	−.002 (.181)	−.027 (.183)
60–69	−.130 (0.193)	.015 (.220)	.024 (.169)	.006 (.207)
70+	−.109 (0.185)	.010 (.202)	.099 (.170)	−.020 (.202)
	1981.3	**1981.4**	**1982.1**	**1982.2**
23–29	−.050 (.187)	−.007 (.183)	−.115 (.182)	.031 (.175)
30–39	.056 (.181)	.017 (.189)	−.061 (.185)	−.055 (.193)
40–49	−.060 (.199)	.031 (.199)	−.076 (.179)	−.024 (.201)
50–59	−.074 (.180)	.004 (.181)	−.020 (.180)	−.032 (.179)
60–69	−.038 (.204)	−.071 (.223)	−.023 (.173)	−.094 (.199)
70+	−.154 (.198)	.105 (.236)	−.123 (.174)	.140 (.196)
	1982.3	**1982.4**	**1983.1**	**1983.2**
23–29	−.006 (.182)	.020 (.184)	.029 (.179)	−.048 (.177)
30–39	−.014 (.201)	−.010 (.197)	.111 (.182)	−.052 (.178)
40–49	−.008 (.200)	.008 (.195)	.088 (.177)	−.038 (.181)
50–59	−.062 (.180)	−.016 (.188)	.052 (.174)	−.020 (.209)
60–69	−.035 (.193)	−.077 (.202)	.049 (.175)	−.101 (.200)
70+	−.108 (.209)	.009 (.219)	.112 (.179)	−.110 (.222)
	1983.3	**1983.4**	**1984.1**	**1984.2**
23–29	.032 (.184)	−.003 (.175)	.015 (.176)	−.076 (.205)
30–39	−.031 (.181)	.011 (.230)	.008 (.187)	−.061 (.183)
40–49	−.004 (.183)	.065 (.180)	−.011 (.176)	−.060 (.181)
50–59	.042 (.207)	.012 (.183)	.011 (.174)	−.027 (.186)
60–69	−.020 (.221)	.012 (.217)	−.064 (.173)	−.003 (.181)
70+	−.020 (.212)	.019 (.196)	−.012 (.178)	.009 (.190)
	1984.3	**1984.4**	**1985.1**	
23–29	−.021 (.213)	.046 (.207)	−.011 (.188)	
30–39	.020 (.185)	.027 (.185)	.034 (.185)	
40–49	.025 (.183)	.034 (.185)	.032 (.186)	
50–59	.007 (.191)	−.034 (.194)	−.065 (.181)	
60–69	−.011 (.178)	−.046 (.180)	.014 (.176)	
70+	−.015 (.186)	−.029 (.190)	.016 (.176)	

Note: Standard deviations are in parentheses.

ries: 23–29, 30–39, 40–49, 50–59, 60–69, and 70+. For each of these six age groups we report quarterly values of 100 times the deviation of the weighted average $\hat{Y}_t^a$ from the mean value, $\Sum_{t=1}^{19} \hat{Y}_t^a$, taken over the nineteen quarters in our sample. According to equation 12′ and ignoring measurement and sampling error, these deviations, which we refer to as average adjusted Euler errors, should be identical for each of the six age groups. In addition to presenting these deviations, table 1 reports the standard deviations of these deviations. These standard deviations are based on information on the variation across households in the percentage change in consumption within age-time cells.

Table 1 indicates that these average adjusted Euler errors are typically different across the six age categories. However, these differences could well be due to within cell variation. The standard errors of the entries in table 1 are quite large.

Another informal way to assess the data is to regress $\hat{Y}_t^a$ on a set of age group dummies and time dummies, either quarterly or semiannual.[2] The results from this regression can be compared with the results from regressing the same dependent variable on age dummies and the interaction of each of the time dummies with each of the age dummies.[3] According to equation 13, given a particular time period t, the age-time interactions should have identical coefficients. For purposes of this regression using quarterly data, we constructed six age dummies corresponding to the six age groups of table 1. The F values for quarterly samples 1, 2, and 3 are 1.470, 1.237, 0.746, respectively. Since the $F(90, 987)$, 5 percent critical value is 1.27, the age-time interactions are significantly different in only one of the three quarterly samples. The $F(25, 103)$ values in the corresponding regressions for the six semiannual samples are 0.912, 2.414, 2.538, 1.485, 1.768, and 0.612. The 5 percent critical value in this case is 1.61. Hence, age-time interactions are significantly different in three of the six semiannual samples.

Table 2 presents our maximum likelihood estimates for ρ and ν for the three quarterly data sets based on individual age cohorts from age 23 through age 80. None of the reported estimates of these parameters is significantly different from the values predicted by the null hypothesis of intergenerational altruism. Indeed, in the case of ν, two of the three estimates are equal to 1, to three decimal places, and the third value of 1.002 implies that the variance of

---

2. In this regression time dummies, age dummies, and the residuals account, respectively, for 81.3 percent, 4.2 percent, and 14.5 percent of the variance of the dependent variable.

3. To illustrate these two regressions, consider the case of two age groups, ages 1 and 2, and two time periods, time 1 and 2. Then the initial regression is:
$\hat{Y}_t^a = \delta_1 A_1 + \delta_2 A_2 + \tau T_2$, where the δs and τs are coefficients, and A_1, A_2 and T_2 are dummies for age group 1, age group 2, and time period 2, respectively. The alternative model is: $\hat{Y}_t^a = \delta_1 A_1 + \delta_2 A_2 + \lambda A_1 T_2 + l A_2 T_2$, and the test is whether $\lambda = l = \tau$.

TABLE 2. Maximum Likelihood Estimates and χ^2 Values: Quarterly Samples

	Consumption Measured per Household						
	Unconstrained		$\rho = 0$		$\nu = 1$		$\rho = 0 \ \nu = 1$
Sample	ρ	ν	ν	χ^2	ρ	χ^2	χ^2
Sample 1	0.020	1.002	1.002	0.958	0.003	1.307	2.345
Sample 2	−0.024	1.000	1.000	0.611	−0.024	0.000	0.611
Sample 3	0.031	1.000	1.000	1.066	0.031	0.000	1.066

Note: Five percent critical values for χ^2 are 5.991 for two restrictions and 3.841 for one restriction.

ω_{it} for 70 year olds is only about 15 percent larger than the corresponding variance for 20 year olds. One of the three point estimates for ρ is negative; a negative value of ρ, even were it significant, seems highly unlikely from the perspective of the life-cycle model. The other two nonnegative values of ρ suggest a very small correlation between the consumption of adjacent age groups. Even if these estimates were significant, their values seem quite small.

The likelihood functions associated with table 2 are rather sharply peaked; hence, one can reject values of ρ and ν that are substantially different (in an economic sense) from the maximum likelihood estimates. Table 3 presents the range of values of ρ and ν that fall within 95 percent chi-squared confidence intervals around the maximum likelihood estimates.[4] According to the table, even if one takes the largest values of ρ and ν that cannot be rejected by the data, the resulting estimates provide no strong evidence of substantial departure from the null hypothesis of intergenerational altruism.

Since many of the consumption expenditures included in our definition of nondurable expenditure may not be made each quarter, the results in table 2 may, in part, reflect the lumpiness of nondurable expenditures; that is, the variance in consumption changes due to the lumpiness of expenditures may dominate the results. Hence, it may be useful to repeat the analysis using simply food expenditure, which is much less lumpy than, for example, clothing expenditure or vacation trips. The results based on quarterly food expenditures are quite similar to the results based on total nondurable, non-housing consumption expenditure. The point estimates in the three samples of ρ are −0.059, −0.068, and 0.002. The point estimates of ν in the three samples are 1.001, 0.998, and 1.003. The estimates of ρ and ν are not jointly significantly different from 0 and 1, respectively; the respective x^2 values for

4. These bounds were constructed by holding one of these parameters fixed at its maximum likelihood value and varying the other parameter until the resulting likelihood was significantly (at the 5 percent level) different from the maximum likelihood.

TABLE 3. 95 Percent Confidence Intervals for ρ and ν: Quarterly Estimates

| | Consumption Measured per Household | | | | | |
| | Maximum Likelihood | | ν Range | | ρ Range | |
Sample	ρ	ν	High	Low	High	Low
Sample 1	0.020	1.002	1.005	0.999	.095	−0.030
Sample 2	−0.024	1.000	1.003	0.997	.020	−0.099
Sample 3	0.031	1.000	1.003	0.997	.106	−0.044

the three samples for the joint test that $\rho = 0$ and $\nu = 1$ are 4.087, 4.991, and 4.757—all of which lie below the 5 percent critical value of 5.991.

Another way to consider the lumpiness of expenditures is to repeat the analysis with semiannual data. Table 4 presents the results based on the six semiannual consumption data sets, which, as mentioned, combine three ages into a single-age cohort. Once again, none of the estimates of ρ and ν are separately or jointly significantly different from the null hypothesis values of $\rho = 0$ and $\nu = 1$. Three of the six point estimates of ν lie above 1 and three lie below 1. Three of the six point estimates of ρ are positive and three are negative. Hence, like the quarterly estimates, there is no suggestion in the data that the null hypothesis is strongly disfavored. Unlike the quarterly results, however, several of the estimates of ν are economically more important. For example, the estimate for ν in the sixth sample of 1.022 implies that the variance of ω_{it} for very old households is over 1.7 times the variance for very young households. In addition, for each of the six samples the confidence intervals around ν include economically significant as well as economically insignificant values. Thus the semiannual results do not provide as

TABLE 4. Maximum Likelihood Estimates and χ^2 Values: Semiannual Samples

| | Consumption Measured per Household | | | | | | |
| | Unconstrained | | $\rho = 0$ | | $\nu = 1$ | | $\rho = 0 \; \nu = 1$ |
Consumption Category	ρ	ν	ν	χ^2	ρ	χ^2	χ^2
Sample 1	−0.133	1.007	1.009	2.531	−0.136	0.409	3.101
Sample 2	−0.142	1.008	1.009	2.945	−0.142	0.478	3.490
Sample 3	0.087	0.990	0.991	0.024	0.080	0.706	1.585
Sample 4	0.055	0.991	0.992	0.467	0.049	0.555	0.918
Sample 5	−0.072	0.984	0.984	0.719	−0.069	2.377	3.054
Sample 6	0.050	1.022	1.022	0.353	0.051	3.679	4.048

Note: Five percent critical values for χ^2 are 5.991 for two restrictions and 3.841 for one restriction.

strong evidence against the life-cycle model as do the quarterly results. It may be that quarterly changes and even semiannual changes in consumption reflect quite lumpy expenditures and that testing the equal Euler error proposition on annual or even biannual would be more appropriate. Unfortunately, appropriate data for such an analysis do not currently exist.

One might question whether we have properly controlled for demographic change in treating $\bar{\psi}^a$ as an age-specific, time-invariant constant. One way to consider whether the results are sensitive to treatment of demographics is to reestimate the model defining household consumption as household consumption per household member or per adult equivalent in the household; in forming adult equivalents we treat each child under age 18 as equal to .5 adults. We tried each of these alternative definitions of household consumption. The quarterly results are essentially the same as those in table 2.[5] The semiannual results are only slightly different from those in table 4; when consumption is measured either as household consumption per member or per equivalent adult, the null hypothesis is rejected in only two of the six semiannual samples.[6]

Are Cohort Euler Errors Correlated with Cohort Changes in Income

One question that may be raised with respect to the empirical findings in the above subsection is the power of the tests against the life-cycle alternative. While we have argued that the variance-covariance matrix of cohort Euler errors is likely to be age-dependent under the life-cycle model, there are some combinations of life-cycle preference structures and distributions of cohort-specific resource shocks that also satisfy the null hypothesis of $\nu = 1$ and

---

5. With household consumption defined as consumption per person, the point estimates for ρ for samples 1, 2, and 3 are 0.034, -0.043, and 0.044, respectively. For ν the corresponding point estimates are 1.001, 1.000, and 1.000. With household consumption defined as consumption per equivalent adult, the three point estimates for ρ are 0.032, -0.035, and 0.039, while the three point estimates for ν are 1.001, 1.000, and 1.000. The χ^2 values for testing the null hypothesis that $\rho = 0$ and $\nu = 1$ are 2.094, 1.952, and 0.395 for the three quarterly samples when consumption is measured per person, and 2.240, 1.352, and 1.667 for the three quarterly samples when consumption is measured per equivalent adult.

6. With household consumption defined as consumption per person the point estimates for ρ for semiannual samples 1, 2, 3, 4, 5, and 6 are -0.1260, 0.0450, -0.0840, -0.1360, 0.0570, and -0.0060, respectively. For ν the corresponding point estimates are 1.0010, 0.9710, 0.9700, 1.0140, 0.9970, and 1.023. With household consumption defined as consumption per equivalent adult, the six point estimates for ρ are -0.1270, 0.0770, -0.0900, -0.1310, 0.0480, and .0100, while the six point estimates for ν are 1.0090, 0.9730, 0.9740, 1.015, 0.9940, and 1.0210. The six respective semiannual χ^2 values for testing the null hypothesis that $\rho = 0$ and $\nu = 1$ are 3.0763, 7.3924, 8.710, 3.807, 0.493, and 4.220 when consumption is measured per person, and 3.0441, 6.699, 7.284, 3.735, 0.533, and 3.581 when consumption is measured per equivalent adult.

TABLE 5. Cohort Average Income Change Coefficients

Sample	Regressions with Time Dummies		Regressions without Time Dummies	
	Coefficient	t-statistic	Coefficient	t-statistic
Quarterly sample 1	.035	1.52	.011	.38
Quarterly sample 2	.068	3.58	.027	.85
Quarterly sample 3	.066	2.70	.034	1.19
Pooled sample	.052	3.57	.026	1.53

$\rho = 0$. A potentially more powerful method for testing altruism against the life-cycle alternative is to ask whether, in addition to age dummies and time dummies (that control for common resource shocks), cohort-specific income changes enter significantly in a regression explaining cohort average percentage changes in consumption. Because the CES asked about income only in its first and fourth interviews, we only have two observations on income. Hence, we considered only households with four complete surveys and formed, for each of the three-year age groups, the average percentage change in income and consumption between the first and fourth interviews. We did this for each of the three quarterly samples.

Table 5 reports the income change coefficients for two different sets of regressions. In the first set we control for common resource shocks by including time dummies. In the second set we exclude the time dummies. Table 5 contains the results from the regressions for each of the quarterly samples, plus the results from pooling the three quarterly samples. In the case of the pooled regression with time dummies, we include different time dummies for each quarterly sample since, as described above, the quarterly samples cover somewhat different time intervals.

Consider the regressions including the time dummies. In two of three quarterly samples and in the case of the pooled regression, the coefficients on cohort income changes are statistically significant. In addition, the point estimates are economically large in the sense that they are even larger than the point estimates one obtains if one does not control for common resource shocks through the time dummies. These results constitute evidence against the altruism model and evidence for the life-cycle model.[7]

---

7. The simple Keynesian model, in which consumption depends only on contemporaneous income, also is supported by these findings. But there appears to be more support in the results for the life-cycle model than the Keynesian model. The reason is that the time dummies in the first set of regressions in table 5 are highly significant. Ignoring measurement error, the Keynesian model (at least the simple version of it) predicts that only changes in current income explain changes in consumption. In the Keynesian model, therefore, the time dummies, which control for common

The Implications of the Findings for the Effectiveness of Fiscal Policy

In this essay we have used cohort data to test the standard model of operative altruistic linkages. The altruism model in contrast to the standard (no-risk-sharing) life-cycle model suggests that (1) after controlling for demographics, consumption changes for different cohorts should, on average, be identical and (2) that, after controlling for demographics, differences across cohorts in their changes in consumption should not be correlated with their income changes. The life-cycle model plus the assumption of perfect risk sharing also delivers these two testable propositions. We tested the first implication by asking whether, after controlling for demographics and common resource shocks, the variance-covariance matrix of consumption changes is age-dependent; we tested the second implication by determining whether differences across cohorts in consumption changes depend on differences across cohorts in their income changes.

We were not able to reject the first implication of the altruism model, but we were able to reject the second. Hence, on balance, our results reject the altruism model and, by extension, the life-cycle model with risk sharing in favor of the standard (no-risk-sharing) life-cycle alternative. An important attribute of these results is that they are nonparametric in nature; specifically, in comparing the average change in consumption across age groups, we place no restrictions on preferences beyond the assumptions of homotheticity and time separability. Our rejection of risk sharing based on cohort data accords with the findings on microdata of Altonji, Hayashi, and Kotlikoff (1992).

While our findings rule out the standard model of altruism in which information is symmetric, one can construct more elaborate models of altruism with information asymmetries in which clan member Euler errors do depend on the clan members' particular income realizations. For example, Kotlikoff and Razin (1988) present a model in which altruistic parents cannot observe their children's work efforts. To avoid being manipulated by children who take it easy and claim their earnings are low because they have low ability, parents will condition their transfers on the observable earnings of their children. In this model, government redistribution between parents and

---

resource shocks, should not enter the regression explaining changes in cohort consumption. In contrast, the life-cycle model would suggest that the time dummies as well as the income change variable would be significant. The reason is that the income change variable does not, under the life-cycle hypothesis, control perfectly for the cohort's change in resources; if the life-cycle model holds and the Euler errors of different age groups are correlated, then the time dummies should pick up that component of the common shock to the different cohorts' Euler errors that are not captured by the change in income. This point was first made in Altonji, Hayashi, and Kotlikoff 1989.

children, assuming it is observable, would not change the parents' information sets and would, therefore, be completely offset by the parents in their private transfer behavior.

However, for this asymmetric information model to be plausible one would expect to see annual or at least periodic inter vivos transfers to children, with these transfers depending on the donor's income. But all the cross-section studies of U.S. private transfers suggest that, apart from the very wealthy, the vast majority of U.S. citizens neither receive nor make transfers on a routine basis. In addition, the evidence on U.S. bequests indicates that they are almost always divided equally among children with no regard to their children's current, let alone past, earnings. These facts seem strong evidence against altruism models with asymmetric information.

If one rejects, as do we, the standard as well as more elaborate varieties of the altruism model, one is left with the following implication: government redistribution between cohorts will raise the consumption of cohorts receiving the transfers and lower the consumption of those making the transfers. But what is the implication of this for national consumption and national saving? In the case of policies that redistribute from future generations to current generations, the implication is clearly an increase in national consumption and a decline in national saving. Even policies that simply redistribute between currently living cohorts will lower national saving if the redistribution runs from younger to older cohorts. The reason is that older cohorts, at least in the United States, appear to have substantially higher propensities to consume than do younger cohorts out of their remaining lifetime resources.[8]

The deleterious impact of intergenerational redistribution on national saving is more than a theoretical possibility. In the past four decades the U.S. government has engineered a massive intergenerational redistribution toward older generations of the day and away from all generations coming behind them (see Kotlikoff 1992). Simulation studies of life-cycle models suggest that such redistribution would seriously lower U.S. savings and capital formation. This is indeed what has transpired. Since 1980 the United States has been saving at about two-fifths the rate observed in the prior three decades. This reduced saving cannot be attributed to increased government consumption since government spending on goods and services relative to NNP has remained roughly constant since the mid-1950s. Rather it reflects an increase in the rate of private sector consumption out of the annual output left over after government consumption is netted out. If this increase in private sector consumption is due to redistribution toward the elderly, one would expect to observe a shift since the 1950s in the shape of the cross-section, age-consumption profile, with the relative consumption of the elderly increasing

---

8. This statement is based on research in progress by Jagadecsh Bokhala and Laurence J. Kotlikoff to measure how the propensity to consume varies with age.

over time. This is precisely what is emerging from preliminary analysis of the 1962–63, 1972–73, and the 1980s Consumer Expenditure Survey (see Kotlikoff, Gokhala, and Sabelhaus forthcoming).

To conclude, this essay contributes to a growing body of findings that document the effectiveness of intergenerational redistribution in raising the consumption of generations receiving income from the government and lowering the consumption of generations giving income to the government. While the precise effect of postwar U.S. intergenerational redistribution on U.S. saving may never be known, the available evidence from this and other studies suggest that past and present U.S. intergenerational redistribution may well be the main reason for the long term and continuing decline in U.S. saving.

APPENDIX: THE LIKELIHOOD FUNCTION AND THE DERIVATION OF THE ESTIMATORS

Under our assumption that the η_t^as are normal and independent across time, the log of the likelihood function, L, is given by:

$$L = \log K - \frac{1}{2} \sum_{t=1}^{T} \log|V_t| - \frac{1}{2} \sum_{t=1}^{T} \eta_t' V_t^{-1} \eta_t \qquad (A.1)$$

where $\eta_t = Y_t - \psi - \mu_t^i$. The term Y_t is a column vector whose elements are $\hat{Y}_{t_r}^a$. The vector ψ captures the time-invariant, age-specific constants arising in equation 13 when $\bar{\psi}_t^a$ is time invariant. The vector i is a column vector of 1s. The term T equals the number of time periods in our data set.

The matrix V_t equals $H_t'VH_t$, and V is defiined by

$$V = \sigma^2 \begin{vmatrix} \nu^2 & \rho\nu^3 & & & \cdot & & \cdot \\ \rho\nu^3 & \nu^4 & & \cdot & & \cdot & \\ \cdot & & \cdot & & \cdot & & \cdot \\ \rho^{N-2}\nu^N & \rho^{N-3}\nu^{N+1} & \cdot & & \cdot & \nu^{2N-2} & \rho\nu^{2N-1} \\ \rho^{N-1}\nu^{N+1} & \rho^{N-2}\nu^{N+2} & & & & \rho\nu^{2N-1} & \nu^{2N} \end{vmatrix}$$

where N is the number of age cohorts (58 in the case of quarterly data and 19 in the case of semiannual data) in our data, and

$$H_t = \begin{vmatrix} h_{1t} & 0 & \cdot & \cdot & \cdot & 0 \\ 0 & \cdot & & & & \cdot \\ \cdot & & \cdot & & & 0 \\ 0 & \cdot & \cdot & 0 & \cdot & h_{nt} \end{vmatrix} \qquad \text{where } h_{at} \text{ equals } \sum_k w_{atk}^2 / \left(\sum_k w_{atk}^2 \right) \text{ and}$$

where w_{atk} is the CES population weight of household k, which is age a at time t.

The first-order conditions resulting from maximizing equation A.1 with respect to ψ, μ_t, and σ^2 are given respectively in equations A.2, A.3, A.4:

$$\sum_{t=1}^{T} V_t^{-1}\,\eta_t = 0 \tag{A.2}$$

$$iV_t^{\prime-1}\,\eta_t = 0 \tag{A.3}$$

$$NT = \sum_{t=1}^{T} \eta'_t V_t^{-1} \eta_t \tag{A.4}$$

From equation A.3 we have

$$\mu_t = (iV_t^{-1}i)^{-1}(Y_t - \psi) \tag{A.5}$$

Equations A.5 and A.2 imply

$$\sum_{t=1}^{T} V_t^{-1}\,[I - (i'V_t^{-1}\,i)ii'](Y_t - \psi) = 0 \tag{A.6}$$

Normalizing the sum of the μ_ts to zero yields

$$s^2 \sum_{t=1}^{T} (iV_t^{\prime-1}i)^{-1}i'V_t^{-1}(Y_t - \psi) = 0 \tag{A.7}$$

Multiplying equation A.7 by i and adding the resulting expression to equation A.6 leads to

$$\hat{\psi} = \sum_{t=1}^{T} [V_t^{-1} - (iV_t^{\prime-1}i)^{-1}(V_t^{-1} - I) i'V_t^{-1}]^{-1}$$

$$\left\{ \sum_{t=1}^{T} [V_t^{-1} - (i'V_t^{-1}i)^{-1}(V_t^{-1} - I)ii'V_t^{-1}]Y_t \right\} \tag{A.8}$$

Given knowledge of the V_ts, we can use equation A.8 plus equation A.5 to determine estimates of the μ_ts and the elements of ψ. Rather than solve analytically for the estimates of ν and ρ, we searched over a grid of alternative pairs of these parameters. For each choice of these parameters we formed the V_t matrices and used equations A.8 and A.5 to calculate the corresponding values of ψ and the μ_ts.

REFERENCES

Altonji, Joseph, Fumio Hayashi, and Laurence J. Kotlikoff. "Is the Extended Family Altruistically Linked? New Tests Based on Micro Data." *American Economic Review* (Dec. 1992): 1177–98.

Altonji, Joseph, and Aloysius Siow. "Testing the Response of Consumption to Income Changes with (Noisy) Panel Data." *Quarterly Journal of Economics* 102 (May 1987): 293–328.

Aschauer, David. "Fiscal Policy and Aggregate Demand." *American Economic Review* 75, no. 1 (March 1985): 117–27.

Auerbach, Alan J., and Laurence J. Kotlikoff. "An Examination of Empirical Tests of Social Security Savings." In *Social Policy Evaluation: An Economic Perspective,* ed. Elhanan Helpman et al. New York: Academic Press, 1983.

Barro, Robert J. "Are Government Bonds Net Wealth?" *Journal of Political Economy* 82, no. 6 (Nov./Dec. 1974): 1095–1117.

Bernheim, B. Douglas, and Kyle Bagwell. "Is Everything Neutral?" *Journal of Political Economy* 96 (1988): 308–38.

Boskin, Michael J., and Laurence J. Kotlikoff. "Public Debt and U.S. Saving: A New Test of the Neutrality Hypothesis." *Carnegie-Rochester Conference Volume Series,* February, 1986.

Boskin, Michael J., and Lawrence Lau. "An Analysis of U.S. Post War Consumption and Saving." 2 parts. National Bureau of Economic Research Working Paper, no. 2605; no. 2606. National Bureau of Economic Research, 1988.

Cochrane, John. "A Simple Test of Consumption Insurance." *Journal of Political Economy* 99 (October 1991): 957–76.

Cox, Donald. "Motives for Private Income Transfers." *Journal of Political Economy,* 95 (June 1987): 508–46.

Darby, Michael R. *Effects of Social Security on Income and the Capital Stock.* Washington, DC: Amer. Ent. Inst., 1979.

Feldstein, Martin. "Social Security, Induced Retirement, and Aggregate Capital Accumulation." *Journal of Political Economy* 82, no. 5 (Sept./Oct. 1974): 905–26.

Flavin, Marjorie A. "The Adjustment of Consumption to Changing Expectations about Future Income." *Journal of Political Economy* 89, no. 5 (October 1981): 974–1009.

Hall, Robert E. "Stochastic Implications of the Life Cycle–Permanent Income Hypothesis: Theory and Evidence." *Journal of Political Economy* 86, no. 6 (December 1978): 971–87.

Hall, Robert E., and Frederic Mishkin. "The Sensitivity of Consumption to Transitory Income: Estimates from Panel Data on Households." *Econometrica* 50, no. 2, (March 1982): 461–81.

Hayashi, Fumio. "The Effects of Liquidity Constraints on Consumption: A Cross Sectional Analysis." *Quarterly Journal of Economics,* no. 1 (Feb. 1985): 183–206.

King, Mervyn A., and Jonathan I. Leape. "Wealth and Portfolio Composition: Theory and Evidence." National Bureau of Economic Research Working Paper, no. 1468, 1984.

Kormendi, Roger. "Government Debt, Government Spending, and Private Sector Behavior." *American Economic Review* 73, no. 4 (December 1983): 994–1010.

Kotlikoff, Laurence J. "Intergenerational Transfers and Savings." *Journal of Economic Perspectives* 2, no. 2 (Spring 1988): 41–58.

———. "Altruistic Extended Family Linkages, A Note." In *What Determines Savings?*, by Kotlikoff. Cambridge, MA: MIT Press, 1989.

———. *Generational Accounting*. New York, NY: Free Press, 1992.

Kotlikoff, Laurence J., and Assaf Razin. "Making Bequests without Spoiling Children." National Bureau of Economic Research Working Paper, no. 2735, 1988.

Kotlikoff, Laurence J., Jagadecsh Bokhala, and John Sabelhaus. "Understanding Postwar Changes in U.S. Saving." Forthcoming.

Lawrence, Emily. "Do Transfers to the Poor Reduce Savings?" Yale University, 1983. Mimeo.

Leimer, Dean R., and Selig D. Lesnoy. "Social Security and Private Saving: A Reexamination of the Time Series Evidence Using Alternative Social Security Wealth Variables." Working Paper, no. 19. Washington, DC: Social Security Administration, Office of Research and Statistics, 1980.

Mace, Barbara. "Full Insurance in the Presence of Aggregate Uncertainty." *Journal of Political Economy* 99 (October 1991): 928–56.

Mankiw, N. Gregory, Julio J. Rothenberg, and Lawrence H. Summers. "Intertemporal Substitution in Macroeconomics." *Quarterly Journal of Economics* 48: 1983.

Menchik, Paul L. "Unequal Estate Division: Is it Altruism, Reverse Bequests, or Simply Noise?" Paper presented to the 1984 Seminar on Modeling the Accumulation and Distribution of Wealth, Paris, France, 1984.

Rosenzweig, Mark R. "Risk, Implicit Contracts, and the Family in Rural Areas of Low Income Countries." *Economic Journal* 98 (December 1988): 1148–70.

Samuelson, Paul. "Lifetime Portfolio Selection by Dynamic Stochastic Programming." *Review of Economics and Statistics* 51, no. 3 (August 1969): 239–46.

Shapiro, Matthew. "The Permanent Income Hypothesis and the Real Interest Rate: Some Evidence from Panel Data." *Economics Letters* 14 (1984): 93–100.

Townsend, Robert M. "Risk and Insurance in Village India." University of Chicago, 1989. Mimeo.

Williamson, Samuel H., and Warren L. Jones. "Computing the Impact of Social Security Using the Life Cycle Consumption Function." *American Economic Review* 73, no. 5 (December 1983): 1036–52.

Zeldes, Stephen. "Consumption and Liquidity Constraints: An Empirical Investigation." *Journal of Political Economy* 97 (1989).

CHAPTER 8

Bequest and Asset Distribution: Human Capital Investment and Intergenerational Wealth Transfers

Toshiaki Tachibanaki and Seiji Takata

The role of bequests and inheritances is a controversial subject in economics. We delve into two main issues. First we investigate whether or not bequests are important to the wealth accumulation process. This is strictly related to whether or not a bequest motive is important to the personal saving rate. Second we examine whether or not bequests and human capital are substitutes. Parents can transfer their resources to their children through the following three forms: (1) human capital investment (i.e., expenditure on education to children), (2) bequest as a form of physical asset, and (3) bequest as a form of financial asset. If the last two are combined into one category as bequest, we can consider two forms of intergenerational transfers: (1) human capital, and (2) bequest. The economics of family investigated the substitution possibility of the two and presented several interesting propositions for the role of both human capital and bequest in the determination of savings and bequests.

The purpose of this essay is to study these two subjects for Japan. The nature of the studies, however, is considerably different between the two subjects in the following way. The role of bequests in wealth distribution is investigated empirically by analyzing various statistical data, while the role of human capital in comparison with material and financial bequests is investigated analytically by employing theoretical models and simulation methods.

Bequests and Wealth Distribution

The best known controversy about the role of bequests in the determination of wealth for the United States is represented in Modigliani 1988a, 1988b and

The authors are grateful to J. Davies, Y. Harada, C. Horioka, M. Hurd, T. Ito, L. Kotlikoff and N. Takayama for their useful comments and criticisms on an earlier version of this paper. The authors are fully responsible for possible errors and opinions in this paper.

Kotlikoff and Summers 1981, 1988 along with Kotlikoff 1988. The former proposes the importance of life-cycle saving motivation with a much lesser emphasis on a bequest motive, while the latter proposes that intergenerational transfers are the most important source of net wealth. Davies in this volume provides a useful survey on the literature in many countries. It is useful to mention an idea that is supported by several authors such as Davies (1981), Abel (1985), and Hurd (1989): bequests can be consistent with life-cycle saving motives coupled with uncertain lifespan and imperfect annuity markets. Also, it is possible that a bequest motive based on gift-exchange (as proposed by Bernheim, Shleifer and Summers 1985), may be one of the life-cycle saving motives, because testators expect returns from giving bequests to beneficiaries. We intend to shed light on these issues for Japan by referring to several existing studies and analyzing the available data.

Wealth Distribution and Bequests

Although studies on income and wage distributions have been fairly popular in Japan, those on wealth distribution have been considerably rare. In particular, the relationship between bequests and wealth distribution has not been investigated seriously because data for the two variables were not easily available. Also, figures of both wealth and bequests even in available sources are unreliable since they are largely measured by respondent selfassessment of both physical and financial assets. In addition to the fact that there have been no serious data collection for bequests, what figures we have of bequests may be biased due to respondents' fear of tax inquiry.

In sum, we understand that the numbers and figures of both wealth and bequest include measurement errors, and thus that the numbers and figures that appear in the subsequent sections are also not free from errors. It may be useful, nevertheless, to refer to Togashi (1979) who concluded that the measurement errors caused by selfassessment of wealth are within a range of 10 percent of true figures when he examined the data source that is used in this essay. Therefore, selfassessment is not entirely useless but provides us with fairly acceptable figures.

Table 1 gives a rough idea of the state of wealth distribution in Japan. Table 1 allows us to examine a time-series change in wealth distribution, because figures were calculated for the data that were collected by a common methodology within a common institution, namely, the Japanese Ministry of Posts and Communication. Thus, the figures in table 1, specifically, Gini coefficients, are comparable among different sampling years and are fairly robust. The estimated result for the United States was also presented to compare it with Japan, although we do not have any intention of making a rigorous comparison. As is well known, an international comparison in wealth is a difficult task.

Japan experienced a rapid increase in land prices in the late 1980s particularly in large urban areas (although these prices have started to show a minor decrease in several areas quite recently). The sky-rocketing increase in land prices contributed to widening wealth inequality considerably. See, for example, Tachibanaki 1989 for the case in the Tokyo metropolitan area, and Tachibanaki 1992 for an increasing inequality in many fields in Japan. Table 1 supports such an increasing inequality in both gross and net wealth from 1985 to 1990. Since there had been a minor declining trend in inequality in wealth holding at least until 1985 as is obvious from table 1, the dramatic increase in wealth inequality in the late 1980s was a shocking phenomenon; it has had a great impact on society and economy in Japan. Since Tachibanaki (1989, 93) discussed the event extensively, we need not explore it here.

Contribution of Bequests to Wealth Accumulation and Distribution

We examine the contribution of bequests and inheritances to both wealth accumulation and inequality in wealth distribution. First we focus on the role of bequest motives in relation to life-cycle saving motives, and second we address the importance of bequests in the determination of wealth inequality.

There is a fairly solid consensus that a bequest motive is crucially important in comparison with a life-cycle saving motive in Japan. In fact, one of the most important reasons for the high personal saving rate is a strong bequest motive (see Hayashi 1986; Hayashi, Ando, and Ferris 1988). Tachibanaki and

TABLE 1. Time-Series Change in Inequality of Wealth Distribution in Japan (Gini Coefficient)

	1977	1981	1985	1990	USA (1983)
Employees					
Income	0.313	0.258	0.267		
Monetary wealth	0.661	0.546	0.696		
Physical wealth		0.623	0.625		
Gross wealth	0.614	0.549	0.513		
Net wealth			0.527		
All Households					
Gross wealth		0.553	0.549	0.601	0.703
Net wealth		0.584	0.568	0.617	0.728

Source: Tachibanaki and Shimono 1991, and Tachibanaki 1993.

Shimono (1986, 91) presented evidence of various degrees of bequest motives that are differentiated by various demographic groups such as income class, and employee class (which was divided by the size of firms or by life-long commitment to a firm or not).

Although nearly all economists support the importance of a bequest motive for the Japanese economy, there remains disagreement with respect to whether a strong bequest motive is altruistic or strategic (i.e., gift-exchange oriented). If the strategic motive dominates the altruistic one, a great part of bequest motives can be understood as a life-cycle saving motive rather than as a pure bequest motive, because the gift-exchange motive evaluates the donor's utility highly, and expects a high return from the recipient. If the strategic motive were stronger, the contribution of the life-cycle saving motive would be higher, and at the same time the life-cycle saving hypothesis would be a more relevant one than is commonly believed, as Modigliani (1988a, 1988b) supposes. Horioka (1990) thinks that the Japanese are gift-exchange motivated rather than altruistically motivated in the determination of a bequest motive. In addition, the recent study by Cox (1987) proposes the superiority of gift-exchange motives over altruism for the United States, although prior studies preferred altruistic motives. It is not an easy task to quantify the relative importance of a gift-exchange motive versus altruistic motive. Since it is certainly true that part of the Japanese bequest motive is gift-exchange, the conventional wisdom of a pure life-cycle saving motive being inferior to a bequest motive should be discounted to a certain extent. The latter part of this essay, in fact, proposes that a gift-exchange motive is important in certain cases in Japan.

Another important element, which possibly reduces the importance of an altruistic bequest motive and thus raises the importance of a life-cycle saving motive in Japan is the importance of precautionary savings in fear of uncertainty in both earnings and death. Tachibanaki and Takata (1991) found that a considerable part of savings in Japan was precautionary because the Japanese are afraid of uncertainty in income and death. Thus, it is possible to guess that some part of bequest left is unintended as a result of unexpected events. Unintended bequest may be consistent with life-cycle saving motives. Provided that the study of Tachibanaki and Takata is correct, the reliability of life-cycle saving motives is higher even in Japan than is commonly believed.

In sum, it is likely that the importance of life-cycle saving motives would be higher than were believed previously, if the argument of both a gift-exchange motive and a precautionary saving motive were relevant for Japan. It should be emphasized, however, that the preceding argument does not necessarily imply that the *amount* of intergenerational transfers plays a minor role in wealth accumulation. The arguments mentioned merely imply that the motivations of intergenerational transfers must be modified when we take into

TABLE 2.   Shares in Total Wealth in 1990

Shares	Gross Wealth	Net Wealth
Shares by top 1%	13.69%	14.14%
top 5%	31.57%	32.53%
top 10%	44.25%	45.35%
top 25%	67.37%	68.63%

Source: IPTP 1990; Tachibanaki 1993.

account both precautionary savings and gift-exchange bequest motives. The amount of intergenerational transfers (or bequests) is not altered even if both precautionary savings and gift-exchange bequest motives are introduced.

It would be interesting to examine the inequality in total wealth, and the share of inheritances over total wealth, before analyzing the contribution of inheritances to total wealth inequality. Tables 2 and 3 give these figures. Table 2 shows that the top 1 percent of wealth holders have the largest share of wealth, about 13 to 14 percent, and the top 5 percent hold about 31 to 33 percent of the wealth. These figures are considerably lower than those in Western countries (see Davies in this volume). Thus, wealth concentration in Japan is not as strong as in other developed nations. Table 3 shows that about 45 percent of wealth in Japan is occupied by inheritances (i.e., intergenerational wealth transfers). In other words, about 55 percent of wealth is explained by the contribution of life-cycle wealth accumulation. This number for Japan can be compared with the works of Modigliani and Kotlikoff for the United States, and that of Davies for Canada and the United Kingdom. The differentiation in estimation methods make it risky to draw firm conclusions about the contribution of intergenerational wealth transfers to total wealth. Forty-four point five percent is only a preliminary number for Japan based on statistical evidence without adjusting for the element of precautionary savings and gift-exchange bequest motives.

TABLE 3.   Household Wealth and the Share of Inherited Wealth (ten thousand yen)

Wealth	Mean	Households Who Received Bequests	Mean Value of Inherited Wealth	Share of Inherited Wealth
Financial Wealth	1,051.2	4.3%	1,150	4.7%
Physical Wealth	5,196.3	23.7%	11,500	52.6%
Total Wealth	6,247.5	26.4%	10,530	44.5%

Source: IPTP 1990.
Note: Households who inherited either financial or physical wealth; Sample number = 3,478.

We attempt a decomposition analysis to estimate the contribution of bequests and inheritances to inequality in wealth distribution by analyzing statistical data. There are two conflicting views on the contribution of bequests and inheritances to wealth distribution. The first view stipulates a compensating role of bequests, proposing that the family is characterized as an income-equalizing institution, and thus that bequests are compensatory in that (*ceteris paribus*) low-income children inherit more than advantaged children. In other words, the bequest received is inversely related to recipient income. Thus, the contribution of bequest may be minor in wealth distribution. This view has been proposed by Ishikawa (1975), Becker and Tomes (1979), and Tomes (1981) all of whom support the importance of human capital investment in intergenerational transfers.

The second view postulates an agnostic opinion of the family objective function, proposing that bequests need not respond to the characteristics of potential recipients. Thus, the contribution of bequests to wealth inequality is likely to be high. This view is supported by Blinder (1973), Menchik (1980), Davies (1982), Tachibanaki and Shimono (1991), and others. It would be possible to describe that this view is a variant or a complement of an altruistic bequest motive. In the latter part of this essay we will examine whether the first view or the second view is more relevant for Japan coupled with the introduction of a gift-exchange motive. A decomposition of wealth into the contribution of inheritances and that of noninheritances provides us with an idea on how we can understand these conflicting views. Thus, the statistical result of a decomposition is worthwhile.

Before presenting the empirical results, the data source is described and explained. The Institute for Posts and Telecommunications Policy conducted a survey on household asset choice in 1990. The original sample number of 6,000 were randomly selected from all over Japan. The response rate was 58.0 percent, and thus the available number of households is 3,478. Ages of households are 20 to 80 years old, including single families. Figures on income, wealth, and others are per-household based. Figures on these variables were obtained through selfassessment. As was mentioned previously, we understand that measurement errors caused by selfassessment are relatively minor (within 10 percent).

Table 4 shows the result of a decomposition analysis. This table requires some explanation. The questionnaire queried (1) the present value of inheritance received, and (2) the current wealth-value held by a respondent. These two items include both financial assets and physical (real) assets. By employing appropriate estimation methods, it is possible to measure the contribution of inheritances and that of noninheritances (i.e., life-cycle motives) to total current wealth. Table 4 is its empirical implementation.

Three important reservations must be described. First, besides the general problem of selfassessment, the assessment of the *present* value of inheritance received is problematic because the discount rates evaluated by individual respondents differ considerably from individual to individual. It would be possible to obtain a better estimate by asking the current value at the time of receiving inheritance and then calculating the present value on the basis of an appropriate discount rate. Anyway, we have to keep in mind considerable measurement errors in the value of inheritance received. Second, somewhat related to the first point, we do not know how each respondent treated interest

TABLE 4. Decomposition of Wealth Inequality into Inheritances and Noninheritances

	Financial Wealth		Physical Wealth	
	Inheritance	Noninheritance	Inheritance	Noninheritance
		Case 1[a]		
RV	0.017	0.983		
RG	0.014	0.986		
RT	0.016	0.984		
N		(2,907)		
RV			0.463	0.537
RG			0.319	0.681
RT			0.401	0.599
N			(3,186)	
RV	0.006	0.145	0.433	0.416
RG	0.004	0.281	0.251	0.462
RT	0.004	0.087	0.405	0.503
N		(2,693)		
		Case 2[a]		
RV	0.093	0.907		
RG	0.136	0.864		
RT	0.066	0.934		
N	(131)			
RV			0.617	0.383
RG			0.631	0.369
RT			0.595	0.405
N			(427)	
RV	0.007	0.090	0.581	0.322
RG	0.004	0.134	0.537	0.326
RT	−0.004	0.017	0.617	0.370
N		(480)		

Source: IPTP 1990.

Note: RV is relative variance, RG is pseudo-Gini coefficient, and RT is relative Theil measure; there are some rounding errors.

[a] Samples include households whose received inheritances are zero.

that was yielded from inheritance received. Some counted it, while others did not. Also, it is important to consider the contribution of interest to total current wealth. A similar problem occurs for capital gains on land. Since this information is unavailable in the original data source, no serious consideration of it is attempted. We have to rely on the present value of inheritance received and the current value of wealth, which are comparable because they are evaluated at a common time. Third, it was necessary to assume that no transactions (i.e., selling or buying) of both financial and physical assets, which arose from inheritances received, occurred. We understand that this assumption is too stringent. Unless we have cohort data that report annual transactions of both financial and physical assets since a household received inheritance, it is impossible to omit this assumption. Thus, it should be appropriate to describe the figures in table 4 as being only hypothetical and indicative of only very rough contributions of both inheritances and noninheritances.

We employ three measurements to estimate relative contributions: (1) relative variances (RV), (2) pseudo-Gini (RG), and (3) relative Theil (RT). These measures are written briefly as

$$RV = \frac{\mu_k}{\mu} \sqrt{\frac{\bar{V}(Y_k)}{V(Y)}},$$

$$RG = \frac{\mu_k}{\mu} \cdot \frac{\bar{G}(Y_k)}{G(Y)},$$

$$RT = \frac{\mu_k}{\mu} \cdot \frac{\bar{T}(Y_k)}{T(Y)},$$

where μ is the average, and μ_k is the average of kth component. Thus, $\mu = \Sigma_{k=1}^{K} \mu_k$ holds. $\bar{V}$ stands for the usual relative variance, $\bar{G}$ stands for the usual pseudo-Gini coefficient, and

$$\bar{G}(Y_k) = \frac{r(y_i^k, i)}{r(y_i^k, k)} G(Y_k),$$

where $G(Y_k)$ is the Gini coefficient for the kth component, and r is the correlation coefficient between the kth component and the total wealth. Equivalently, the usual pseudo-Theil ($\bar{T}$) is given by

$$\bar{T}(Y_k) = \frac{1}{n} \sum_{i=1}^{n} \frac{y_i^k}{\mu_k} \log \left(\frac{y_i}{\mu} \right).$$

The reason why we multiplied μ_k/μ to the usual measures is that it would be preferable to eliminate the effect of the share of each source over the total wealth as emphasized by Shorrocks (1983). Thus, the figures in table 2 indicate the *relative* contribution of each component to total inequality, and thus the sum is equal to unity. (See Atoda and Tachibanaki 1985 concerning the methodology and its empirical implementation in the case of income distribution.)

Table 4 contains two cases: case 1 includes households who received no inheritances, while case 2 excludes samples whose inheritances are zero. The distinction is important because the former is concerned with all households regardless of their conditions of inheritance, while the latter is concerned only with households who received some inheritance.

We can observe the following results. First, there is no significant difference in the relative importance of inheritance and noninheritance (i.e., life-cycle motives) between case 1 and case 2 with respect to financial assets. Noninheritance parts dominate inequality in financial asset distribution almost exclusively. Second, inequality in physical wealth distribution provides us with a considerably different outcome from the case for financial wealth. The contribution of inheritance is more important for explaining inequality in physical wealth than that of noninheritance (i.e., life-cycle motives) in case 2, while inverse relative importance is observed in case 1. Among households who received some physical assets as inheritance, "How much did a household receive?" is crucial, while "How much did a household save and accumulate?" is critical among all households. More importantly, figures in physical assets suggest the considerable importance of the contribution of inheritance received. The minimum is over 30 percent by RG, and the average contribution is 40 percent. These numbers very roughly correspond to the shares of bequest over total life-time resources estimated by Tachibanaki and Shimono (1991). We find that this contribution is fairly significant, and thus it is concluded that inheritance and bequest—in particular, physical wealth—determine a considerable share of wealth inequality. Finally, when both financial wealth and physical wealth are combined, the greater part of wealth inequality is determined by physical wealth, as the contribution of physical wealth is over 70 to 90 percent in the three measures. The physical asset is an instrument that is transferred intergenerationally.

Bequest Function

A brief empirical estimation of the bequest function is presented to approximate the determination of bequest in Japan. The type 2 Tobit model is estimated, taking the amount of intended bequest as the dependent variable. This variable is not the truly intended bequest because it indicates merely the "desired" level of bequest. In other words, the amount of bequest that the current generations would like to leave to their heirs (i.e., beneficiaries) is the dependent variable. This is close to the intended bequest, but it is not exactly equivalent to the intended bequest because the transfer has not yet been realized. Nevertheless, this model is able to show the bequest behavior, in particular, the intended one, of the Japanese to a certain extent.

Table 5 shows the empirical result. Variables that are significant at the first stage (i.e., a discrete choice [unity if a respondent wants to leave some bequest, zero otherwise] estimation) are: (1) the number of children, (2) income, (3) real assets, (4) inheritance received from a respondent's parent, (5) a dummy variable for extended family (unity if a respondent lives together with his or her parents together, zero otherwise). The probability of having an intention of leaving bequests is higher as (1) the number of children is smaller, (2) the income level is higher, (3) the amount of real-asset holding is larger, (4) the amount of inheritance received is larger, and (5) the possibility of extended family is higher. We find several variables that seem to contradict intuitive understandings.

Before arguing several of these contradictions, it is necessary to examine the second stage, for example, the question, "How much does a respondent want to leave bequest, if he or she intends to do so?" Variables that are significant are (1) the number of children, (2) a dummy variable for spouse's working status (unity if a spouse works, zero otherwise), (3) income, (4) the amount of debt, (5) real asset, (6) inheritance received from a respondent's parent, (7) a dummy variable for extended family, and (8) a hazard rate. The statistical significance of the hazard variable supports the reliability of Heckman's two-step procedure for the Tobit estimation in this paper. The result shows that the intended amount of bequest is larger, as (1) the number of children is larger, (2) the possibility of working spouse is lower, (3) the income level is lower, (4) the amount of debt is higher, (5) the amount of real-asset holding is larger, (6) the amount of inheritance received is larger, and (7) the possibility of extended family is lower.

Signs of the estimated coefficients of several variables such as the number of children, income, and a dummy for extended family are different between the first stage and the second stage, while those of real asset and inheritance received are positive at both stages. The preceding comparison has been made only for the statistically significant variables at both stages.

Several variables that showed different signs between the first and second stages are appealing, and some are quite plausible. For example, take the number of children. If the number of children is large, expenditures on them are large. Thus, there is no room for leaving a bequest, or the probability of leaving a bequest is lower. Once a family decides to leave a bequest, the wage-earner(s) tries to earn a lot even if the family has a larger number of

TABLE 5.   Tobit Estimates of Bequest Functions

Variables	First stage	Second stage
Constant	−0.521	−2065.4
	(1.249)	(−0.674)
AGE	0.003	−52.4
	(0.546)	(−1.557)
KID	−0.135*	819.7*
	(2.127)	(2.068)
UNIVD	−0.092	1379.9
	(0.548)	(1.444)
HIGHD	−0.088	1327.2
	(0.568)	(1.509)
SPOUSED	0.315	−4282.5*
	(1.255)	(−2.718)
INCOME	0.0004*	−1.904*
	(2.636)	(−2.164)
FINASSET	0.00002*	0.583*
	(0.986)	(5.971)
DEBT	−0.00008*	0.979*
	(1.073)	(2.091)
REALASSET	0.00002*	0.471*
	(1.745)	(14.75)
INHERIT	0.00007*	0.157*
	(2.836)	(6.005)
LIVED	0.725*	−2511.6*
	(4.899)	(−2.202)
SELFD	0.147	−463.3
	(0.991)	(−0.566)
HAZARD		17372.1*
		(3.310)
χ^2 (D.F.)	114.4 (12)	
Adj-R^2		0.527

Note: The sign (*) signifies a statistical significance at the 5 percent level; figures in parentheses are the estimated ratios of the coefficient over the standard error.

Variables: AGE, age of a respondent; KID, number of children; UNIVD, a dummy for university education; HIGHD, a dummy for senior high school education; SPOUSED, a dummy for spouse's working status (unity if a spouse works); INCOME, annual income; FINASSET, amount of financial asset; DEBT, amount of debt; REALASSET, amount of real asset; INHERIT, amount of inheritance received; LIVED, a dummy for extended family (unity if adult children live with parents), SELFD, a dummy for self-employment; HAZARD, hazard ratio.

children. Then, the amount of bequest may be larger. We can provide similar explanations for other variables.

The most convincing result based on table 5 is the strong statistical significance of the real asset and inheritance received. Both the probability and the amount of the intended bequest are positively related to these variables. The implication of the real asset is that the capability of leaving a bequest is indicated by real-asset holding in Japan. The received inheritance suggests a successive intergenerational transfer from grandparent to parent, from parent to children, from children to grandchildren, and so forth. This is consistent with Tachibanaki and Shimono (1991) who showed the possibility of intergenerational transmission of wealth inequality for Japan. This transmission is realized through real assets such as land and house. Table 4 in this paper also supports the preceding mechanism.

The question then arises as to whether we can derive any implications for a bequest motive in Japan from the preceding interpretations of tables 2, 3, 4, and 5, particularly with regard to whether an altruistic motive or a gift-exchange motive dominates. A further question appears as to whether there is any possibility of substitution between human capital and material wealth. Unfortunately, it is impossible to draw any direct conclusions at this stage, but a direct test is made in the next part. The analyses in this part were performed to ascertain the status of wealth distribution, the share of inheritances over total wealth, the contribution of both inheritances and noninheritances (i.e., life-cycle saving motives), and a simple estimation of the bequest function in Japan. The empirical results suggested that bequests play an important role in determining the saving rate and thus wealth accumulation. Wealth accumulation is also affected strongly by bequest and inheritance.

Human Capital, Gift-Exchange, and Bequest

In this part we construct a model of the bequest behavior that takes account of both human capital investment and services to parents by offspring as a gift exchange. There are three types of forms when intergenerational transfers are made, as explained previously. We combine financial asset and real asset into one category, say "material wealth." The third one is human capital investment by parents to children. The substitution possibility between parental bequests of material wealth and human capital investments was argued by Ishikawa (1975), Becker and Tomes (1976, 1979), and Tomes (1981). Also, the most striking empirical finding is that the inheritance received by children is inversely related to the recipient's income as emphasized by Tomes (1981). The quality of a child may be influential, as Becker and Tomes (1976) and Sheshinski and Weiss (1982) note. Since human capital investment is probably the most important form of investment in Japan, it is interesting to examine these issues.

Strategic bequest motives (or gift-exchange motives) are important when we investigate intergenerational wealth transfers, as Bernheim, Shleifer, and Summers (1985), Cox (1987), and some others propose. Transfers represent payments made in exchange for services provided by family members. Services provided by children, measured by the frequency of visits and telephone calls in the United States, are positively related to the size of the potential estate. Cox (1987) presented useful survey evidence of gift-exchange motivated transfers in the United States.

In Japan, an extended family is a typical example of a gift-exchange motive. Adult children live together with their parent, and they receive the major part (or all) of the bequest. The oldest son is responsible for this extended family, a custom quite common in rural areas and less common in urban areas, as Noguchi et al. (1991) found. Adult children pay their parents' living costs, and they have to give up their own time and resources to take care of them. It is very likely that adult children offer various kinds of services to their parents even if they do not live together. However, bequests or inter vivos transfers are made frequently between these two generations. In fact, Noguchi et al. (1991) presents such empirical evidence in many families who do not even live together. Therefore, it is useful to examine the effect of the gift-exchange motive on intergenerational wealth transfers.

A possible contribution of this essay is that we combine two aspects— namely, human capital investment versus material wealth and a gift-exchange motive—in the analysis of bequests and wealth. Also, the ability (or earning capacity) of the child is explicitly taken into account. Finally, the effect of tax policies (i.e., whether wage [income] tax or bequest tax) is examined because they are influential on the course of wealth accumulation and inequality.

Model Specification

We consider, first, a two period, two individual model. The second half of the parent (a bequest donor) and the first half of the child (a bequest recipient) overlap. The parent cares about the education of the child and possibly leaves a bequest. The child provides services to the parent in exchange for education and a bequest. Although tradition supports the services in exchange for the bequest, this model specifies two conditions for the exchange because both educational expenditure to the child and material wealth transfer (i.e., bequest) are sacrifices from the parent's point of view, and equivalently costly.

The utility functions of the parent and of the child are

$$U^p = u(c_1^p) + \frac{1}{1 + \theta} v(c_2^p, s), \tag{1}$$

and

$$U^k = u(c_1^k) + \frac{1}{1 + \theta} u(c_2^k), \tag{2}$$

where U^p is parent's utility, U^k is child's utility, c_i is the ith period consumption, θ is discount rate, and s is the rate of services provided by the child. Equation 1 suggests that the parent receives services, and that those services raise the utility of the parent. The child has to give up his or her wage income by sw, because he or she provides s percent of the total available time and resources. Thus, the child wage income is $(1 - s)w$ where w is his or her wage income. The child receives a human capital investment of x from the parent, and its investment produces a wage income of $w(x)$. Denoting the wage income tax rate by τ_w and the bequest tax rate by τ_b, the budget constraints for both the parent and the child are written as

$$W_0 = c_1^p + \frac{1}{1 + r} c_2^p + x + \frac{1}{(1 + r)^2} b \tag{3}$$

$$(1 - \tau_w)(1 - s)w + \frac{1 - \tau_b}{1 + r} b = c_1^k + \frac{1}{1 + r} c_2^k \tag{4}$$

where W_0 is the parent's after-tax wage income and received inheritance, and r is the interest rate. Thus, W_0 stands for the initial wealth. The maximization problem is solved by the parent and the child jointly and is the sum of the two utility functions

$$\text{Max}(U^p + \beta U^k) \tag{5}$$

$$\text{subject to equations 3 and 4, and } b \geq 0 \tag{6}$$

where β is the weight for the child. This parameter may be called the degree of "altruism" because it indicates how seriously the child's utility is evaluated compared with the parent's. The condition $b \geq 0$ signifies that a negative bequest is prohibited.

The usual Kuhn-Tucker conditions can be derived under the Lagrangian multipliers λ_1 for the parent budget constraint, λ_2 for the child budget constraint, and λ_3 for bequest b. They are written as

$$\frac{\partial L}{\partial c_1^p} = \frac{\partial u}{\partial c_1^p} - \lambda_1 = 0, \tag{7}$$

$$\frac{\partial L}{\partial c_2^p} = \frac{1}{1 + \theta} \cdot \frac{\partial v}{\partial c_2^p} - \frac{1}{1 + r_1} \lambda_1 = 0, \tag{8}$$

$$\frac{\partial L}{\partial x} = -\lambda_1 + \lambda_2(1 - \tau_w)(1 - s)\frac{dw}{dx} = 0, \tag{9}$$

$$\frac{\partial L}{\partial s} = \frac{1}{1 + \theta}\frac{\partial v}{\partial s} - \lambda_2(1 - \tau_w)w = 0, \tag{10}$$

$$\frac{\partial L}{\partial c_1^k} = \beta\frac{\partial u}{\partial c_1^k} - \lambda_2 = 0, \tag{11}$$

$$\frac{\partial L}{\partial c_2^k} = \beta\frac{1}{1 + \theta}\frac{\partial u}{\partial c_2^k} - \lambda_2\frac{1}{1 + r} = 0, \tag{12}$$

$$\frac{\partial L}{\partial b} = -\frac{1}{(1 + r)^2}\lambda_1 + \frac{1 - \tau_b}{1 + r}\lambda_2 + \lambda_3 = 0, \tag{13}$$

$$\frac{\partial L}{\partial \lambda_1} = \frac{\partial L}{\partial \lambda_2} = 0. \tag{14}$$

We consider two cases. In both cases, equation 3 and equation 4 are always binding. The first case assumes that interior solutions for any variables are available. Thus, constraint 5 is nonbinding, and, thus, $\lambda_3 = 0$. The second case is the case in which constraint 5 is binding, and, thus $\lambda_3 > 0$.

Nonbinding Case
In this case, $\lambda_3 = 0$ holds. Thus, we obtain the following identity:

$$\lambda_2 = \frac{1}{(1 - \tau_b)(1 + \lambda)}\lambda_1. \tag{15}$$

By utilizing the above identity, we can rearrange the first-order conditions as follows:

$$\frac{\partial v}{\partial c_2^p} = \frac{1 + \theta}{1 + r} \cdot \frac{\partial u}{\partial c_1^p}, \tag{16}$$

$$(1 + r)(1 - \tau_b) - (1 - \tau_w)(1 - s)\frac{dw}{dx} = 0, \tag{17}$$

$$\frac{1}{1 + \theta}\frac{\partial v}{\partial s} - \frac{(1 - \tau_w)w}{(1 - \tau_b)(1 + r)}\frac{\partial u}{\partial c_1^p} = 0, \tag{18}$$

$$\beta \cdot \frac{\partial u}{\partial c_1^k} - \frac{1}{(1 - \tau_b)(1 + r)} \cdot \frac{\partial u}{\partial c_1^p} = 0, \tag{19}$$

$$\frac{\partial u}{\partial c_2^k} = \frac{1 + \theta}{1 + r} \frac{\partial u}{\partial c_2^k}. \tag{20}$$

We specify the following three functions to enable a numerical evaluation of the solutions as follows:

$$u(c) = \frac{c^{1-\gamma}}{1 - \gamma}, \tag{21}$$

$$v(c, s) = \frac{c^{1-\gamma}}{1 - \gamma} + k \frac{s^{1-\gamma}}{1 - \gamma}, \tag{22}$$

$$w(x) = dx^p, \tag{23}$$

where γ is the elasticity of marginal utility (or the relative aversion parameter), k is the weight for services, and dx^p is the constant elasticity human capital production function. Parameter d represents the level of efficiency that is kept constant. Parameter ρ signifies the degree of earnings capacity produced by human capital investment, and thus indicates the ability of the child. It is called "ability" for the sake of simplicity.

The solutions for equations 16, 17, 18, 19, and 20 may be written after simple manipulations as

$$c_2^p = \left(\frac{1 + r}{1 + \theta} \right)^{1/\gamma} c_1^p, \tag{24}$$

$$x = \left[\frac{(1 + r)(1 - \tau_b)}{(1 - \tau_w)(1 - s)d\rho} \right]^{1/\rho - 1}, \tag{25}$$

$$s = \left[\frac{k(1 - \tau_b)(1 + r)}{(1 + \theta)(1 - \tau_w)w} \right]^{1/\gamma} c_1^p, \tag{26}$$

$$c_1^k = [\beta(1 - \tau_b)(1 + r)]^{1/\gamma} c_1^p, \tag{27}$$

$$c_2^k = \left[\frac{\beta(1 - \tau_b)(1 + r)^2}{1 + \theta} \right]^{1/\gamma} c_1^p. \tag{28}$$

Binding Case
In this case, $b = 0$ holds, and, thus, $[1/(1 + r)^2]\lambda_1 > [(1 - \tau_b)/(1 + r)]\lambda_2$ holds. The budget constraints are reduced to the following forms:

$$W_0 = c_1^p + \frac{1}{1 + r} c_2^p + x, \tag{29}$$

and

$$(1 - \tau_w)(1 - s)w(x) = c_1^k + \frac{1}{1 + r} c_2^k. \tag{30}$$

By employing the same functional specifications as equations 21, 22, and 23, we obtain the following solutions:

$$c_2^p = \left(\frac{1 + r}{1 + \theta} \right)^{1/\gamma} c_1^p, \tag{31}$$

$$x = \left[\frac{1}{\beta d\rho(1 - \tau_w)(1 - s)} \left(\frac{c_1^k}{c_1^p} \right)^\gamma \right]^{1/\rho - 1}, \tag{32}$$

$$s = \left[\frac{k}{(1 + \theta)\beta(1 - \tau_w)w} \right]^{1/\gamma} c_1^k, \tag{33}$$

$$c_2^k = \left(\frac{1 + r}{1 + \theta} \right)^{1/\gamma} c_1^k. \tag{34}$$

Equations 16–20 for the nonbinding case, and equations 31–34 for the binding case are used to evaluate solutions numerically under given parameter values, because it is not easy to derive the comparative statics properties of the two cases.

Comparative Statics
Some attempts for comparative statics are possible when we simplify the model further. The comparative statics result is obtained for a multigenerational model.

$$\text{Max } U = \sum_{t=1}^{\infty} \beta^{t-1} \left[u(c_{1t}) + \frac{1}{1 + \theta} v(c_{2t}, s_t) \right], \tag{35}$$

subject to $(1 - \tau_w)(1 - s_t)w_t + \frac{1 - \tau_b}{1 + r} b_t = c_{1,t+1} + \frac{1}{1 + r} c_{2,t+1}$

$$x_{t+1} + \frac{1}{(1 + r)^2} b_{t-1}, \tag{36}$$

where the parent is called the tth generation, and the child is called the $(t + 1)$th generation. The preceding model assumes that one generation takes account of the next generations unlike the previous two models of individuals. We consider only a nonbinding case here for the comparative statics result.

The first-order conditions are given after some manipulations as follows:

$$\lambda_t = \frac{1}{(1 - \tau_b)(1 + r)} \lambda_{t-1}, \tag{37}$$

$$\frac{\partial v}{\partial c_{2,t}} = \frac{1 + \theta}{1 + r} \frac{\partial u}{\partial c_{1,t}}, \tag{38}$$

$$\frac{\partial u}{\partial c_{1,t+1}} = \frac{1}{\beta(1 - \tau_b)(1 + r)} \frac{\partial u}{\partial c_{1,t}}, \tag{39}$$

$$\frac{\partial w}{\partial x_t} = \frac{(1 - \tau_b)(1 + r)}{(1 - \tau_w)(1 + s_t)}, \tag{40}$$

$$\frac{\partial v}{\partial s_t} = \frac{(1 + \theta)(1 - \tau_w)w(x_t)}{(1 - \tau_b)(1 + r)} \frac{\partial u}{\partial c_{1t}}. \tag{41}$$

We would like to evaluate $\partial x/\partial c$, and $\partial s/\partial c$, based on the preceding equations. After tedious calculations we obtain the following simultaneous equation by assuming $\partial^2 v/\partial s \partial c = 0$:

$$\begin{pmatrix} (1 - s)w'' & -w' \\ -\dfrac{(1 + \theta)(1 - \tau_w)}{(1 - \tau_b)(1 + r)} w'u' & v_{ss} \end{pmatrix} \begin{pmatrix} \dfrac{\partial x}{\partial c} \\ \dfrac{\partial s}{\partial c} \end{pmatrix} = \begin{pmatrix} 0 \\ \dfrac{(1 + \theta)(1 - \tau_w)}{(1 - \tau_b)(1 + r)} wu'' \end{pmatrix} \tag{42}$$

or

$$\begin{pmatrix} A & B \\ C & D \end{pmatrix} \begin{pmatrix} \dfrac{\partial x}{\partial c} \\ \dfrac{\partial s}{\partial c} \end{pmatrix} = \begin{pmatrix} 0 \\ E \end{pmatrix}. \tag{43}$$

The determinant of the matrix (i.e., the numerator) cannot be evaluated easily because it is impossible to evaluate the sign of $(AD - BC)$. However, the signs of the denominator for the Cramer equation are easily determined.

Therefore, it is impossible to evaluate the sign of $\partial x/\partial c$ and $\partial s/\partial c$ exactly. We can propose, nevertheless, that their signs are opposite.

By simplifying the functional of $v(c, s)$ as

$$v(c, s) = \frac{c^{1-\gamma}}{1 - \gamma} - k(1 - s)^2. \tag{44}$$

We can obtain the exact solution of $c_{1,t+1}$, x_t and s_t as follows:

$$c_{1,t+1} = [\beta(1 - \tau_b)(1 + r)]^{1/\gamma}c_{1t}, \tag{45}$$

$$x_t = \left[\frac{k(1 + r)^2(1 - \tau_b)^2}{d^2\rho(1 - \tau_w)^2(1 + \theta)} c_{1t}^{\gamma} \right]^{1/2\rho-1}, \tag{46}$$

$$s_t = 1 - \frac{(1 - \tau_b)(1 + r)}{d\rho(1 - \tau_w)} x_t^{1-\rho}. \tag{47}$$

These solutions suggest the following properties:

$$\frac{\partial x}{\partial c} \gtreqqless 0 \Leftrightarrow \rho \gtreqqless \frac{1}{2},$$

and

$$\frac{\partial c}{\partial t} \gtreqqless 0 \Leftrightarrow \beta(1 - \tau_b)(1 + r) \gtreqqless 1.$$

When the "ability" is higher (or lower) than one-half, an increase in consumption raises (or lowers) the amount of human capital investment. Since we already know that the signs of $\partial x/\partial c$ and $\partial s/\partial c$ are opposite, an increase in consumption decreases (or increases) the amount of services to the parent when the same inequality is held with respect to the preceding. The present property has some interesting economic implications, although it has been derived under special circumstances.

Simulation Results

We have already presented the model and have examined several properties analytically under several assumptions. This subsection presents some simulation results under given parameters to demonstrate more general results that can be achieved only through numerical simulation techniques. It is necessary to introduce specific parameter values that enable us to obtain numerical solutions. These parameter values are expected to be close to the plausible values in Japan. The real interest rate r is equal to 0.5, and the discount rate also takes the same value. Since one generation lives for twenty years to bear another generation, the value of 0.5 was chosen. The relative aversion parameter γ is equal to 3.0, which is common in many studies. Other parameters are somewhat arbitrary but were chosen to assure plausible calibrations. The efficiency for human capital production, d, is 150, and k, the weight for utility derived from services provided by the child, is 2×10^{-7}. The wage tax rate, τ_w, is 0.1, and the bequest tax rate, τ_b, is 0.2 for the basic simulation, although these tax parameters are changed later to examine the effect of tax policies. We perform two basic simulations. The first one is for a two-generations model, and the second one is for a multigenerations model but assumes the steady state. The first model assumes $\beta = 0.8$, the weight for the child in comparison with the parent. The steady state case endogenously solves the value of β. Obviously, the steady state solution produces a common value for the parent's consumption and the child's consumption.

One of the important concerns in this study is the impact on income and wealth distribution. Two possible effects are examined, namely, the difference in the child's ability and the parent's initial endowments (i.e., the sum of the received bequest) and the child's income during the child's working life. We do not distinguish the source of endowments between these two. We assume that both the child's ability and the parent's initial wealth distribute normally with constant averages and variances. This assumption enables us to examine changes in distributions of consumption, income, bequest, and other variables, because the original distributions are known.

Table 6 shows the results based on various child ability levels. The average of abilities is 0.1 and the standard deviation is 0.0248. Thus, the coefficient variation is equal to 0.248. We can observe the following results based on table 6. First, both the parent's and child's consumptions increase as the ability of the child increases. This is due to the fact that the increase in educational attainment of the child is considerable, and thus wage earnings of the child increase. Also, it is interesting to note that although the child's consumption is lower than the parent's when the ability is lower, it becomes higher when the ability is higher. This happens because the child's earnings capacity increases fairly rapidly, as the ability of the child increases.

Second, the amount of bequest is a decreasing function of the child's ability, and thus a decreasing function of the child's wage income. At some point the parent does not leave any bequest to the child. This is corresponding to the binding case, that is, $b = 0$. Thus, inequality in bequest distribution is very large, since the coefficient of variation is 0.659. An interesting result is that the rate of services provided by the child is a decreasing function of the child's ability up to $\rho = 0.14$, and thus the child's earning capacity. The child

TABLE 6. Basic Simulation Based on Various Ability Parameters (ρ), and τ_w (wage tax rate) = 0.1, τ_b (bequest tax rate) = 0.2, W_0 (initial resource) = 200 under the Two-Generation, Two-Period Model

ρ	0.04	0.06	0.08	0.1	0.12	0.14	0.16	Average	SD	CV
C_p	99.7	100.9	102.6	104.6	107.0	108.4	108.2	104.7	2.43	0.023
C_k	98.3	99.5	101.2	103.2	105.6	110.8	117.4	103.8	3.57	0.034
x	4.28	6.79	9.69	13.07	17.06	19.35	19.62	13.20	4.03	0.305
$s(\%)$	10.34	10.28	10.22	10.16	10.11	9.61	9.98	10.09	0.24	0.023
W	159.0	168.3	179.9	194.0	210.8	227.1	241.5	195.6	18.4	0.094
$Y = (1 - s)W$	142.5	151.0	161.5	174.3	189.5	205.3	217.4	175.9	17.0	0.096
$(1 - t_w)Y$	128.3	135.9	145.4	156.8	170.5	184.7	195.7	158.3	15.3	0.096
B	66.7	56.3	43.6	28.4	10.2	0.0	0.0	27.6	18.2	0.657
$(1 - t_b)B$	53.3	45.0	34.9	22.7	8.2	0.0	0.0	22.1	14.5	0.657

Note: C_p, consumption of parents; C_k, consumption of children; x, human capital investment; s, rate of services for parent; w, wage; Y, income; B, bequest; SD, standard deviation; CV, coefficient of variation.

responded quite cooly to the parent because the amount of bequest to be received from the parent declines constantly and finally becomes zero. In other words, we find that the bequest received moves parallel to the services for the child. This is one of the properties implied by the gift-exchange bequest motive, which our simulation seems to support. If we are allowed to use intuitively appealing words, we can state, "The more intelligent the person is, the cooler and more rational he is." It should be pointed out, however, that the rate of services provided by the child turns out to increase at the highest ability, and thus the highest wage earning level. This indicates the fact that the most capable wage earners become altruistic rather than exchange-motivated. If we are allowed to use intuitively appealing words again, we can state that the extremely rich have room for providing the parent with services.

Table 7 presents the result for the case in which the parent's initial wealth is varied with the constant ability parameter (i.e., $\rho = 0.1$). The lowest wealth is 110, and the highest is 290. The average of initial wealth is 200 with a standard deviation of 33.4. Thus, the coefficient of variation is 0.167. We observe the following results based on table 7. First, both the parent's consumption and the child's consumption are increasing functions of the parent's initial wealth. This is quite natural. However, the difference between the parent's and the child's consumption is inverse, unlike the previous table, because the former is higher than the latter when the initial wealth is lower, while the inverse is true when the initial wealth is higher.

Second, the degree of human capital investment increases at least until the average (i.e., $W_0 = 200$) as the parent's income increases. It starts to decline after the average, however, although the degree of the decrease is fairly minor. This gives us an interesting interpretation of education. When the parent's resource is limited (i.e., lower), the parent attempts to increase human capital expenditure to the children. When the parent's resource is considerably high, the parent wants to increase his own expenditure (i.e., consumption) by marginally cutting the educational expenditure to the child. A poor family is more anxious to provide their children with education in order to compensate their poor initial condition, or may be more ambitious in expecting a higher status of their future generation. This may be called a compensatory role of education, which hopefully cancels the poor initial condition of the parent and expects a higher earning of the child. This is one of the symptoms of the famous "regression toward the mean." A rich family takes the opposite policy because an increase in educational expenditure is very marginal even when their initial wealth increases.

Third, the preceding scenario is clearly understood when we review bequest figures. At the lower level of the parent's initial resource, the amount of bequest is zero. It starts to be positive at the middle level, and increases fairly rapidly when the parent's initial wealth is higher than the average. In

TABLE 7. Basic Simulation Based on Various Parents' Initial Resources (W_0), and τ_w (wage tax rate) = 0.1, τ_b (bequest tax rate) = 0.2, ρ (children's ability) = 0.1 under the Two-Generation, Two-Period Model

W_0	110	140	170	200	230	260	290	Average	SD	CV
C_p	63.3	79.2	94.5	104.6	114.0	123.5	132.9	103.8	11.99	0.115
C_k	86.5	91.2	95.1	103.2	112.5	121.8	131.1	104.1	9.02	0.087
x	4.52	7.97	12.44	13.07	12.92	12.77	12.62	12.39	1.54	0.125
$s(\%)$	8.19	8.48	8.71	10.16	11.08	12.00	12.93	10.12	1.06	0.105
W	174.4	184.6	193.0	194.0	193.7	193.5	193.3	192.7	3.05	0.016
$Y = (1 - s)W$	160.1	168.9	176.2	174.3	172.3	170.3	168.3	173.2	2.42	0.014
$(1 - t_w)Y$	144.1	152.0	158.6	156.8	155.0	153.3	151.5	155.9	2.18	0.014
B	0.0	0.0	0.0	28.4	60.8	93.3	125.7	32.9	29.6	0.899
$(1 - t_b)B$	0.0	0.0	0.0	22.7	48.7	74.6	100.6	26.3	23.6	0.899

Note: C_p, consumption of parents; C_k, consumption of children; x, human capital investment; s, rate of services for parent; w, wage; Y, income; B, bequest; SD, standard deviation; CV, coefficient of variation.

this range, the amount of human capital investments showed only a minor increase. The above phenomenon suggests the existence of a higher degree of substitution possibility between human capital investment and material wealth as a form of bequest. We thus confirm the proposition advocated by the human capital school concerning such a substitution possibility. This is also supported by table 6.

Fourth, the rate of services provided by the child increases as the parent's initial wealth increases. This is corresponding to the zero amount of bequest at the lower level. In this range, the rate of services performed by the child is fairly low. However, when the amount of bequest becomes nonzero, the rate of services jumps from the 8 percent level to the 10 percent level. The rate of services increases on a fairly straight curve, as the amount of bequest increases. This constitutes verification for the gift-exchange motive of bequest.

Fifth, an interesting observation related to this phenomenon is that the wage income and the after-tax income decrease as the amount of bequest increases. This was mainly caused by two outcomes. First, the human capital expenditure has started to decline. Second, the rate of services by the child increases. Thus, the child gives up his or her working time by providing the parent with services. Obviously, these outcomes were produced in exchange for the increase in bequest received.

The above scenario is not beneficial to a macroeconomy because the growth rate in an economy is likely to be reduced. The reason is that the workers' productivity would be lowered because of a lesser degree of human capital investment. Also, working hours of workers would be declining because the child provides the parent with more services. Therefore, an increase in capital accumulation through a form of bequest is not good for a *growth* economy.

We have examined the two-generation, two-period model. The model was capable of producing several interesting results regarding the relationship between bequests and other economic variables. Needless to say, the real world is multigenerational and multiperiod. Thus, we extend our model to a multigeneration, multiperiod model. It is necessary, however, to assume the steady state for technical reasons. Thus, the consumption level of the parent and that of the child are the same. The steady state assumption, however, enables us to solve the value of β, the weight for the child endogenously. Therefore, the model in the steady state is more general than that in the previous section in the sense that the intergenerational cooperation is taken into account more seriously.

Tables 8 and 9 show the simulation results based on the steady state assumption. Since the qualitative results—such as the positive bequest versus zero bequest, the effect on human capital investment, wage earnings, the rate of services provided by the child, and so on—are not so different from those

TABLE 8. Basic Simulation Based on Various Ability Parameters (ρ), and τ_w (wage tax rate) = 0.1, τ_b (bequest tax rate) = 0.2, W_0 (initial resource) = 200 under the Steady State Assumption

ρ	0.04	0.06	0.08	0.1	0.12	0.14	0.16	Average	SD	CV
C	82.9	85.1	88.1	91.7	96.1	101.2	106.4	92.3	5.02	0.054
x	4.37	6.93	9.87	13.3	17.3	22.0	22.6	13.7	4.56	0.334
$s(\%)$	8.55	8.62	8.73	8.87	9.04	9.25	10.07	8.90	0.23	0.026
W	159.1	168.5	180.1	194.3	211.2	231.3	247.1	196.3	19.4	0.099
$Y = (1 - s)W$	145.5	153.9	164.4	177.0	192.1	209.9	222.2	178.8	17.2	0.096
$(1 - t_w)Y$	131.0	138.6	148.0	159.3	172.9	188.9	200.0	160.9	15.5	0.096
B	129.5	115.2	97.5	76.2	50.9	20.8	0.0	73.3	29.1	0.397
LS	65.6	69.8	75.1	81.5	89.3	98.5	106.4	82.5	8.90	0.108
$(1 - t_b)B$	103.6	92.2	78.0	61.0	40.7	16.6	0.0	58.6	23.3	0.397
Ratio	0.612	0.569	0.510	0.428	0.313	0.145	0.0	0.402	0.133	0.332

Note: C, consumption; x, human capital investment; s, rate of services for parent; w, wage; Y, income; B, bequest; LS, life-cycle savings; Ratio, ratio of after-tax bequest to total wealth (i.e., after-tax bequest plus life-cycle savings); SD, standard deviation; CV, coefficient of variation.

TABLE 9. Basic Simulation Based on Various Parents' Initial Resources (W_0), and τ_w (wage tax rate) = 0.1, τ_b (bequest tax rate) = 0.2, ρ (children's ability) = 0.1 under the Steady State Assumption

W_0	110	140	170	200	230	260	290	Average	SD	CV
C	65.6	81.2	88.9	91.7	94.5	97.2	100.0	91.2	4.58	0.050
x	0.75	4.66	13.32	13.28	13.23	13.19	13.14	12.57	2.39	0.190
s(%)	16.1	11.09	8.59	8.87	9.14	9.42	9.70	9.14	0.94	0.103
W	145.7	175.0	194.3	194.3	194.2	194.1	194.0	192.5	6.77	0.351
$Y = (1 - s)W$	122.2	155.6	177.6	177.0	176.4	175.8	175.0	175.0	7.59	0.043
$(1 - t_w)Y$	110.0	140.0	160.0	159.3	158.8	158.3	157.5	157.5	6.83	0.043
B	0.0	0.0	19.0	76.2	133.5	190.8	267.1	79.6	57.6	0.722
LS	65.6	81.2	86.4	81.5	76.7	71.8	65.3	80.6	4.79	0.059
$(1 - t_b)B$	0.0	0.0	15.2	60.99	106.8	152.6	213.7	63.8	46.1	0.722
Ratio	0.0	0.0	0.149	0.428	0.582	0.680	0.765	0.381	0.213	0.559

Note: C, consumption; x, human capital investment; s, rate of services for parent; w, wage; Y, income; B, bequest; LS, life-cycle savings; Ratio, ratio of after-tax bequest to total wealth (i.e., after-tax bequest plus life-cycle savings); SD, standard deviation; CV, coefficient of variation.

based on the previous two-generation, two-period model, we do not repeat the qualitative result for the multigeneration, multiperiod model. The quantitative differences, however, between the previous tables 6 and 7, and tables 8 and 9 based on the steady state assumption are considerable. Thus, these points are described briefly.

The most important difference appeared in the figures of consumption, the rate of services, and the amount of bequest, which, for the consumption figures, showed considerable decreases in comparison with the previous tables. The rates of services provided by the child also showed minor decreases. The largest increases occurred in the figures of bequests for families who decided to leave some bequest (i.e., the nonbinding case). The amount of bequest almost doubled in comparison with the two-generation, two-period model. Some people provide a higher than 50 percent rate of bequest over their total lifetime saving. This is largely due to the following fact. Since a multigeneration, multiperiod model takes more significant account of the utilities of future generations than does the previous model, it is natural that each generation consumes less and leaves a larger bequest more. One interesting contrast is the considerable decrease in inequality in bequest distribution. The estimated coefficient of variation in bequest distribution decreased from 0.657 to 0.332, and from 0.899 to 0.559, respectively.

The Effect of Tax Policies

We consider two forms of taxes in this model framework: wage income and bequest. Several parameter values are examined in order to draw the effect of tax policies. The examination is somewhat special in that, first, somewhat extreme values of tax parameters are adopted; namely, (1) the wage tax rate is 0.4, and the bequest tax rate is 0.0 (i.e., no bequest tax), and (2) the wage tax rate is 0.0 (i.e., no wage tax), and the bequest tax rate is 0.4. Second, no tax revenue neutrality is assumed. Thus, the simulation is not realistic but intends to draw only the qualitative effect of tax policies.

Table 10 shows the simulation result of consumption, after-tax income, and after-tax bequest when the tax parameters are changed. Figures in the first and fourth column are the same as those of the basic simulations reported formerly (i.e., $\tau_w = 0.1$ and $\tau_b = 0.2$). Two important observations are summarized based on table 10. First, changes in consumption figures that are represented by the child's figures are fairly minor even when the tax parameters are changed. This arises partly because the changes in the two tax parameters are nearly revenue neutral. Second, the effect of income tax, and the effect of bequest tax are straightforward. For example, when the tax rate for income is zero and the tax rate for bequest is high (i.e., 0.4) families increase wage income and decrease bequest. These changes are fairly dramatic. The

TABLE 10. The Effect of Taxations on Consumption, Income, and Bequest, a Two-Generation, Two-Period Model

ρ	0.04	0.06	0.08	0.1	0.12	0.14	0.16	Average	SD	CV
$\tau_w = 0.1$, $\tau_b = 0.2$										
c_k	98.3	99.5	101.2	103.2	105.6	110.8	117.4	103.8	3.57	0.034
$(1 - \tau_w) Y$	128.3	135.9	145.4	156.8	170.5	184.7	195.7	158.3	15.3	0.096
$(1 - \tau_b) B$	53.3	45.0	34.9	22.7	8.2	0.0	0.0	22.1	14.5	0.657
$\tau_w = 0.4$, $\tau_b = 0.0$										
c_k	94.3	94.7	95.4	96.2	97.2	98.5	99.9	96.4	1.18	0.012
$(1 - \tau_w) Y$	82.3	85.9	90.6	96.3	103.2	111.4	121.0	97.2	7.99	0.082
$(1 - \tau_b) B$	112.4	107.9	102.5	96.0	88.3	79.1	68.3	95.1	9.05	0.095
$\tau_w = 0.0$, $\tau_b = 0.4$										
c_k	95.8	97.8	101.3	107.3	113.7	120.3	127.2	107.9	7.18	0.067
$(1 - \tau_w) Y$	145.9	156.0	168.8	178.9	189.4	200.5	212.0	178.8	13.6	0.076
$(1 - \tau_b) B$	20.6	10.5	0.0	0.0	0.0	0.0	0.0	1.47	4.00	2.712
W_0	110	140	170	200	230	260	290	Average	SD	CV
$\tau_w = 0.1$, $\tau_b = 0.2$										
c_k	86.5	91.2	95.1	103.2	112.5	121.8	131.1	104.1	9.02	0.087
$(1 - \tau_w) Y$	144.1	152.0	158.6	156.8	155.0	153.5	151.5	155.9	2.18	0.014
$(1 - \tau_b) B$	0.0	0.0	0.0	22.7	48.7	74.6	100.6	26.3	23.6	0.899
$\tau_w = 0.4$, $\tau_b = 0.0$										
c_k	63.6	74.5	85.4	96.2	107.1	117.9	128.8	96.2	12.1	0.125
$(1 - \tau_w) Y$	100.9	99.4	97.9	96.4	94.8	93.3	91.8	96.4	1.69	0.017
$(1 - \tau_b) B$	7.75	37.2	66.6	96.0	125.4	154.8	184.2	96.0	32.7	0.341
$\tau_w = 0.1$, $\tau_b = 0.4$										
c_k	94.2	99.4	103.7	107.3	110.9	118.5	126.2	107.6	5.06	0.047
$(1 - \tau_w) Y$	156.9	165.6	172.8	178.9	181.5	179.9	178.3	177.1	5.09	0.029
$(1 - \tau_b) B$	0.0	0.0	0.0	0.0	4.92	26.5	48.0	3.49	8.38	2.401

Note: ρ, ability parameter; W_0, parent's initial wealth; τ_w, wage income tax rate; τ_b, bequest tax rate; Y, income; B, bequest; c_k, child's consumption level; SD, standard deviation; CV, coefficient of variation.

zero tax rate on bequest and the high income tax rate give a completely different scenario. Having only one tax revenue, say relying only on a bequest tax or on a wage income tax, has an enormous effect on the family behavior regarding the determination of the bequest. From the economic policy point of view, specializing in bequest tax rather than specializing in wage income tax is preferable because it has a positive effect on economic growth. When the tax rate for wage income is higher, a negative effect on human capital investment and labor supply is possible. Consequently, the growth rate in an economy is lowered. This is not good for a *growth* economy.

Concluding Remarks

In closing, this essay examined various aspects of the relationship between bequests and wealth in the Japanese case. The first part examined a time-series change in wealth distribution, including both financial and physical assets. Then, the concentration on wealth holding, the share of inheritances over total wealth, and the contribution of inheritance and of noninheritance (i.e., life-cycle saving motives) to both wealth accumulation and inequality in wealth distribution is estimated by applying various methods. Finally, a simple bequest function is estimated by the type 2 Tobit estimator. These examinations enabled us to evaluate quantitatively the effect of bequest on wealth accumulation and inequality in wealth distribution in Japan.

The second part constructed a theoretical model of the bequest and saving behaviors by taking into account both the effect of human capital investment and the contribution of services to the parent provided by the child. The latter aspect is strictly related to a gift-exchange (or strategic) motive. First, we presented some comparative statics results derived under several simplified assumptions. Second, when we adopted a more realistic model than the previous model that is used to derive some comparative statics results, it is impossible to solve the model analytically. Then, we applied a numerical simulation method to derive some meaningful implications. The results achieved suggest that both human capital investment and a gift-exchange motive are important in the determination of savings and bequests in Japan. In particular, the influence of the child's ability (i.e., earnings capacity) is crucial to education, saving, and bequest. Finally, the effect of tax policies was examined briefly.

Several future works are suggested. We obtained the results based on theoretical works and/or simulation techniques with respect to the implication of human capital investment and a gift-exchange motive for the determination for saving (thus consumption), education, and wealth accumulation. Although several interesting observations were proposed, we have not examined them empirically. Also, we have not presented any evidence on how human capital investment, services by the child, and gift-exchange motives are quantitatively important in the determination of the saving rate and other economic variables in Japan. Finally, it would be necessary to take into account the number of children (or no children versus some children) when these issues are examined.

REFERENCES

Abel, A. B. 1985. "Precautionary Saving and Accidental Bequest." *American Economic Review* 75 (September): 777–91.

Atoda, N., and T. Tachibanaki. 1985. "Decomposition of Income Inequality by Income Sources" (in Japanese). *Quarterly of Social Security Research* 20 (Spring): 330–40.

Becker, G. S., and N. Tomes. 1976. "Child Endowments and the Quantity and Quality of Children." *Journal of Political Economy* 84, no. 4 (August): S143–62.

Becker, G. S., and N. Tomes. 1979. "An Equilibrium Theory of the Distribution of Income and Intergenerational Mobility." *Journal of Political Economy* 87, no. 6 (December): 1153–89.

Bernheim, B. D., A. Shleifer, and L. H. Summers. 1985. "The Strategic Bequest Motive." *Journal of Political Economy* 93, no. 6 (December): 1045–76.

Blinder, A. S. 1973. "A Model of Inherited Wealth." *Quarterly Journal of Economics* 87 (November): 608–26.

Cox, D. 1987. "Motives for Private Income Transfers." *Journal of Political Economy* 95, no. 3 (June): 508–46.

Davies, J. B. 1981. "Uncertain Lifetime, Consumption, and Dissaving Behavior." *Journal of Political Economy* 89, no. 3: 561–77.

———. 1982. "The Relative Impact of Inheritance and Other Factors on Economic Inequality." *Quarterly Journal of Economics* 96 (August): 471–98.

Hayashi, F. 1986. "Why is Japan's Saving Rate so Apparently High?" In *NBER Macroeconomics Annual*, ed. S. Fischer, 147–210. Cambridge, MA: MIT Press.

Hayashi, F., A. Ando, and R. Ferris. 1988. "Life Cycle and Bequest Saving: A Study of Japanese and U.S. Households Based on Data from 1984 NSFIE and the 1983 Survey of Consumer Finance." *Journal of the Japanese and International Economies* 2, no. 2 (June): 450–91.

Horioka, C. Y. 1990. "The Importance of Life Cycle Saving in Japan: A Novel Estimation Method." Osaka University ISER Discussion Paper, no. 225.

Hurd, M. D. 1989. "Mortality Risk and Bequests." *Econometrica* 57 (July): 779–813.

Institute for Posts and Telecommunications Policy (IPTP). 1990. *Household Asset Choice*. IPTP.

Ishikawa, T. 1975. "Family Structures and Family Values in the Theory of Income Distribution." *Journal of Political Economy* 83, no. 5 (October): 987–1108.

Kotlikoff, L. J. 1988. "Intergenerational Transfers and Savings." *Journal of Economic Perspectives* 2 (Spring): 41–58.

Kotlikoff, L. J., and L. H. Summers. 1981. "The Role of Intergenerational Transfers in Aggregate Capital Accumulation." *Journal of Political Economy* 89 (August): 706–32.

———. 1988. "The Contribution of Intergenerational Transfers to Total Wealth: A Reply." In *Modelling the Accumulation and Distribution of Wealth,* ed. D. Kessler and A. Masson, 53–67. Oxford: Clarendon Press.

Menchik, P. L. 1979. "Intergenerational Transmission of Inequality: An Empirical Study of Wealth Mobility." *Economica* 46 (November): 349–62.

———. 1980. "Primogeniture, Equal Sharing, and the U.S. Distribution of Wealth." *Quarterly Journal of Economics* 94 (March): 299–316.

Modigliani, F. 1988a. "Measuring the Contribution of Intergenerational Transfers to Total Wealth: Conceptual Issues and Empirical Findings." In *Modelling the Accumulation and Distribution of Wealth,* ed. D. Kessler and A. Masson, 21–52. Oxford: Clarendon Press.

———. 1988b. "The Role of Intergenerational Transfers and Life Cycle Saving in the Accumulation of Wealth." *Journal of Economic Perspectives* 2 (Spring): 15–40.

Noguchi, Y. et al. 1991. *A Study on Bequests and Wealth Accumulation.* Tokyo: Keizai-Seisaku Kenkyusho.

Sheshinski, E., and Y. Weiss. 1982. "Inequality Within and Between Families." *Journal of Political Economy* 90 (February): 105–27.

Shorrocks, A. F. 1983. "The Impact of Income Components on the Distribution of Family Income." *Quarterly Journal of Economics* 97:311–26.

Tachibanaki, T. 1989. "Japan's New Policy Agenda: Coping with Unequal Asset Distribution." *Journal of Japanese Studies,* Summer, 15:345–69.

———. 1992. "Higher Land Prices as a Cause of Increasing Inequality: Changes in Wealth Distribution and Socio-economic Effects." In *Land Issues in Japan: A Policy Failure?,* ed. J. H. Haley and K. Yamamura, 175–94. Seattle, Washington: Society for Japanese Studies.

———. 1993. "Housing and Savings." In *Economics of Housing,* ed. Y. Noguchi and J. Poterba. Chicago: NBER and University of Chicago Press.

Tachibanaki, T., and K. Shimono. 1986. "Saving and the Life-Cycle." *Journal of Public Economics* 31:1–24.

———. 1991. "Wealth Accumulation Process by Income Class." *Journal of the Japanese and International Economies* 5 (September): 239–60.

Tachibanaki, T., and S. Takata. 1993. "Wealth Accumulation Under Uncertainty in Income and Bequest Motive." Kyoto Institute of Economic Research, Discussion Paper, no. 381.

Togashi, M. 1979. "A Study on Wealth Distribution of Employees" (in Japanese). *Hitotsubashi Ronso* 81: 114–25.

Tomes, N. 1981. "The Family, Inheritance, and the Intergenerational Transmission of Inequality." *Journal of Political Economy* 89, no. 5 (October): 928–58.

CHAPTER 9

The Effect of Bequest Motives on the Composition and Distribution of Assets in France

Luc Arrondel, Sergio Perelman, and Pierre Pestieau

The relation between bequests and savings is pervasive in economics. Witness to this link is the recent debate on the proportion of accumulated wealth that can be imputed to bequest motives. Though far from being settled, this debate is currently pausing around the figures of 0.2 and 0.8. For Modigliani 1988, 20 percent is the share of inheritance in aggregate capital accumulation and 80 percent that of life-cycle saving; whereas for Kotlikoff 1988, it is just the other way around. Note that even if we take the former more conservative figure, a fifth of total accumulated wealth is due to inheritance, which is not negligible. In this essay, we do not want to address the issue of level but rather that of structure: what is the effect of inheritance on the structure and distribution of wealth?

The issue of the effect of bequest motives on the composition of wealth has received little attention in the literature in spite of its paramount importance. It is indeed not indifferent for an economy to have a wealth structure biased toward real estate or toward productive capital. International comparisons of capital structure reveal quite striking differences in this area and these differences can have decisive implications in terms of growth, employment, and social welfare.

The second issue, the effect of inheritance on inequalities in the distribution of wealth, has been widely studied. In this essay, we focus on the relative contribution of intended bequests as opposed to unplanned bequests on wealth distribution.

People leave bequests for a number of reasons that allow us to develop a taxonomy of bequests, including unplanned bequests, altruistic bequests, stra-

This paper was presented at the IPTP International Conference on Savings and Bequests, Tokyo, March 17 and 18, 1992. We have benefited from helpful conversations with A. Masson and E. Wolff and from the excellent discussions with T. Ito and Y. Aso.

tegic bequests, or more generally bequests as exchange, and paternalistic bequests, to pick the most usual. Each of these concern specific assets and hence one can expect that if the relative importance of these different motives for bequests varies over time or across countries, this will indeed imply varying wealth patterns.

This essay is organized as follows. In the next section, we define the concept of intended bequests and present the data to be used. In the third section, we use this data to see how wealth structure can be explained by variables acknowledged to reflect bequest intent. In the fourth section, the same data is used to assess the extent to which inequalities in the distribution of assets can be explained by bequest motives.

Concepts and Data

Intended Bequests Motives

The purpose of this essay is to analyse the effect of bequest intent on the composition and the distribution of wealth. Thus we are not interested by all types of bequests, but just by intended bequests. Indeed not all bequests are planned. As forcefully noted by Modigliani 1988, a substantial portion of the observed bequest flow undoubtedly reflects the precautionary motive arising from the uncertainty of the time of the death. Unless people can manage to put all their retirement reserves into life annuities, people tend to die with some wealth, the amount of which reflects risk aversion and the cost of running out of wealth.[1] As to why households do not use most of their wealth to buy annuities, one often cites the very unfavorable rates that are currently offered on such annuity contracts.

Two models of intended bequests are generally distinguished depending on whether they are based on altruistic or on gift-exchange motives.[2] The gist of the altruistic models is that bequests are an instrument in a dynastic utility maximization process in which a parent arranges for equity across and within generations.[3] Bequests are compensatory forms of transfers that aim at equalizing incomes among children as well as those between parents and children. But before bequeathing, parents who are careful to invest in children in the most productive way first allocate funds for schooling on the basis of respective rates of return among children. Eventually the rate of return to these human capital expenditures will fall and reach the market interest rate. Then,

---

1. Davies 1981.
2. For a survey of models of inheritance, see Masson and Pestieau 1991.
3. Barro 1974; Becker and Tomes 1976, 1979.

all further parental transfers will be financial ones, gifts or bequests, since the market interest rate is not subject to diminishing returns.

This is the unconstrained version of the altruistic model, that is, the version in which parents are so wealthy or so altruistic that they can afford transferring first human capital and then financial assets. This version has powerful implications in a wide range of areas, notably as to the neutrality of public debt. For the purpose at hand, it implies that the greater the number of children parents have, the less they will bequeath because of the greater opportunity to make productive human capital transfers. In the constrained version of this model, altruistic parents cannot afford reaching the level of transfers for which the rates of return of human capital invested in their children reach the market rate of interest. Then, there are no bequests.[4]

The other class of intended bequests is based on the idea of exchange: parents expect during their old age some sort of support from their children, the price of which is a bequest at the end of their lives. The terms of that exchange can be determined in a more or less harmonious way. A now classical example of a nonharmonious exchange is the so called model of strategic bequest.[5] According to this model, parents will use the threat of disinheritance, playing one potential heir against another to acquire attention and services from them. To be credible, this manipulative behavior requires that there be at least two children who do not cooperate and who trust their parents when they announce at the beginning of their old age the bequest rules that state how much of a bequest each child will receive as a function of the attention supplied by each of them.

Clearly bequests originating from precautionary motives are quite different by nature from those dictated by altruistic or strategic motives. They come from pure life-cycle accumulation considerations. The level of wealth so bequeathed must thus tend to be on the average proportional to life resources. Assuming that one can distinguish intended bequests from unplanned ones, one faces two problems when looking at their influence on wealth composition and wealth distribution. First, depending on whether they are motivated by altruism or exchange considerations, the influence can be different. This is particularly true for wealth distribution. One generally expects that altruistic bequests increase wealth inequality whereas exchange-motivated bequests are rather neutral toward wealth distribution. Second, one quickly realizes that most households exhibit mixed behavior toward inheritance; they save with a

---

4. We are here just talking of nonpaternalistic bequests. There are also bequests that are based on altruistic but paternalistic motives. Analytically, these bequests are treated as terminal consumption.

5. Bernheim, Shleifer, and Summers 1985.

combination of precautionary, altruistic, and strategic motives. To sort out those different motives, the quality of data is clearly a crucial question.

Data

The data set comes from the INSEE (French National Institute of Statistics) 1986 survey on households' financial assets. This survey covers 5,600 French households and includes detailed socioeconomic characteristics, information on intergenerational transfers, wealth-holding motives, and bequests intents, as well as information on total gross wealth and holding of particular assets. The fifteen assets considered in this survey are given in table A.1 along with holding frequency. Those assets are divided in four subsets:

1. liquid assets: checking accounts, saving accounts (tax- and nontax-exempt), saving plans for housing, annuities and life insurance, savings certificates and time deposits;
2. stock values: bonds, stocks, mutual funds;
3. primary housing;
4. other properties: secondary residences, income property, commercial real estate (land, farm, business).

As to the households' characteristics or rather those of the households' heads, we focus on those that are inheritance specific: age, wealth, spouse, children, education, bequest intent, inheritance. In most of the essay, we use a subset of households whose head is over 60. We indeed believe that at that age people have a clearer idea as to the motives for which they are holding particular baskets of assets. There are 1,278 such households that have in common that they had been asked the two following questions in the INSEE survey:

1. You have not dipped into your savings since you became a retiree or a widow(er); is it to bequeath them to your heirs?
2. Are you planning to leave your children or grandchildren all or part of what you own as gifts inter vivos?

We also focus on a narrower subset of households, those aged over 60 and having at least one child. There are 1,053 such households.

We use the positive responses to at least one of these two questions as an indicator of their intent to bequeath. This variable "bequest intent" will be used to reflect an intended bequest motive.[6]

A third question was asked to the same households and concerns the

---

6. On this see Perelman and Pestieau 1991.

existence of a will. It was phrased as follows: "One often worries about the consequences of passing away; have you in that respect written a will?"

A positive answer to that question does not really reflect a genuine bequest motive but rather an intention to partially circumvent the quasi-mandatory equal sharing rule or to look after the surviving spouse. As another indicator, we will follow Hurd 1987 who bases the strength of bequest motive on whether the people have living children. The number of children as well as the presence of a spouse will also be used as proxy of bequest intent. We also have some information as to whether people have made gifts to their heirs that has to be interpreted with caution. It is surely indicative of altruism but it can be viewed as a substitute for bequests.

Note that all these indicators of bequest motives are used in explaining wealth composition. We indeed expect that people with bequest motives hold a wealth structure that is different from that held by people without such motives. When dealing with wealth distribution, we would like to know whether the parents of wealth owners had bequest intents. Such information being unavailable, we use as proxies for bequest intent the number of siblings, the fact of having inherited a house, and the fact of having benefited from gifts, with the same caveat as previously mentioned for the latter.

Bequest Motives, Accumulation, and Wealth Composition

We first look at the effects on gross wealth of a range of variables pertaining to characteristic of households and of variables reflecting bequest intent. The results of an OLS regression[7] are given on table 1 for the aged sample with and without children. Besides the independent variables there presented, we also controlled for education, occupation, and income. The negative relation between wealth and age beyond 60 is expected. Having children has no effect on wealth except for households with more than three. In this case the negative effect probably is due to the cost of rearing children. Note however that this effect is only significant for more than three children. All variables reflecting some bequest motive—spouse, inherited house, bequest intent, and will—have all a positive incidence on the level of wealth. There are however two exceptions: having received or having made a gift has a negative yet nonsignificant effect on cumulated wealth.

We now turn to the issue of diversification, that is, the number of assets held by households. This issue is generally dealt with on the basis of conventional portfolio theory and life-cycle hypothesis. One of the standard results obtained in that literature is a very striking life-cycle pattern with a pro-

---

7. Heteroscedasticity-consistent standard errors are calculated.

TABLE 1. Wealth accumulation: OLS model; Dependent variable: ℓn (wealth)

Explanatory Variables	Aged Sample	Aged Sample with Children Only
Constant	4.67 (0.183)*	4.81 (0.191)*
Bequest related variables[a]		
Spouse	0.557 (0.099)*	0.464 (0.110)*
Inherited house	0.544 (0.095)*	0.411 (0.101)*
Received inter-vivos gifts	−0.071 (0.123)	−0.012 (0.132)
Transferred inter-vivos gifts	−0.023 (0.104)	−0.064 (0.110)
Bequest intent	—	0.489 (0.101)*
Will	—	0.446 (0.108)*
Number of children		
none	RG	—
1	0.034 (0.136)	RG
2	0.041 (0.133)	0.012 (0.120)
3	0.044 (0.142)	−0.033 (0.128)
4 or more	−0.344 (0.137)*	−0.350 (0.125)*
Age[b]		
61–65	RG	RG
66–70	−0.141 (0.119)	−0.155 (0.122)
71–75	−0.123 (0.125)	−0.216 (0.136)
>75	−0.478 (0.112)*	−0.608 (0.117)*
R^2	0.339	0.379
Number of households	1,278	1,053

Note: Heteroscedasticity-consistent standard errors are given in parentheses. RG: Reference group corresponding to the constant term. * Significant at a 5 percent level (t-test).
[a] Binary variables.
[b] Household head.

nounced "hump-shaped" profile that peaks at the age of 60.[8] The number of assets owned increases rapidly in the early stages of life, reaches a plateau in the age ranges of forty through sixty and then declines rapidly in old age. It also appears that the reduction in the number of assets after retirement varies across households, which can be explained partially by differential motives of bequest.

In that respect, we want to see the influence of variables pertaining to inheritance on the number of assets held by households older than 60. Those assets are the fifteen presented in table A.1. To do so, we use a Poisson model for count data.[9] The results are given in table 2 for the main explanatory variables: age, wealth, children, and the bequest indicators. We also con-

8. See, e.g., Dicks-Mireaux and King 1984; King and Leape 1987; Arrondel and Masson 1989.

9. See, e.g., Maddala 1983, 51–54.

trolled for education, income, and occupation. Not surprisingly wealth has a positive effect on diversification. As it is known, diversification implies transaction costs that are only justified for high amounts of investment. Diversification decreases with age and with the number of children, though not significantly for the latter. Both results can be explained by the concern to avoid risks. All the variables pertaining to bequest motives have a positive and significant effect on diversification with only one exception: having made gifts.

We now come to the gist of this section, that is, the effect of bequest motives on the structure of assets. Two preliminary remarks are in order on this. First, to keep the analysis tractable, one has to consider broad categories of assets and look at particular combinations of those categories. Second, we

TABLE 2.   **Wealth diversification: Poisson model; Dependent variable: number of assets**

Explanatory Variables	Aged Sample	Aged Sample with Children Only
Constant	−6.71 (0.083)*	−6.47 (0.092)*
Bequest related variables[a]		
Spouse	0.049 (0.034)	0.037 (0.038)
Inherited house	0.100 (0.033)*	0.081 (0.036)*
Received inter-vivos gifts	0.113 (0.039)*	0.116 (0.042)*
Transferred inter-vivos gifts	0.012 (0.035)	0.011 (0.037)
Bequest intent	—	0.086 (0.037)*
Will	—	0.026 (0.039)
Number of children		
none	RG	RG
1	−0.020 (0.047)	—
2	−0.034 (0.047)	−0.013 (0.042)
3	−0.045 (0.049)	−0.026 (0.045)
4 or more	−0.074 (0.050)	−0.049 (0.046)
Wealth (ℓn)	0.175 (0.011)*	0.161 (0.012)*
Age[b]		
61–65	RG	RG
66–70	−0.036 (0.042)	−0.041 (0.045)
71–75	−0.068 (0.045)	−0.087 (0.049)
>75	−0.083 (0.041)*	−0.085 (0.044)*
Log-likelihood test (degrees of freedom)	765.3 (23)	651.5 (24)
Number of households	1,278	1,053

Note: Standard errors are given in parentheses. RG: Reference group corresponding to the constant term.
* Significant at a 5 percent level (*t*-test).
  [a] Binary variables.
  [b] Household head.

expect that households with either altruistic or strategic motives of bequest
will hold assets less liquid and more physical than households with pure
precautionary motives. Four categories of assets are considered: liquid assets,
stock values, primary housing, other properties. We then use a multinomial
logit model[10] to explain five alternative combinations of assets: (*a*) liquid
assets and primary housing; (*b*) liquid assets, stock values, primary housing;
(*c*) liquid assets, primary housing, and other properties; (*d*) the four categories
plus the reference combination that only comprises liquid assets.

Table 3 presents the coefficients for the variables of interest in this paper.
Income, occupation, and education, which have also been used, are not mentioned in table 3, but one has to keep in mind that they were controlled for.
There are two ways of looking at this table. First, one can focus on a given
combination. Second, one can compare coefficients between two columns to
see the relative effect of each explanatory variable on holding one combination rather than another. The reference combination is liquid assets that are
held by almost every household.

Age has no effect on combinations (*a*) and (*b*) but a negative, though
weakly significant, effect on combinations (*c*) and (*d*) including other properties, which makes sense. Wealth has an important effect on all combinations
especially the complete one. A large number of children seems to call for the
least diversified combination. One has to remember that here all households
have at least one child and that hence the presence of children implies more
pressure on resources.

Not surprisingly in view of the results on diversification, all variables
pertaining to bequest motives induce one to hold more than just liquid assets.
The only exception concerns households having already made some inter-
vivos gifts. If we think that going from (*a*) to (*d*) means more diversification
and less liquidity we see that the reaction to those variables is mixed. Having
inherited a house clearly favors the complete combination of assets. Having a
spouse leads to two different combinations: a simple one and the most complete one possible. Those who have received inter-vivos gifts will surely hold
more than just liquid assets; they will tend to rather hold a combination with
other properties.

We now come to the last two variables, the most interesting from our
viewpoint. The indicator of bequest intent reveals a strong preference for the
type (*b*) portfolio with liquid assets, stocks, and primary housing. In other
words, the portfolio with other properties would be held by people with
motives other than just that of bequeathing. Finally, households having written a will tend to own a combination with other properties. This is not

---

10. In a companion paper (Perelman and Pestieau 1992), we have studied the issue of asset
composition using a log-linear model with multiple dependent variables.

TABLE 3. Wealth Diversification: Multinomial model, Aged sample

| | Alternative Asset Combinations | | | |
Explanatory variables	(a) —Liquidities —Home	(b) —Liquidities —Home —Stock values	(c) —Liquidities —Home —Other properties	(d) —Liquidities —Home —Stock values —Other properties
Constant	-5.19 (4.94)	-5.15 (6.10)	0.260 (5.33)	-2.33 (6.26)
Bequest related variables[a]				
Spouse	0.587 (0.241)*	0.012 (0.304)	0.273 (0.258)	0.633 (0.316)*
Inherited house	0.499 (0.331)	0.894 (0.367)*	1.181 (0.326)*	1.292 (0.359)*
Received inter-vivos gifts	1.195 (0.400)*	1.085 (0.456)*	1.509 (0.398)*	1.264 (0.443)*
Transferred inter-vivos gifts	-0.027 (0.262)	-0.058 (0.329)	0.126 (0.272)	0.133 (0.321)
Bequest intent	0.806 (0.373)*	1.680 (0.394)*	1.282 (0.376)*	0.947 (0.405)*
Will	0.532 (0.338)	0.047 (0.406)	0.578 (0.356)	0.755 (0.381)*
Number of children				
1	RG	RG	RG	RG
2	-0.208 (0.311)	-0.397 (0.353)	-0.573 (0.316)	-0.417 (0.371)
3	-0.049 (0.328)	-0.798 (0.400)*	-1.034 (0.359)*	-0.539 (0.396)
4 or more	-0.594 (0.314)	-1.250 (0.398)*	-1.053 (0.328)*	-1.033 (0.395)*
Age[b]	0.150 (1.120)	0.058 (1.391)	-1.140 (1.215)	-1.609 (1.425)
Wealth (ℓn)	1.006 (0.087)*	0.833 (0.108)*	1.164 (0.097)*	1.694 (0.134)*

Log-likelihood 2,389.4
Number of households: 1,053

Note: Asymptotic standard errors are given in parentheses. RG: Reference group corresponding to the constant term. * Significant at a 5 % level (t-test).
[a] Binary variables.
[b] Household head.

surprising; these are the assets for which sharing often leads to conflicts. Through that effect one also sees that there is an interaction between the nature of assets and the existence of a will. In other words, a will is not really an exogenous variable.[11]

Bequest Motives and Wealth Inequality

The role of bequests on wealth inequality has been a controversial subject for a long time. Since the 1970s, this issue has motivated a number of models. Even though the impact of inheritance on the distribution of wealth remains a debated question, it seems that a certain consensus has been reached.

The first models are based on the life-cycle hypothesis and consider a society without inheritance. The role of transmissions is measured by the inequality gap between observed wealth distribution and simulated distribution. Atkinson 1971 and especially Oulton 1976 and Russel 1979 conclude that life-cycle factors (differences in age and in both human and nonhuman income) contribute only a minor part to current wealth inequality. Oulton attributes most of this inequality to the residual factor, that is, inheritance; whereas Russel bases his explanation on factors pertaining to differential attitudes toward risk and dispersion in ratios of return. Those estimates are nevertheless questionable as the gap between actual and simulated distribution can also come from inadequate modelling, from missing variables, or from the interaction between inheritance and life-cycle factors.

Bevan 1979, Flemming 1979, and especially Blinder 1976 and Davies 1982 propose more comprehensive models that embody accumulation from both life-cycle and wealth transfers and that are capable of generating, or at least reproducing, the observed wealth distribution. The influence of each factor is assessed by comparing the observed distribution with that simulated without this factor. Without being in total agreement, those models reach some common conclusions. Life-cycle variables (including differences in time preference) only play a limited role, yet more important than in the previously mentioned models. Those variables cannot explain wealth holding among the top brackets. For these, wealth holding is mainly explained by bequests and gifts. Davies 1982 shows that wealth concentration is due to the mere existence of bequests and not to their unequal distribution. The contribution of intergenerational transfers to wealth inequality among households not belonging to the top brackets is much lower, if not negligible.[12]

Instead of dealing with simulation models, one can instead study directly

---

11. See Barthold and Ito 1992 which compares attitude toward writing wills in the United States and in Japan. France is in that respect closer to Japan than to the United States.
12. See also Davies and Shorrocks 1978; Davies 1982; Jenkins 1987.

the degree of wealth immobility between generations. Evidence appears conflicting here. In the United States, wealth immobility, measured by the correlation between parents' and their children's wealth, is high, on the order of 0.7 (Menchik 1979), much higher than income immobility (0.25). In the United Kingdom, wealth and income immobility appear much closer, about equal to 0.5.[13] These two approaches, simulation models and intergenerational wealth correlation, are not possible in France for lack of reliable data on wealth holding by parents and children.

Consequently, we consider two subsets of households in the INSEE survey: those with heads aged between 20 and 60, and those with heads aged 60 and over who have at least one child. We believe that for the first subset, having received inter-vivos gifts or having inherited a house can reflect intentional bequest motives as well as the number of siblings. For the subset of aged, we use as our indicator of bequest intent these bequest-related variables: the existence of a will, the number of children, and the fact of having inherited a house. In this case, we look at the relation between bequest motives and wealth inequality for the same generation; we implicitly assume that there will be some correlation between the distribution of wealth of that generation and the distribution of wealth of the following generation.

As indicator of wealth inequality, we use Theil's index and decompose it. Table 4 provides for the sample of young households (between 20 and 60) the values of Theil's coefficient for bequest related characteristics. It also gives a decomposition of this inequality measure.[14] Even though households having inherited a house or having benefited from gifts are on average wealthier than the other households, the distribution of their wealth is relatively less unequal. Bequests and gifts seem to have an equalizing effect on the population receiving them, which is a bit surprising. Note that the effect of siblings is negligible, even though, as expected, wealth decreases with the number of siblings.

The contribution of those three variables to inequality is negligible. Combining them with life-cycle variables does not bring additional explanation. That is, the cross effect of, say, "having received a gift" and "age" is not larger than the sum of the simple effects of those two variables.

Turning to the sample of aged households, the results of which are given in table 5, one notes that wealth inequality is lower among households with bequest intent than among households without bequest intent, even though the former own more wealth than the latter. The effect of the variable "will" is quite different: those who write a will have more wealth and a more unequal distribution of wealth. Households with two children have the most unequal wealth whereas households with three children have the highest level of

---

13. Harbury and Hitchens 1979; Atkinson, Maynard, and Trinder 1983.
14. See Bourguignon and Morrison 1985; Masson and Arrondel 1989.

wealth. Those having inherited a house are much wealthier than the others and their wealth is slightly more unequally distributed.

As to the decomposition of Theil's index, the variables "having inherited a house," and "having written a will," explain respectively 7.6 and 13.6 percent of wealth inequality. The effect of "bequest intent" or of the "number of children" is very small. Overall those results are disappointing and somehow paradoxical. Many analysts of French wealth distribution indeed believe that bequests are an important determinant of wealth inequality. Yet, this does not appear in data such as that used here.

What is clearly happening is that wealth inequality is generated by a number of factors including those of the life-cycle hypothesis such as age, income, or occupation. When inheritance is added it has two effects: a direct disequalizing effect linked to the simple fact that the distribution of bequests is itself highly unequal, and an indirect equalizing effect linked to those intentional transfers that are aimed at offsetting market disparities.

TABLE 4.   Wealth Distribution: Theil coefficients, Age 21 to 60

		Theil Coefficient	Mean Wealth (1,000 FF)
Total		0.794	494.3
Inter-vivos gifts received	yes	0.455	778.7
	no	0.869	441.2
Inherited house	yes ·	0.548	982.2
	no	0.800	440.9
Number of siblings[a]	0	0.747	663.5
	1	0.762	578.7
	2	0.778	536.9
	3	0.759	438.8
	4 and more	0.808	380.9

	Theil Decomposition (in percentage)				
	Simple Effects	Cross Effects			
		Age	Occupation	Education	Income
Inter-vivos gifts received	3.4	14.9	20.0	7.9	15.4
Inherited house	5.4	16.1	20.4	10.0	17.4
Number of siblings[a]	2.4	15.7	18.7	6.3	14.1
Age[a]	12.5	1.0	25.9	20.8	23.1
Occupation[a]	17.8		1.0	19.3	24.8
Education[a]	4.2			1.0	15.0
Income[b]	12.3				1.0

Note: All the observations are weighted in order to be representative of the whole French population.
[a] Household head.
[b] Income does not include capital returns or gains.

Conclusion

To what extent bequest motives influence the composition and the distribution of wealth is an interesting and important topic, but one that has received little attention in empirical work because of data problems. We definitely need better, expanded data sets on the various assets held by households and on the characteristics and motives of these households. With enlarged data, there could be progress toward more definite conclusions than merely the exploratory ones presented in this essay.

What emerges from this essay is that not only inheritance but also bequest-related variables such as the number of children, bequest intent, the number of siblings, and the presence of a spouse imply particular wealth patterns. That they contribute to wealth inequality is less clear.

TABLE 5. Wealth Distribution: Theil coefficients, Aged sample (with children only)

		Theil Coefficient	Mean Wealth (1,000 FF)
Total		1.041	480.8
Bequest intent	yes	0.776	753.8
	no	0.869	441.2
Will	yes	1.086	1125.9
	no	0.780	351.6
Number of children	1	0.781	451.4
	2	1.183	547.6
	3	1.031	584.1
	4 and more	1.043	350.9
Inherited house	yes	1.022	857.0
	no	0.920	368.8

| | | Theil Decomposition (in percentage) | | | |
| | Simple Effects | Cross Effects | | | |
		Age	Occupation	Education	Income
Bequest intent	3.3	5.6	24.6	18.7	21.6
Will	13.6	15.3	30.7	28.5	27.7
Number of children	1.7	6.8	26.1	21.5	23.6
Inherited house	7.6	11.1	27.6	22.2	25.9
Age[a]	2.5	1.0	26.1	20.2	31.7
Occupation[a]	21.7		1.0	27.2	30.3
Education[a]	17.3			1.0	26.6
Income[b]	19.4				1.0

Note: All the observations are weighted in order to be representative of the whole French population.
[a] Household head.
[b] Income does not include capital returns or gains.

TABLE A.1. Summary Statistics for Assets

	Total Sample[a]		Aged Sample[b] (with children)	
	Percent of households owning asset	Asset owner's mean wealth[c]	Percent of households owning asset	Asset owner's mean wealth[c]
Financial assets				
Liquid assets				
Checking accounts	95.8	637.9	90.7	627.0
Tax exempt savings accounts	74.8	642.2	79.4	614.8
Other savings accounts	12.8	917.1	18.3	797.9
Saving plans for housing	32.2	849.2	17.8	992.0
Annuities and life insurance	33.1	819.9	15.5	835.7
Savings certificates and time deposits	5.6	1441.2	8.8	1031.1
Stock values				
Bonds	11.1	1377.9	17.5	1373.0
Mutual funds	16.8	1288.1	18.8	1371.0
Stocks	9.9	1472.4	9.6	1853.5
Physical assets				
Primary housing				
Primary residence	55.2	893.3	63.2	782.0
Other properties				
Secondary residence	12.3	1441.2	12.1	1544.2
Income property	12.0	1388.1	14.4	1130.1
Investment in land	18.1	977.8	22.4	789.0
Farm enterprise	6.9	1002.3	6.8	561.3
Business enterprise	9.9	1499.9	6.2	1759.3
Total	100.0	616.9	100.0	578.9

[a]Household's head aged > 20 years old.
[b]Household's head aged > 60 years old, retired or widow(er).
[c]In thousands of 1986 FF. 1 $ = 6 FF.

REFERENCES

Arrondel, L., and A. Masson. 1989. "Hypothèse du cycle de vie, diversification et composition du patrimoine: France 1986." *Annales d'économie et de statistique* 17:1–45.

Atkinson, A. B. 1971. "The distribution of wealth and the individual lifecycle." *Oxford Economic Papers* 23:239–54.

Atkinson, A. B., A. K. Maynard, and C. G. Trinder. 1983. *Parents and Children.* London: Heinemann.

Barro, R. J. 1974. "Are government bonds net wealth." *Journal of Political Economy* 82:1095–1117.

Barthold, T., and T. Ito. 1992. "Bequest taxes and accumulation of household wealth: US-Japan comparison." In *Political Economy of Tax Reforms,* ed. T. Ito and A. O. Krueger. Chicago: University of Chicago Press.

Becker, G., and N. Tomes. 1976. "Child endowments and the quantity and quality of children." *Journal of Political Economy* 84:S143–62.

———. 1979. "An equilibrium theory of the distribution of income and intergenerational mobility." *Journal of Political Economy* 87:1153–89.

Bernheim, B., A. Shleifer, and L. H. Summers. 1985. "The strategic bequest motive." *Journal of Political Economy* 93:1045–76.

Bevan, D. L. 1979. "Inheritance and the distribution of wealth." *Economica* 46:381–402.

Blinder, A. S. 1976. "Inequality and mobility in the distribution of wealth." *Kyklos* 29:607–38.

Bourguignon, F., and C. Morrison. 1985. "Une analyse de l'inégalité des revenus individuels en France." *Revue économique* 36:741–77.

Davies, J. B. 1981. "Uncertain lifetime, consumption and dissaving in retirement." *Journal of Political Economy* 89:561–77.

———. 1982. "The relative impact of inheritance and other factors on economic inequality." *Quarterly Journal of Economics* 97:471–98.

Davies, J. B., and A. F. Shorrocks. 1978. "Assessing the quantitative importance of inheritance in the distribution of wealth." *Oxford Economic Papers* 30:138–49.

Dicks-Mireaux, L. D. L., and M. A. King. 1984. "The effect of pensions and social security on the size and composition of household asset portfolio." In *Financial Aspects of the U.S. Pensions System,* ed. Z. Bodie and J. Shoven, 399–439. Chicago: University of Chicago Press.

Flemming, J. S. 1979. "The effects of earnings inequality, imperfect capital markets, and dynastic altruism on the distribution of wealth in life cycle models." *Economica* 46:363–80.

French National Institute of Statistics (INSEE). 1986. "Survey on household's financial assets."

Harbury, C. D., and D. M. W. N. Hitchens. 1979. *Inheritance and Wealth Inequality in Britain.* London: Allen and Unwin.

Hurd, M. D. 1987. "Saving of the elderly and desired bequests." *American Economic Review* 77:298–312.

Jenkins, S. 1987. "The distribution of wealth: A survey." In *Economic perspectives: An annual survey of economics 6,* ed. D. W. Pearce and N. J. Rau. New York and London: Harwood Academic Publishers.

King, M., and J. Leape. 1987. "Asset accumulation, information and the life-cycle." NBER Working Paper, no. 2392. Typescript.

Kotlikoff, L. J. 1988. "Intergenerational transfers and savings." *Journal of Economics Perspectives* 2:41–58.

Maddala, G. S. 1983. *Limited-Dependent and Qualitative Variables in Econometrics.* Cambridge: Cambridge University Press.

Masson, A., and L. Arrondel. 1989. "Hypothèse du cycle de vie et accumulation du patrimoine: France 1986." *Economie et Prévision* 90:11–30.

Masson, A., and P. Pestieau. 1991. "Tests des modèles d'héritage: Inventaire critique." *Economie et Prévision* 100–101:73–91.

Menchik, P. L. 1979. "Inter-generational transmission of inequality: An empirical study of wealth mobility." *Economica* 46:349–62.

Modigliani, F. 1988. "The role of international transfers and life cycle saving in the accumulation of wealth." *Journal of Economic Perspectives* 2:15–40.

Oulton, N. 1976. "Inheritance and the distribution of wealth." *Oxford Economic Papers* 28:86–101.

Perelman, S., and P. Pestieau. 1991. "Les legs volontaires en France: Évaluation et explication." *Economie et Prévision* 100–101: 129–35.

———. 1992. "Inheritance and wealth composition." *Journal of Population Economics* 5:305–18.

Russel, T. 1979. "The share of the top wealth holders: The life cycle, inheritance, and efficient markets." *Annales de l'Insée* 33–34:159–80.

CHAPTER 10

Inheritance and the Distribution of Wealth in Britain and Canada

James B. Davies

In this essay I overview what is known about inheritance and the distribution of wealth in Britain and Canada. While these countries are of independent interest, their comparison also has some fascinating features. There are strong contrasts in the kind of data available as well as contrasts in substantive aspects of inheritance and wealth distribution. These differences are sufficient to span much of the range that would be observed in a larger cross-section of countries. Many lessons for other countries, such as Japan, are apparent in the experience of Britain and Canada.

Britain has fairly consistent annual estimates of wealth distribution going back to 1923, based on the estate multiplier method. It has very little sample survey evidence. Canada, in contrast, has no estate multiplier estimates, and has not even had an estate tax that would make such estimates possible since 1972. Instead it has had sample surveys of wealth holding at roughly seven-year intervals since the 1950s. The British evidence shows decreasing wealth concentration throughout the century, whereas the Canadian provides no evidence of trend.

Turning to inheritance, to cite the most obvious difference between the countries, Britain has a landed aristocracy whose bequest practices have had an important impact and retain some importance to this day. In Canada there is no such phenomenon. On the data side, a series of studies have been carried out in Britain, first by Wedgwood in the 1920s and more recently by Harbury and Hitchens in the 1950s, 1960s, and 1970s, that study the relationship between the wealth left by wealthy decedents and that left on death by their predecessors or successors. In Canada, on the other hand, two large-scale microsimulation exercises have estimated the distribution of inherited wealth

This essay was presented at the International Conference on Savings and Bequests, held in Tokyo on March 17 and 18, 1992, under the sponsorship of the Institute for Posts and Telecommunications Policy (IPTP) of Japan. I would like to thank John Burbidge, Pierre Pestieau, Tsuneo Ishikawa, Tony Shorrocks, Toshiaki Tachibanaki, and the conference participants for comments and assistance. Responsibility for all errors or omissions is my own.

and its contribution to wealth inequality by synthetic means. Researchers in both countries have constructed pure life-cycle models to see how much wealth concentration might be obtained in the absence of inheritance.

In this essay I will study the British and Canadian evidence on wealth distribution and inheritance in turn. Before doing so, however, we should consider our motivation. As pointed out by Shorrocks (1987), while much effort has been devoted to improving estimates of the distribution of wealth in many countries, there have been critics who question the value of this enterprise. One criticism is that physical and financial wealth is swamped in aggregate importance by human capital (including pension rights). It is also argued that intergenerational transfers in the form of human capital investments dwarf conventional bequests.

Ideally, wealth and inheritance should not be studied in isolation. If we are interested in getting an idea of the distribution of economic well-being, for example, then wealth and human wealth should be aggregated. If we are interested in understanding saving motives, perhaps because of lagging national saving and investment, the choice between saving in human versus nonhuman form should similarly be studied, and the focus should probably be on the flow (saving) rather than the stock (wealth). Thus, it *might* be argued that studies of wealth distribution and inheritance can only be justified as providing background information for more comprehensive studies.

In fact, stronger motives for studying wealth and inheritance can be found. It is true that, in aggregate, human wealth is about three times as important as nonhuman. However, nonhuman wealth is much more unequally distributed, and forms a high proportion of total wealth for those at the very top. Its importance in determining the extreme upper tail of the distribution of lifetime wealth (lifetime earnings plus inheritances) is therefore disproportionate. A substantial equalizing trend in the wealth distribution will generally imply a considerable reduction in inequality in the upper reaches of the lifetime wealth distribution. In my view, this provides sufficient reason to be interested in statistics on the distribution of (narrowly defined) wealth. An associated reason why *inheritance* is so interesting is that, for many observers, the legitimacy of the observed income and wealth distributions depends very much on the degree to which wealth differences result from inheritance rather than effort.

From this viewpoint, there is considerable merit in continuing to collect, and analyze, statistics on narrowly defined wealth. In recent years there have been several studies of the effect of including social security and private pension wealth, as well as human wealth. While these are valuable, their purposes are distinct from those of conventional studies of wealth distribution, and they should not be regarded as replacing the latter.

In addition to the equity issue, there is legitimate concern about lagging saving rates in many countries. Over the last two decades economists have become very interested in the role of the bequest motive for saving. This stems in part from the claim of Kotlikoff and Summers (1981) that inherited wealth makes up about 80 percent of household wealth in the United States. While this claim has been hotly contested, there is now a consensus that both bequest and life-cycle saving are important.

The remainder of this essay is organized as follows. In the next section I review what is known about wealth ownership in Britain; then I perform a similar exercise for Canada. The British evidence on the role of inheritance is then studied, followed by that for Canada. The final section concludes my investigation.

The Distribution of Wealth in Britain

There are several excellent recent summaries of the evidence on the distribution of wealth in Britain. There is no attempt here to provide a comprehensive guide to the methods used to generate the wealth distribution estimates. The reader is referred instead to Atkinson and Harrison 1978; Royal Commission on the Distribution of Income and Wealth 1977, 1979; Shorrocks 1987; and Good 1990.

The main source of evidence on wealth distribution in Britain is provided by the estate multiplier method. This familiar technique takes decedents in a year as a sample of the living, and estimates the distribution of wealth by applying population weights equal to age-sex specific inverse mortality rates —that is, "mortality multipliers." Table 1 presents two time series of estimated shares of top wealth holders in Britain since 1923: the Atkinson and Harrison series for 1923–81, and the new Inland Revenue Series C for 1976–89. (Gini coefficients are also reported for the Inland Revenue series.) Both series adjust for missing persons and missing wealth, but differences in procedure lead to significant differences in the estimates for the period 1976–81 where the two series overlap.[1] These differences act as a reminder of the

---

1. The differences between Atkinson and Harrison's (1978) numbers and the new Series C estimates are illuminated to some extent by the explanation in Good 1990, 148–49, of the difference between the old and new Series C numbers. The old Series C estimates were roughly similar to the Atkinson and Harrison figures. (See, e.g., Atkinson, Gordon, and Harrison 1989, table 2, 319.)

The four most important factors accounting for the decline in estimates of top shares from the old to the new Series C (in order of importance) were (i) new estimates of joint property (i.e., assets owned jointly by spouses and therefore not recorded for estate tax purposes) that increased the imputations for this item, (ii) new estimates of the value of small estates (i.e., those not identified by the estate multiplier method), (iii) technical improvements allowing the use of estates of those *dying* in the year in question, rather than those estates assessed during that year (this improvement was already made in some of the old Series C numbers—some time after 1976 but before 1981), (iv) new mortality multipliers based on owner occupancy rather than social class.

TABLE 1. Shares in Total Wealth, England and Wales, 1923–89

	Top 1%	Top 5%	Top 10%	Top 20%
	a) Atkinson and Harrison Estimates, 1923–81			
1923	60.9%	82.0%	89.1%	94.2%
1924	59.9	81.5	88.1	93.8
1925	61.0	82.1	88.4	93.8
1926	57.3	79.9	87.4	93.2
1927	59.8	81.3	88.3	93.8
1928	57.0	79.6	87.2	93.1
1929	55.5	78.9	86.3	92.6
1930	57.9	79.2	86.6	92.6
1936	54.2	77.4	85.7	92.0
1938	55.0	76.9	85.0	91.2
1950	47.2	74.3	—	—
1951	45.8	73.6	—	—
1952	43.0	70.2	—	—
1953	43.6	71.1	—	—
1954	45.3	71.8	—	—
1955	44.5	71.1	—	—
1956	44.5	71.3	—	—
1957	43.4	68.7	—	—
1958	41.4	67.8	—	—
1959	41.4	67.6	—	—
1960	33.9	59.4	71.5	83.1
1961	36.5	60.6	71.7	83.3
1962	31.4	54.8	67.3	80.2
1964	34.5	58.6	71.4	84.3
1965	33.0	58.1	71.7	85.5
1966	30.6	55.5	69.2	83.8
1967	31.4	56.0	70.0	84.5
1968	33.6	58.3	71.6	85.1
1969	31.1	56.1	67.7	83.3
1970	29.7	53.6	68.7	84.5
1971	28.4	52.3	67.6	84.2
1972	31.7	56.0	70.4	84.9
1973	27.3	50.8	66.8	84.9
1974	22.6	47.8	64.1	83.1
1975	22.7	45.8	61.9	80.8
1976	24.4	48.7	65.1	83.7
1977	22.1	46.5	62.5	81.0
1978	21.9	45.6	62.4	81.5
1979	21.5	45.2	61.2	80.3
1980	19.4	42.4	59.3	79.4
1981	22.7	45.9	62.6	82.3

TABLE 1—*Continued*

	Top 1%	Top 5%	Top 10%	Top 25%	Top 50%	Gini
			b) Inland Revenue Series C Estimates, 1976–89			
1976	21%	38%	50%	71%	92%	.66
1977	22	39	50	71	92	.66
1978	20	37	49	71	92	.64
1979	20	37	50	72	92	.65
1980	19	36	50	73	91	.65
1981	18	36	50	73	92	.65
1982	18	36	49	72	91	.64
1983	20	37	50	73	91	.65
1984	18	35	48	71	91	.64
1985	18	36	49	73	91	.65
1986	18	36	50	73	90	.64
1987	18	37	51	74	91	.66
1988	17	38	53	76	93	.67
1989	18	38	53	75	94	.67

Sources: Atkinson, Gordon, and Harrison 1989, table 1. Inland Revenue 1991, table 11.5.

inherent difficulties in estimating wealth distribution generally, and by the estate multiplier method in particular.

The most notable feature of table 1 is the long decline in wealth inequality from 1923 to 1981. On average, there was a 0.7 percentage point decline in the share of the top 1 percent, for example, *per year* over the period 1923–81 according to the Atkinson and Harrison series. This decline was most rapid in the 1920s and 1970s, and slowest in the 1960s. Further points to note are as follows.

1. There is a break point in the Atkinson and Harrison time series between 1959 and 1960. Atkinson and Harrison (1978, 167) devoted some attention to this, and found that some of the discontinuity (less than half) might be explained by their having made too small an allowance for the wealth of missing persons in the 1950s. In any case, this discontinuity exaggerates the recorded decline in inequality, and perceptions of long-term trends should be adjusted for this.
2. The more exclusive the group the greater is the decline in its wealth share over time, both in percentage points, and proportionally. Thus, for example, in the Atkinson and Harrison series while the share of the top 1 percent fell from 34 percent in 1960 to 19 percent in 1980, the share of the top 20 percent hardly declined at all. And in the Series C estimates, while the share of the top 1 percent fell from 21 to 18

percent between 1976 and 1989, the shares of the top 10 percent and 25 percent actually increased. To a large extent what has happened is a redistribution of wealth among the top quintile rather than a spread in wealth holding to the bottom 80 percent. Some believe that part of the decline in concentration is more apparent than real. A significant part of the decline could simply be due, for example, to wealthy families dividing wealth more equally between spouses.

There are many difficulties in applying the estate multiplier method in Britain as elsewhere. Twenty years ago these severely affected the quality of the available British statistics. However, since that time, due to intensive research by the Royal Commission on the Distribution of Income and Wealth (1977, 1979; hereafter referred to as the Royal Commission), Atkinson and Harrison (1978), and officials of the Inland Revenue (1991), these difficulties have been seriously addressed, and the published data now embody attempted corrections for the various sources of error. The discussion of difficulties that follows provides an indication of the amount of effort that has to be put into developing high quality estate multiplier estimates, and the degree of uncertainty attached to these numbers. It does not constitute a criticism of the current British data.

A first difficulty in developing good estate multiplier estimates is that size of estate is not known for decedents who leave too little on death for a grant of representation to be required. This leads to the problem of "missing persons." Since the real value of the basic estate tax exemption varies over time this means that the portion of the population caught by the method fluctuates over time. However, in the British case the exemption level has been sufficiently low that a substantial portion of the population *is* caught by estate tax, so that this is less of a concern than in many other countries, for example, the United States. It is now standard practice in Britain to make an imputation for the wealth of missing persons based on independent balance sheets of the household sector.

Another notable problem in the estate multiplier approach is that of "missing wealth." Some wealth is missing from the estate tax estimates because it is not taxable on death. Well-known examples are property settled on a surviving spouse (with no power to dispose of the capital) and discretionary trusts. Under the latter, benefits paid are at the discretion of the trustees. When a beneficiary dies, the assets held in trust are effectively passed on to new beneficiaries of the trust without being taxed. An imputation is made in the Inland Revenue Series C statistics for such omissions. An idea of the magnitude of the required correction is given by Atkinson and Harrison (1978, 162) who found that including nondutiable settled property raised the share of the top 5 percent from 57.2 to 59.3 percent in 1972.

An interesting feature of "missing wealth" is that for one asset category —life insurance—it is negative. That is because life insurance is valued for estate tax purposes at the amount assured (since the latter enters the estate), which is considerably in excess of the cash surrender value of the typical policy. The excess of insured value over cash surrender value exaggerates the wealth of the life insured, and, in particular, likely exaggerates the relative wealth of smaller wealth holders, for whom life insurance is a more important asset. Again, the British wealth distribution estimates discussed here correct for this problem.

A further difficulty with the estate multiplier method lies in the construction of mortality multipliers. It is known that there are considerable differences in mortality rates not only by age and sex, but also by income, wealth, and social class. Alternative multipliers have been experimented with by various investigators, most notably by Atkinson and Harrison (1978). Atkinson and Harrison also investigate the *theoretical* impact of using different multipliers, finding that it is in principle ambiguous (see Atkinson and Harrison 1978, chap. 3). It is therefore perhaps not surprising that the experiments with different multipliers generally fail to alter greatly the degree of estimated concentration. Further, if a consistent type of multiplier is used over time we may once again hope that estimates of *change* are little affected by the choice of multiplier.[2]

Explaining Changes in Wealth Distribution

One approach to analyzing the causes of changes in wealth distribution might be referred to as an "accounting approach." It breaks down changes in the share of the top 1 percent, for example, into components due to price and quantity changes of particular kinds of assets. This type of study has been done for Britain by the Royal Commission (1979). But, in addition, the fact that a long time series of annual observations are available has allowed an econometric approach to be used as well by Harrison (1976), Atkinson and

---

2. The Inland Revenue's current practice in estimating the Series C distributions is described as follows:

> In practice two multipliers are used within each stratum. Mortality is affected not only by age, sex, and marital status but also by other factors including social class. In order to allow for this, very approximately, different sets of multipliers are used for estates above and below a cut-off point which has been increased in steps from £10,000 in 1976 to £25,000. The multipliers are derived from data provided by the Office of Population Censuses and Surveys Longitudinal Study of social class and occupational mobility. The mortality rates of people with estates greater than the cut-off are assumed to be similar to those of people living in owner occupied housing. For the estates under the cut-off, the multipliers are half way between those used for the larger estates and those appropriate to the population as a whole. (1991, 100)

Harrison (1978), Harbury and Hitchens (1987), and Atkinson, Gordon, and Harrison (1989). As far as I am aware, no comparable studies have been performed, or are possible, with other countries' intermittent time series.

Before looking at the evidence from some of the British studies, let us consider briefly what factors could, in principle, affect the shape of the wealth distribution, and in particular the shares of top wealth groups over time. One that has already been referred to is the wider dispersal of wealth ownership among the members of wealthy families, in part for estate tax avoidance reasons. This wider dispersal can be largely cosmetic—as perhaps in the splitting of assets between husband and wife, but it may also contribute to a real equalization in the distribution of wealth over time—for example, when the practice of primogeniture is replaced by more equal division among offspring.

Another class of factors whose impact on wealth concentration has been studied extensively is price changes. Stock market booms tend to increase top shares, while increases in house prices do the opposite since housing is relatively more important for the less wealthy. A further influence is taxation. Stringent application of estate tax or capital transfer tax ought to reduce wealth concentration over time, as should high rates of effective income taxation for high income groups.

Harrison (1976) estimated the impact of a range of factors including share prices, house prices, extent of owner occupation, and estate duty on the shares of the top 1 percent, top 2 to 5 percent, and top 5 to 10 percent for the period 1923–69. He found that the two price indexes had some explanatory power for all three groups, but that adding extent of owner occupation and estate duty only helped for the top 2 to 5 percent. The strongest finding was that most of the explanatory power simply came from time trend, a dummy for World War II, and a further dummy for the break in the time series in 1959–60.

Atkinson and Harrison (1978) did further work with similar data, extended to 1972. They also set out a theoretical model of the determinants of top wealth shares and used this to motivate a number of alternative estimating equations for the share of the top 1 percent. (The other top groups were not studied.) Their two best-fitting equations provided competing explanations for the decline in wealth inequality in Britain in the mid-twentieth century:

> According to equation B, the decline has been associated with the spread of "popular" wealth, coupled with an exogenous downward trend (possibly reflecting differential rates of accumulation or changes in marriage and inheritance customs), with an upward movement in share prices working in the opposite direction. In equation F there is no exogenous downward trend, and the effect of popular wealth is insignificant. Ac-

cording to this, the main motive forces have been estate duty, either directly through transferring money to the Treasury or indirectly via family rearrangements of wealth, and—in the opposite direction—the rise in share prices. (Atkinson and Harrison 1978, 239–40)

Thus, a clearcut explanation did not emerge. Note that in Atkinson and Harrison (1978) the separate influences of house prices and extent of owner occupation are combined in the "popular wealth" variable—the value of owner occupied housing and consumer durables relative to other wealth. The fact that estate duty is significant in one of the favored specifications but was not in Harrison 1976 is due to the removal of the time trend in that specification. (Dummies for the war and the 1959–60 discontinuity are still included.)

Harbury and Hitchens (1987) also employed the regression approach, focussing on the impact of asset price changes. In a relatively unstructured regression of top shares of five groups on four specific asset price indexes they found that only three of the twenty asset price coefficients were significant. However, when a single weighted asset price index was used for the top 1 percent it proved to be highly significant. In both the Harbury and Hitchens specifications the time trend also does a great deal of work, echoing the finding of Harrison (1976).

Atkinson, Gordon, and Harrison (1989) first updates Atkinson and Harrison's specification *B*, using a time series extended to 1981. (The reason for abandoning specification *F* was not discussed.) The results were quite similar to the original ones. An improved, log-logistic specification using the same variables was also estimated. A valuable application was the use of the estimated equations to explain the observed decline in the share of the top 1 percent from 31.7 to 22.7 percent between 1972 and 1981. The original Atkinson and Harrison equation (with minor corrections), for example, predicts a share in 1972 of 31.1 percent and in 1981 of 20.7 percent. The time trend contributed 2.4 percentage points of the predicted decline, and the spread of popular wealth a further 12 percentage points. A rise in share prices toward the end of the period had the opposite effect of raising the share of the top 1 percent by about 5 percentage points.

What can we conclude from these econometric studies? The consensus seems to be that there is a strong "exogenous" influence showing up in the time trend. This may reflect changes in patterns of estate division and estate tax avoidance, the redistributive impact of taxes, and demographic factors such as fertility of the wealthy and mate selection in marriage. In addition to the influence of "time," share prices and the spread of popular wealth are very important influences.

Supplementing these regression studies, the Diamond Royal Commission used an accounting approach to decompose changes in the shares of top groups into price and quantity changes by type of asset. They found that both kinds of change were important, but that their relative importance changed considerably over time. The most important price changes were those in shares and housing, confirming an important theme of the econometric studies (see Royal Commission 1979, 129–30).

Wealth Composition

Table 2 compares the balance sheet of the household sector in Britain implied by the crude estate multiplier technique—"identified wealth"—with the full balance sheet that allows for missing persons and missing wealth. In some important aspects the balance sheets are in considerable agreement. First, they both indicate that housing makes up 41 to 43 percent of total household assets. There is also comparability in bank deposits and liquid assets (about 12 percent of total assets), and company shares (7 to 9 percent). However, "identified wealth" considerably underestimates the importance of consumer durables and exaggerates the value of life insurance policies greatly.

Shorrocks (1982) has studied how portfolio composition varies in Britain with age and wealth. Rather than looking merely at differences in wealth composition by age or wealth group, he uses a regression approach that allows him to isolate the *partial* impact of age and wealth. His major conclusions

TABLE 2.   "Identified Wealth" versus Balance Sheet Household Wealth, Britain, 1987

Asset Type	Identified Wealth		Balance Sheet Household Wealth	
	Amount (£ billions)	% of Total Assets	Amount (£ billions)	% of Total Assets
Dwellings	409	42.6%	670	41.2%
Buildings, Trade Assets and Land	66	6.9	77	4.7
Consumer Durables	25	2.6	121	7.4
Bank Deposits and Liquid Assets	114	11.9	197	12.1
Government Bonds	28	2.9	49	3.0
Company Shares	89	9.3	117	7.2
Life Policies	169	17.6	146	9.0
Other Assets	61	6.3	248	15.3
Total assets	961	100.0	1,625	100.0
Debts	86	8.9	217	13.4
Net worth	875	91.1	1,408	86.6

Source: Inland Revenue 1991, table 11.2.

concern patterns of wealth holding for five main asset groups. He found that cash and saving deposits have a strong positive relationship with age and a strong negative relationship with wealth level. Stocks and listed shares vary positively and strongly with age and wealth, but wealth has more influence. Unlisted shares, trade assets, and personal debts, all associated with assets held in private businesses, show a strong tendency to decline with age and to increase with wealth. Illiquid assets—insurance policies, household goods, and other personal assets—show a strong negative trend with age, but little variation with wealth. Finally, dwellings and property debts tend to fall with age, but wealth level has the dominant effect—an initial rise followed by a subsequent decline.

Shorrocks (1982) results imply that, at a particular wealth level, rises in share prices increase the relative wealth of older groups, while an increase in housing prices has the opposite effect. Also note that, controlling for age, dwellings are not monotone in wealth. Hence, while it is true that a rise in housing prices reduces the shares of the top 1 percent and 5 percent it likely does so also for bottom groups.

Age and Wealth

The debate about the life-cycle model (LCM) of saving has focussed much attention on the age profile of wealth holding. Several studies have asked whether the "hump saving" predicted by the LCM is actually observed. In Britain, as elsewhere, the cross-sectional evidence is mixed (Shorrocks 1987, 43).[3] But cross-sectional evidence could not be decisive, in any case, because the age profile is contaminated by cohort and differential mortality effects. Panel data are needed to see if "hump saving" really occurs. There are no true panel data on wealth holding in either Britain or Canada. However, the availability of a long time series on wealth distribution makes possible "pseudo" panel studies.[4] Such a study was carried out for Britain by Shorrocks (1975), who found that once appropriate adjustments were made for changes in cohort composition over time there was evidence of a hump-shaped age profile of wealth. However, at the 95th and 99th percentiles this tendency was weaker than at a lower level in the distribution. This agrees with the Canadian evi-

---

3. Dunn and Hoffman (1983) adjust the cross-section age profile to take into account pension as well as marketable wealth. As argued by Shorrocks (1987) this guarantees that the age profile will be hump shaped, which is not very interesting. The LCM predicts that marketable wealth, as well as pension wealth, should be decumulated toward the time of death. What happens to marketable wealth is the relevant empirical issue.

4. A pseudo-panel is constructed from successive cross sections by noting that those aged, say, 25–29 in 1970 were aged 30–34 in 1975. With good sampling, and corrections for attrition bias, this is a good way to construct grouped panel data.

dence, to be discussed later, that the LCM fits the behavior of lower income groups better, and may not provide a good description of the behavior of top groups. Since the top groups in fact do most of the saving, this implies that saving for bequest is important.

The Distribution of Wealth in Canada

The best answer to the question "How is wealth distributed in Canada?" may be "We do not know." It is more difficult than generally appreciated to establish the distribution of *any* economic characteristic. In Canada the major source of information on the distributions of income and wealth among individuals and families is Statistics Canada's Survey of Consumer Finance (SCF). This survey provides estimates of income distribution every year, and has provided estimates of wealth distribution at roughly seven-year intervals.[5] But, like all surveys the SCF is subject to sampling and nonsampling error, as Statistics Canada itself continually reminds its data users.

Sampling error is, of course, the difference between the *sample* value of a statistic—for example, average wealth—and its true *population* value, given that all those in the sample respond fully and correctly to the survey. The larger the sample the smaller this error is likely to be. For characteristics like national means it is generally small, since the sample sizes used by Statistics Canada are large. When it comes to estimating the shape of the overall *distribution* of a highly skewed variable like wealth, however, sampling error can be significant. Most samples will select too few genuinely rich households, and a few will have too many. This problem can be addressed by heavily oversampling in the upper tail, for example by using income tax records to select a supplementary sample. However, such an approach has only been used on one occasion in Canada (the 1977 SCF).[6]

Nonsampling error is more troublesome. It takes two forms. First, some people refuse to be interviewed. Studies indicate that the likelihood of this nonresponse varies systematically with characteristics like age, region, and income. These systematic differences can be corrected through the assignment of different weights to families according to their likelihood of being included

---

5. The most recent wealth surveys were conducted in 1970, 1977, and 1984. Unfortunately, at present it is not known when, or indeed whether, the SCF wealth survey will be conducted again. Under current planning at Statistics Canada the SCF will become part of a short-term rolling panel survey, the Survey of Labour and Income Dynamics (SLID). There is active interest both at Statistics Canada, and in the academic community, in surveying wealth more frequently under SLID than has been done in the past.

6. The 1977 SCF had 12,734 respondent families in total, 184 of whom were from a special high income sample. This compares with an overall sample of 4,102 and a high income sample of 438 in the 1983 U.S. SCF survey (Avery, Elliehausen, and Kennickell 1988). While introducing the high income sample in 1977 increased the estimated income shares of top groups slightly, it had a negligible effect on the estimated wealth distribution (Oja 1986).

in the sample. Differential response across age groups, for example, can be almost entirely corrected since we have good prior information on the distribution of Canadians by age. However, we do not have prior information about the true distribution of wealth. (If we did, we would not need the survey.) Therefore, it is only if differential response according to these variables is highly correlated with that according to observable characteristics (age, region, size of urban area, etc.) that it can be fully corrected by weighting procedures. Since the correlation is, in fact, far from perfect, differential response remains a serious problem.

Another form of nonsampling error—misreporting—occurs because people sometimes refuse to report certain items or make mistakes. In cases where people report that they own an asset, but not its value, an imputation is generally made. However, no correction is possible if the interviewers do not know that the family *owns* a particular type of asset or if its value is merely underreported. U.S. validation studies indicate that, on average, common financial assets like bank accounts are typically underreported by 40 to 50 percent. Other assets are more accurately reported. The value of owner-occupied houses, for example, is, on average, reported with surprising accuracy (see Davies 1979b).

Some of the results of these combined errors are well-known for the SCF *income* distribution. While wages and salaries are on average reported fairly accurately, SCF estimates of average transfer payments are about 20 percent less than the true figures, and the shortfall is about 50 percent for investment income (Statistics Canada 1990, 52). The situation is even worse for wealth surveys. The spring 1984 SCF, for example, produced estimates of stock ownership for Canadian families that were only about 14 percent of the year-end 1983 independent national balance sheet totals. Other assets are not so badly underrepresented, and some assets, such as housing, appear to be fairly accurately represented.

Keeping all these reservations in mind, let us look at table 3, which shows the SCF estimates of the distribution of wealth in Canada for 1970, 1977, and 1984. A quick look at the table suggests that inequality dropped from 1970 to 1977–84. However, there were significant changes in the survey procedure over this period that make any assessment of trend unreliable. For example, in part due to liberalization of the criteria for keeping families with incomplete responses in the sample, response rates rose from 75 to 80 percent between 1970 and 1977, and then to 87 percent in 1984. The ratio of mean wealth to income also rose from 2.4 in 1970 to 2.9 in 1977 and 1984. It is difficult to say to what extent the increase in wealth relative to income, and the decline in concentration, are due to the increased response rate (and other changes) versus real underlying changes in wealth distribution. This is a question that deserves more careful attention than it has so far received.

One attractive feature of the survey approach is that it provides informa-

TABLE 3. SCF Wealth Distribution, Canada

Share of	1970	1977	1984
top 1%	18.0%	n.a.	16.8%
top 5%	39.2	n.a.	37.5
top 10%	53.3	50.7%	51.3
Quintile 1	70.9	68.3	68.8
Quintile 2	20.1	20.7	19.8
Quintile 3	8.4	9.4	9.3
Quintile 4	1.6	2.1	2.4
Quintile 5	−1.0	−0.5	−0.3
Gini Coefficient	0.716	0.689	0.686
Mean	$18,189	$46,273	$85,344
Median	7,575	21,754	39,876

Sources: Shares of top 1 percent and 5 percent computed by author (see text). All other figures: Oja 1986, 25 and 26.

tion on many characteristics *other* than wealth. One knows about the respondent family members' education, labor force status, income components, etc. This advantage over estate multiplier data has been exploited by both Canadian and foreign researchers interested in the determinants of wealth holding. (See the subsequent discussion about the age wealth profile in Canada.) More crudely, we can readily compare the Canadian distributions of income and wealth since they are both estimated in the same survey. As generally observed, there is much more dispersion in the distribution of wealth than in income. In 1984, for example, the SCF indicates that the share of the top 10 percent of families (where the families are arranged according to wealth) was 51.3 percent. The corresponding income share (when the families are sorted by income) was 26.3 percent.

As noted above, in both the 1977 and 1984 SCF mean wealth equals about three times average income. This allows us to guess roughly how much wealth would have been found per family if the SCF wealth survey had been repeated more recently. In 1989, for example, mean income was $41,083. If the wealth-income ratio were 3:1, then mean wealth in spring 1990, as estimated by the SCF, would have been about $123,000. Median wealth, which gives a better idea of the wealth of the "typical" family,[7] would have been only about $57,500 according to a similar calculation.

---

7. The median is the level of wealth such that one half of the families have less and one half more. In sampling from a heavily skewed distribution like that of wealth it is likely to be much more reliable than the average. Also, it is a better indicator of the wealth of the "typical" family. A family with wealth equal to the average would be at about the seventieth percentile. That is, it would be at an "upper middle" wealth level rather than "in the middle."

It is also interesting to note some of the characteristics of the top 1 percent of wealth-holding families. There were approximately 100,000 families in this category in 1984, and their average wealth was $1,434,000 according to the SCF. Only about half of those in the top 1 percent were millionaires. Even allowing for the difficulties with the SCF, it is thus clear that the "top 1 percent" and the "super rich" are far from the same thing. The latter are a small minority of the top 1 percent.

As has been made clear above, the figures shown in table 3 are affected by important sources of error. This is especially true in the upper tail. To put the matter plainly, the SCF estimates miss a good deal of the upper tail of the wealth distribution entirely. The richest family in 1984, for example, had net worth of only about $6 million, and was a farm family. (In comparison, the 1983 SCF in the United States, which heavily oversampled higher income groups, had a richest respondent with $86 million, and even in this case there was great concern about the portion of the upper tail that had been missed. See Avery, Elliehausen, and Kennickell 1988.) Since it is well-known that Canada has several billionaire families, there is a very long segment of the upper tail of the wealth distribution missing from the survey evidence. This should act as a caution to anyone who believes that knowledge of wealth holding in their country would be radically improved by launching a nationally representative sample survey without oversampling in the upper tail. There has been an awareness of this point for many years in Britain (see, e.g., Harrison 1979), which may help to explain the lack of recent surveys on wealth holding in that country.

The limitations of the SCF sample survey indicate that if we are to get anything like an accurate idea of the Canadian wealth distribution we must turn to alternative sources. In another essay (forthcoming), I have examined a number of these. Also, there is some journalistic evidence and there are two recent private studies on the subject, some of whose results have been publicized in the press.

From time to time *Fortune* magazine publishes a list of the world's superrich. In 1989 *Fortune* (September 11, 1989, 73) estimated that there were 8 billionaire families with partial or complete Canadian residence. This number would fluctuate from year to year, depending on how well the stock market is doing, real estate values, and so forth, but it is clear that some Canadians figure among the world's superrich. Corroboration of the *Fortune* assessment is provided by Francis (1986) who studied the corporate wealthy in Canada, and reported that there were 6 billionaire families. To give an idea of their activities and importance, the wealthiest of these families, the Reichmanns of Canary Wharf fame, were the eighth richest family in the world in 1989 according to *Fortune*. Other Canadian billionaires, as described in the *Fortune* article, include the second Lord Thomson of Fleet (a newspaper magnate and majority owner of the historic Hudson's Bay Company); the Irving family (whose firms dominate many industries in the province of New Brunswick); the Bronfmans (offspring of the distilling giant, Samuel Bronfman); and the Westons (involved in food processing and retailing, and forest products).

Other journalistic evidence provides more information on the sub-billionaires. Newman (1975) attempted to provide a complete list of all Canadian families with wealth over $20 million. There were 160 families on his list. The list of the corporate wealthy provided by Francis (1986) indicated 32 families with wealth over $100 million. Using this evidence I "guesstimate" that the share of the top 1 percent in the Canadian wealth distribution is somewhere in the range of 23 to 27% (Davies forthcoming). This implies considerably more concentration than is suggested by the SCF wealth distribution.

Recently two other fragments of information about the Canadian wealth distribution have surfaced. As reported in *MacLean's* magazine ([November 5, 1990]: 49), a Toronto management consulting company conducted a survey of 1,350 Canadians over 50 in 1989, and found that on average families with at least one person over 50 "had nearly $350,000 in assets." Unfortunately further details of the study (such as average debt, needed to compute mean net worth) have not been made public. For present purposes it is interesting to ask whether this number is consistent with the figure of $123,000, for *all* Canadian families (i.e., young *and* old) that I obtained for 1990 extrapolating from the 1984 SCF. The 1984 SCF itself indicates mean wealth of families over 50 to be about 40 percent higher than the overall average. This would imply a mean wealth for those over 50 of just $172,200 in 1990 if overall average wealth were $123,000. Thus, for what it is worth, the management company's study suggests that the SCF survey probably underestimates overall wealth holding in Canada quite badly.

The last piece of evidence comes from a study done by the accounting firm of Ernst and Young ("Millionaires: They're Not So Rare Any More," *London Free Press,* Dec. 15, 1990, p. A2). This study used a wide variety of published and industry sources to estimate the full balance sheet of the household sector at year end 1989. It then scaled up the 1984 SCF wealth distribution both for inflation and the difference between the SCF balance sheet and the independent 1989 sheet. A longer upper tail was also added using an unspecified form of extrapolation. Finally, a list of the Canadian wealthy was compiled from public and private sources. I am told by the Ernst and Young researchers that this latter exercise confirmed the accuracy of the estimates surprisingly well.

Only partial details of the Ernst and Young results have been publicly released. However, these are of considerable interest. First, the estimated average Canadian family net worth at the end of 1989 was $260,000, about double what the unadjusted SCF would suggest.[8] Second, as reported in the press, it was estimated that Canada had about 425,000 millionaire families. The latter form about 4.5 percent of the population. In private communication I have learned, further, that it was estimated that there were about one million families (around 10 percent of the total number of families) with wealth between $0.5 million and $5 million, and that these held 49 percent of overall net worth. Finally, 12 percent of household net worth was held by 19,000 families with more than $5 million each.

The Ernst and Young study suggests an even higher level of wealth concentration in Canada than the calculations reported in Davies forthcoming and referred to previously. It suggests a share in the top 10 percent of Canadian families of about 62 percent of the wealth. (The 1984 SCF figure was 51%, see table 3.) On the argument that the SCF share for the top 1 percent captures the people below $5 million reasonably well, but those above hardly at all, the Ernst and Young results argue for an upward revision of the SCF share for the top 1 percent (17 percent in 1984) to a figure somewhere around 27 to 29 percent.

Wealth Distribution in Canada Compared with That in Britain

Official estimates of the wealth distributions in Canada and Britain give the appearance of remarkable similarity. Both countries currently show shares of the top 1 percent of wealth holders in the neighborhood of 17 to 18 percent. However, the above discussion of data problems in the two countries indicates that this similarity is superficial.

It is especially difficult to make a valid comparison of wealth distribution in Canada versus Britain because the estate multiplier and survey methods used in the respective countries have different biases. Further, the estate multiplier estimates are for *individuals,* whereas the survey estimates are for *families.*

The difficulties in a Canada versus Britain comparison can be illuminated by looking at the gap between survey and estate multiplier estimates of wealth inequality in the one country that is blessed with both forms of evidence—the United States. There, current estate multiplier estimates of the share of the top 1 percent are similar to those found in Britain. But, both the 1963 Survey of Financial Characteristics and the 1983 Survey of Consumer Finance (SCF) indicate shares of the top 1 percent in the range of 32 to 34 percent. And,

---

8. In (limited) defence of the SCF estimates it should be pointed out that the Ernst and Young study includes several asset categories that are omitted from the SCF—for example, consumer durables and the value of art collections, jewellery, etc.

when a full upper tail is added to the 1983 SCF, the share rises to 37 percent (Avery, Elliehausen, and Kennickell 1988, 356–61). This may be compared to the "guesstimates" made previously on the basis of the Ernst and Young study that with full upper-tail adjustments the Canadian SCF would give a share of the top 1 percent of about 27 to 29%.

The main point that I would like to make on the basis of the U.S. data is that, for reasons that are still not perfectly understood (see Wolff 1989), sample surveys of families give much higher shares for the top 1 percent than do estate multiplier estimates for individuals. Hence, if Britain and Canada both have estimated shares of the top 1 percent in the range 17 to 18 percent with their disparate data sources, it is very likely that if they had the *same* kind of data (both estate multiplier or both survey) the estimated concentration in Canada would be less than in Britain. Since Britain and the United States appear to have a similar degree of wealth concentration (on the basis of estate multiplier evidence) this conclusion is consistent with the approximate 10 percent gap between our guess at a fully adjusted 1984 Canadian SCF share for the top 1 percent, and the comparable share obtained for the 1983 SCF in the United States.

Is the conclusion here that Canada likely has less wealth inequality than Britain or the United States plausible? Many Canadians would regard this conclusion with skepticism. There is a popular belief that the economy is run by a small number of families. Many industries appear to be dominated by a few large firms (i.e., ignoring competition from imports), and when these firms are Canadian owned they are generally controlled by identifiable individuals or families (see Clement 1975; Francis 1986).

It is worth pointing out that in a small country there can be an illusion that wealth and corporate concentration are above levels elsewhere. First, if firms are operating efficiently any industry will tend to have fewer producers in a smaller country. Second, to the extent that there are restrictive practices, trade barriers, etc., as there are in all countries, the large producers in small countries may in fact be smaller than those in large countries, so that they are more readily controlled by particular individuals or families. Third, if there is a high degree of foreign ownership there is a "missing millionaires" effect. The country's business seems to be run by a small group of people partly because many of those who are helping to run it are outside the borders and get left out of enumeration. Since about 35 percent of Canadian business is foreign-owned—the highest figure for any industrialized country—this third point is of some importance here.

The "missing millionaires" may be quite important in accounting for the apparently lower degree of wealth concentration in Canada than in Britain or the United States. Consider the effect of removing 35 percent of British shareholders and putting them in Germany (or removing 35 percent of U.S. shareholders and putting them in Japan). No doubt there would be a sizeable decline in estimated wealth inequality. I would argue that, so to speak, this experiment has already been done in Canada, the only difference being that the missing millionaires are in the United States.[9]

Wealth Composition

Table 4 indicates the relative importance of the different forms of wealth for Canadian households and unincorporated businesses at the end of 1990, as estimated by Statistics Canada's national balance sheets. These estimates are independent of the SCF survey. Note, first, that a bit more than one third (actually 35 percent) of the total value of assets is made up of different forms of real estate, the most important of which is residential housing. There is about an even split between nonfinancial and financial assets. Of the latter, stocks and bonds (excluding Canada Savings Bonds) make up only 11.9 percent of total assets. More widely distributed assets—cash, deposits, Canada Savings Bonds, and life insurance and pensions—make up 35.2 percent of the total.

It is interesting to compare this wealth composition with that found in Britain (see table 2). There are some surprising differences. For example, the value of residential structures owned by households is only 23 percent of total wealth in Canada, but in Britain it is 41 percent. This is especially surprising since 30 to 40 percent of British households live in public housing, whereas a very small proportion of Canadians do so. Canadians appear to hold a much larger fraction of their wealth in cash and deposits (19 percent versus 12 percent in Britain); and also have more in the form of consumer durables and corporate stock.[10] Debt is also more important for Canadians (19 percent versus 13 percent). These differences depend somewhat on which years are used for comparison. However, similar differences for dwellings, cash and deposits, corporate stock, and debt are also evident in a comparison of the

---

9. The figures on the incidence of stock ownership in Canada and the United States are remarkably consistent with this simple story. According to the 1984 Canadian SCF 13.4 percent of families held stock (Statistics Canada 1986, table 25, 67). In the 1983 SCF in the United States the comparable figure was 20.4 percent (Kennickell and Shack-Marquez 1992, table 4, 4).

10. In view of the previous discussion about Canada's missing millionaires, it is surprising to find that corporate stock seems more important in the Canadian household balance sheet. A decade ago an obvious possible explanation would have been the greater degree of public ownership of industry in Britain. This factor may still be important. Despite recent privatizations, a greater fraction of British industry remains in the public sector, and the value of the recently privatized companies may still be depressed by the heritage of low profitability in the state sector that they have yet to overcome.

TABLE 4. Year-End National Balance Sheets—Persons and Unincorporated Business, Canada, 1990

	In Million Dollars	Percent of Assets
I. Nonfinancial Assets		
Residential Structures	$512,958	23.1
Nonresidential Structures	34,030	1.5
Land	240,430	10.8
Consumer Durables	241,678	10.9
Machinery, Equipment, and Inventories	29,170	1.3
Total	1,058,266	47.6
II. Financial Assets		
Cash and Deposits	422,803	19.0
Canada Savings Bonds	35,425	1.6
Other Canadian Bonds	23,041	1.0
Life Insurance and Pensions	324,491	14.6
Stock	241,907	10.9
Miscellaneous	116,941	5.3
Total	1,164,608	52.4
Total assets	2,222,874	100.0
III. Debt		
Mortgages	268,954	12.1
Other Debt	149,671	6.7
Total	418,625	18.9
Net worth	1,804,249	81.2

Source: Calculated from Statistics Canada 1991, table 02-27.

1975 British balance sheet (Shorrocks 1987, table 2.3, 42) with the 1976 Canadian national balance sheet figures.[11] It would be interesting to investigate the extent to which these differences are due to differences in methods of estimation, but that is beyond the scope of this study.

Age and Wealth

Unlike cross-section evidence on wealth holding in some other countries (e.g., the United States) the Canadian data have provided some comfort to the supporters of the life-cycle model. In the United States the cross-section decline in mean wealth past age 65 has tended to be rather small (or negative). The 1963 SCF, for example, found that the mean wealth of families with

11. The four categories listed, as a fraction of total assets were 38.8 percent, 17.7 percent, 8.4 percent, and 11.5 percent for Britain in 1975. The corresponding figures for Canada were 23.3 percent, 17.9 percent, 10.6 percent, and 18.6 percent.

heads aged 65 and above was only 5.2 percent less than that of 54–65 year olds (Projector and Weiss 1966, 110); Greenwood (1987, 128) found that her 65+ group was 5.8 percent *wealthier* than her 55–65 year olds; and in the 1983 Survey of Financial Characteristics of Consumers the 65+ group had a mean wealth 11.4 percent below that of the 55–64 year olds (Avery et al. 1984, 863). In contrast, the 1970, 1977, and 1984 Canadian SCFs show declines in mean wealth from age 55–65 to 65+ of 13.9 percent, 33.0 percent, and 31.7 percent. Thus, at least specifically, the life-cycle model seems to work better in Canada than in the United States. (Are the "missing millionaires" at work again to reduce the amount of saving for bequest in Canada?)

Fortunately, evidence on the age-wealth relationship in Canada is not confined to the cross-section profile. King and Dicks-Mireaux (1982) constructed estimates of the permanent income of 1977 SCF families, and found that the ratio of wealth to permanent income displayed a strongly humped age profile. Burbidge and Robb (1985) found that the hump-shaped profile for the representative family masks interesting detail. They found that although the hump was displayed by "blue collar" families, "white collar" families did not dissave in retirement.[12]

Inheritance in Britain

A person's wealth at a moment in time is the result of past accumulation. This accumulation comes from two main sources: labor income ("earnings"), or gifts and inheritances. Both provide resources that can either be saved or consumed. Resources that are saved can accumulate at different rates. Wise or lucky investors earn high rates of return, while others may "lose their shirts." Finally, given the lifetime path of earnings, savings, etc., at least up to retirement the older the consumer the greater tends to be his or her wealth. Thus, current wealth depends on

1. Past earnings
2. Inheritances (including gifts)
3. Saving rates out of earnings and inheritances
4. Rates of return
5. Age

---

12. Rather than looking at the ratio of wealth to permanent income, Burbidge and Robb regressed wealth on a wide range of characteristics, including, e.g., occupation, education, labor force status, and region. In order to summarize the results they isolated certain family types. The "blue collar" type had a husband in the lowest of three occupational categories, husband and wife with 10 years or less of schooling, and a wife who had not worked in the last five years. In the "white collar" family both spouses had 11 to 13 years of schooling and were in the middle of three occupational categories.

Our interest here centers on just one of these factors—inheritance. Our main task is to assess to what degree wealth concentration depends on this factor rather than the others. In addition, we are interested in knowing what factors affect the level and concentration of inherited wealth.

Impact of Inheritance on Wealth Distribution

It is sometimes suggested that concerns about wealth inequality are misplaced since the last, and most innocuous, of these factors—age—can explain much of the observed inequality. To see whether this is the case, simple examples of societies, which, although egalitarian, would display considerable wealth concentration, can be devised. Atkinson (1971), for example, considered a society in which everyone works for 40 years, retires for 10 years, and then dies with certainty. In a central case, population and earnings both grow at a constant rate of 2 percent per year, desired consumption grows at 3 percent, and the real interest rate is 4.5 percent. With these assumptions the shares of top 1 percent, 5 percent, and 10 percent would be 2.1 percent, 10.1 percent, and 19.6 percent respectively. In contrast, he noted, estimated actual shares in Britain at the time, taking into account state pensions, were 22 percent, 41 percent, and 52 percent. Uniform inheritances received by all at age fifty and passed on unchanged at death, and an allowance for "propertyless women" raised the top shares to 3.4 percent, 17 percent, and 33 percent respectively, still far short of estimated actual shares.

After Atkinson (1971) pointed out that age differences alone explained little of observed wealth inequality, a flurry of papers were written in Britain developing more elaborate examples of pure life-cycle societies where influences other than inheritance were modeled. Oulton (1976) presented examples similar to Atkinson's except that differences in earnings and rates of return were also incorporated. He derived analytic expressions for the coefficient of variation (CV) and variance of logarithms, and claimed that age and earnings differences together would produce a CV equal to only about 10 percent of actual figures. Davies and Shorrocks (1978) criticized Oulton for comparing his predicted CVs with an inappropriate estimate of actual wealth inequality, and for confining attention mainly to a single inequality measure. They presented alternative results indicating that age and earnings differences could account for 60 percent, 82 percent, or 45 to 89 percent of apparent actual wealth inequality according to the Gini coefficient, variance of logarithms, and Atkinson's index (with a range of values for its single parameter, ϵ). The top 1 percent, 5 percent, and 10 percent of wealth holders would have shares of 5.6 percent, 16.7 percent, and 27.2 percent respectively. The latter could be raised to about 9 percent, 28 percent, and 45 percent respectively by allowing uniform inheritance and propertyless women as in Atkinson 1971.

Flemming (1976) also introduced unequal earnings into Atkinson's simple model, but in contrast to Oulton, argued that the results could account for the shape of the wealth distribution except for the top one or two centiles. In fact, Flemming's top shares—5.5 percent and 16.5 percent for the top 1 percent and 5 percent—are very similar to those obtained by Davies and Shorrocks (1978) using the Oulton model. Thus the considerable difference in "results" between Oulton 1976 and Flemming 1976 is due to divergent interpretations of very similar models.

While the work by Oulton (1976), Flemming (1976), and Davies and Shorrocks (1978) is interesting, what it tells us about the role of inheritance in determining wealth distribution is limited. Even if the behavior modeled were realistic the results would only set an upper bound on the influence of inheritance. Davies and Shorrocks (1978) therefore argued that the importance of inheritance would not become clear until a *complete* model was constructed that incorporated in a realistic way all five of the influences on wealth distribution listed previously. This task was undertaken in Davies 1979a, 1982, using Canadian data. A somewhat similar exercise was carried out in Wolfson 1977, 1979, also using Canadian data. The Davies and Wolfson results are discussed in the subsequent section on Canadian evidence on inheritance.

There is another, unique, strand of evidence on the impact of inheritance on wealth holding in Britain. Wedgwood (1928, 1929) pioneered a method of studying the importance of inherited wealth in explaining the wealth held at death; this method was reapplied to data from the 1950s, 1960s, and 1970s by Harbury and Hitchens (1979).

Wedgwood (1929) investigated the sources of wealth held by 99 persons dying with at least £200,000 in a twelve-month period during 1924–25. About 60 percent had a predecessor (usually a parent) who had died leaving at least £50,000, and about 70 percent had predecessors who left at least £10,000 (Wedgwood 1929, 138–39). Wedgwood concluded that

> of the *men* in the upper and middle classes at the present day, about one third owe their fortunes almost entirely to inheritance (including gifts *inter vivos*), another third to a combination of ability and luck with a considerable inheritance of wealth and business opportunity, and the remaining third largely to their own activities. (Wedgwood 1929, 163)

In other words, one-third could clearly be classed as "inheritors," and one-third as "self-made." The remaining one-third were in an intermediate category.

After performing various adjustments to Wedgwood's numbers to achieve comparability with his study for 1956–57, Harbury (1962) found that there was no evidence that the importance of inheritance had declined from the decedents of the 1920s to those of the 1950s. However, the studies reported by Harbury and Hitchens (1979) for 1956–57, 1965, and 1973, some of whose results are presented here in table 5, indicated that there were changes subsequently.

After considering carefully a variety of different methods of establishing whether a son was an "inheritor" or "self made," Harbury and Hitchens concluded that if a father had left more than £25,000 on death (no matter how divided among heirs), on average it would be appropriate to classify the son as an inheritor rather than self-made. By this rule, both the 1956–57 and 1965 data indicated 68 percent of the decedents were inheritors, but by 1973 the fraction had fallen to 58 percent.

The establishment of rules for determining what fraction of people are "self made" or "inheritors" in the Harbury and Hitchens study is somewhat subjective. A systematic investigation of how much a decedent had actually inherited was not carried out. All that we know, for most decedents, is how much their fathers left when they died. In nonsystematic subsamples the division of the father's estate, and wealth left by other relatives, is known, but this information is not very useful. For those men who appeared to be self-made on the basis of the amount left by their fathers, there was a systematic search for the amounts that had been left on death by the fathers-in-law. This search boosted the number of men who could be considered inheritors by an average of about 14 percentage points across the three samples (Harbury and Hitchens 1979, table 4.1, 73).

If a son dies leaving £100,000, and his father died leaving £50,000, was the son an inheritor? If the son was the eldest, and the family was practicing primogeniture then clearly he was. But the son may have been the fourth offspring in a family with eight children. How much did he inherit in that case? Would it have been enough to classify him as an inheritor? None of these questions are addressed in the Harbury and Hitchens technique. What it tells us is whether sons who died wealthy came from similarly wealthy families, or had more humble origins. Exactly how family wealth affected one's eventual fortune is not traced.

An interesting feature of the Harbury and Hitchens 1979 results is the statistically significant postwar period decline in the cumulative proportion of wealthy male decedents with fathers at a given wealth level (see table 5). But the decline in the scale of inheritance for top wealth holders must actually have been greater than suggested by the relatively small changes in table 5. This is because top inheritances were accounting for a smaller share of a *declining* slice of the wealth pie. Between 1923 and 1989 the share of the top 1 percent in Britain fell from 61 to 18 percent (see table 1). If half the wealth of the top 1 percent had been due to inheritance, and there had been no change in the distribution of inherited relative to other wealth over this period, then the share of the top 1 percent in 1989 would have been 30 percent *even if self-*

made wealth had completely evaporated for the top 1 percent. Thus the powerful trend in the wealth distribution time series implies a drop in the importance of inherited wealth in the upper tail much stronger than that indicated by the Harbury and Hitchens results alone.

Harbury and Hitchens (1979) conclude with a chapter that throws some doubt on the declining importance of inheritance. They regress son's estate on father's for five samples and find that the fraction of variance in son's estate explained by variance in father's *increased* from 28 percent for sons dying in 1934 to 67 percent for those dying in 1973. This led Harbury and Hitchens to qualify their results considerably. This is only necessary insofar as the question is how important inheritance is in explaining the assets of the wealthy. There I agree with Harbury and Hitchens that they obtained a mixed result. On the larger question of whether inheritance became a less important influence on the overall shape of the wealth distribution in Britain in the twentieth century, however, there is much less doubt, as previously argued.

Explaining the Distribution of Inherited Wealth

Why is the distribution of inherited wealth so concentrated? Part of the answer lies in the great importance of *human* wealth. The majority of families find that investing in their children's human capital, via upbringing and education, is more effective than providing gifts and bequests. Why are all families not in

TABLE 5.   Estates of Sons' Fathers Dying with ≥ £ 100,000, constant 1973 prices

Father's Estate Over (£)	Sample Years (Cumulative Percentages)		
	1956–57	1965	1973
1,000,000	9	4	7
500,000	19	12	13
250,000	33*	24	21
100,000	51*	45	36
50,000	63*	55	47
25,000	68*	68	58
10,000	75	77	71
5,000	78	80	74
1,000	85	83	79
All	100	100	100
Sample Size	532	94	108

Source: Harbury and Hitchens 1979, table 3.3.
*Significantly different from the 1973 sample at the 5 percent level.

this position? First, some provide for their heirs by passing along family businesses (including farms). Second, some who are sufficiently wealthy (or whose children are sufficiently untalented) exhaust the attractive opportunities for investing in their children's education and upbringing before their benevolence has been used up. Third, the lure of bequests may be used to elicit attention from children in a form of intergenerational exchange. The genuinely wealthy would almost all be in one of these three categories, and we therefore expect to see them making much use of bequest.

The extent of concentration in inheritance depends on the degree of inequality of wealth among the living, practices of estate division, fertility, and choice of marital partner (see Atkinson 1983, 183–89). Interestingly, an initially egalitarian society in which freedom of opportunity allows some people to amass large self-made fortunes will tend to show very unequal inheritance as the self-made men and women pass their fortunes on to their offspring. This scenario seems to fit the United States very well, where the Rockefellers, DuPonts, Morgans, etc. were once self-made, but are now inheritors. In equilibrium it is quite possible to have both substantial, new, self-made fortunes in every generation and considerable inequality of inheritance.

Turning to estate division, at one extreme, in some societies primogeniture is practiced. Under this arrangement, which is still practiced by some wealthy families in Britain, the bulk of the estate passes to the eldest son (or daughter in the absence of a son). This keeps large estates intact, and preserves wealth inequality over time. At the opposite extreme, many families, particularly in "New World" countries like Australia, Canada, and the United States, practice equal division of estates. Especially where families are reasonably large (which was true in Britain and Canada in the nineteenth and early twentieth centuries) this may cause the rapid break down of wealth concentration if there is imperfectly assortative mating.

How are estates generally divided in Britain today, and how has this changed over time? On the basis of his investigations Wedgwood (1928, 48) concluded:

> There is little doubt that, among the very wealthy, equal division of the spoils among the family, irrespective of place and sex, is not the general rule. It appeared to be usual, among wealthier predecessors in my sample for the sons to receive a larger share than the daughters. In the case of the smaller estates, equal division is much more common.

It is unclear whether practices of estate division have become more egalitarian among the wealthy in Britain since Wedgwood's study. In a sample of 281 estates worth £10,000 or more left in 1944–45 Fijalkowski-Bereday (1950) found that there were only 20 cases in which bequests to surviving children were unequal. He wrote that "equal division takes place nearly always if there is more than one child, and . . . unequal division occurs mostly in the largest estates when there is enough to provide adequately for all the dependents without giving them an equal share" (Fijalkowski-Bereday 1950, 183–84). Unfortunately it is difficult to tell precisely how common unequal division was in Fijalkowski-Bereday's top estate class (£400,000+). He records that for 35 of these estates there was "surviving issue," and in 10 cases with more than one child there was unequal division, but we do not know in how many cases there was more than one child. It is thus not clear, on the basis of Fijalkowski-Bereday's evidence, whether Wedgwood's conclusion that equal division was not the general rule for the very wealthy would have needed any modification to bring it up to date in 1944–45.

More recent evidence is provided by the Royal Commission on the Distribution of Income and Wealth (1977), which examined the wills of a sample of decedents leaving at least £15,000. In the 77 cases where there was more than one surviving child equal division was found in 38 cases (Royal Commission 1977, 178). It might seem that this is a high rate of equal division. However, in the largest estate class (£500,000+) unequal division was found in 12 of 17 cases. Also, note that for the full sample, with the £15,000 cutoff, unequal division is much more frequent than in Fijalkowski-Bereday's full sample with its £10,000 cutoff in 1944–45 (higher in real terms than £15,000 in 1977). Thus, on the face of it, the Royal Commission's evidence seems to suggest an increase in unequal division compared with 1944–45.

It is also interesting to note from the Royal Commission (1977) that children were far from being the sole recipients, even when there was no surviving spouse. Only 57 percent of the wealth left by widowed parents passed to children (or "their issue"). Fully 26 percent went to other relatives and 11 percent was left to unrelated individuals. Only 4 percent was left to charity, confirming earlier evidence that the average amount left to charity by wealthy decedents is low—both absolutely and in comparison to the amounts left in the United States (see Atkinson 1972, 64).

That 43 percent of estates left by widowed parents went to persons other than children or grandchildren might seem to indicate a fairly wide diffusion that could lead to progressive break down in the concentration of inherited wealth. This also seems consistent with the observed decline in such concentration in Britain in the twentieth century. However, Atkinson (1972) points out that the relatives and unrelated individuals who share in bequests by the wealthy are often themselves very wealthy.[13] Thus, the net degree of equalization in inherited wealth from this source may be small.

---

13. Atkinson (1972, 64) states, "This was illustrated by the will of Alfred de Rothschild, who in 1918 left his estate to (among other people) Lord and Lady Carnarvon, Lord Porchester, Lady Curzon, Lord Esher and the Marquis de Soveral. A newspaper report at the time commented that 'it is seldom that a rich man distributes his money so widely or so generously.'"

Differences in fertility according to wealth can also, in principle, have a sizeable effect if estates are divided fairly equally among offspring. If the wealthy had smaller families than others, their wealth would be broken up relatively slowly by division among heirs, and wealth concentration would tend to be preserved.[14] While this factor may formerly have been important, in both Britain and Canada today fertility is uniformly very low across income and wealth groups, so that it likely has very little effect.

Finally, the extent of assortative mating is important. If wealthy sons marry wealthy daughters, inherited wealth can remain confined to a small minority of families—even if wealth is equally divided among offspring. While there is positive sorting of mates according to wealth and income in Britain, Canada, and similar countries, the correlation in mates' backgrounds is far from perfect. This fact is sometimes obscured by the way in which evidence on this score is presented. A popular tool is the transition matrix. Atkinson (1972, 66), for example, presents data from a 1949 study of social mobility in Britain shown here in table 6. The clustering of entries on the diagonal gives the impression of a fairly high degree of positive sorting according to social class.[15] However, appearances can be deceiving. Spearman's rank correlation coefficient for husbands and wives in this table is just 0.400. This indicates that only about 16 percent of the variance in a wife's rank is explained by a husband's (or vice versa). This does not represent a high degree of immobility. Thus, there may be a strong tendency for inequality in inherited wealth to be broken down through wealthy children marrying nonwealthy spouses in Britain, as well as through division of estates.

Inheritance in Canada

There is much less direct evidence on inheritance for Canada than for Britain. In part this reflects the fact that Canada, like other New World countries, was regarded historically as quite an egalitarian society. There are no landed

---

14. It has even been claimed that an important way in which families *become* wealthy is through being relatively infertile. This effect could operate not only through wealth being less split up on death, but also through lower child rearing and education costs allowing greater accumulation.

15. Atkinson (1972, 67) presented additional very interesting data on the tendency of sons and daughters of dukes to marry within the aristocracy over the period 1330–1934. Of 513 sons, 255 (or 50 percent) married within the peerage. Of 592 daughters 349 (59 percent) did likewise. There has been a decline in the tendency to marry within the aristocracy, but over the period 1830–1934 40 percent of the sons and 47 percent of the daughters still did so. Atkinson (1972) suggests that when the tendency to marry foreign aristocrats (at least up until 1914) and U.S. heiresses is taken into account, there is good reason to believe that the selectivity in marriage by this group had not really declined much.

aristocratic families. The rapid economic development during the last fifty years, combined with high levels of immigration, has appeared to favor the rise of self-made individuals and industrious immigrant families (e.g., the Batas and the Reichmanns). There has been much less popular concern about the perpetuation of wealth inequality via inheritance than in Britain. This relative lack of concern seems to be reflected in the fact that the federal estate and gift taxes, and all provincial succession duties, have now been abolished.

While there has been less concern about concentration of inherited wealth in Canada than in Britain, this does not mean that there has been *no* concern. In the early days of British Canada there was in fact a great deal of concern about such inequality. In the early nineteenth century both Upper and Lower Canada (Ontario and Quebec today) were controlled by tight-knit establishment cliques. The iniquites of the "family compact" and the "chateau clique" have been rehearsed by generations of Canadian school children. Their power was broken by the disestablishment of the church and the advent of more democratic government. Nevertheless, a close-knit community of powerful families of British origin continued to dominate the nation's business, and some of their descendants remain powerful in this regard to the present day.

Concern about the concentration of corporate and political power in Canada, and the possible lack of social and economic mobility, increased with the publication of sociologist John Porter's immensely influential book, *The Vertical Mosaic,* in 1965. This volume described the membership and behavior of the Canadian "elite" in considerable detail, and argued that Canada was a much less egalitarian country than generally supposed. This theme has been echoed ever since in the Canadian sociological literature.

TABLE 6. Degree of Assortative Mating in Britain in 1949

Husbands' Social Group	Percentage Marrying Wives From Social Group			
	I	II	III	IV
I. Professional and managerial	37	36	21	6
II. Supervisory and other nonmanual	6	34	41	18
III. Skilled manual	3	20	54	24
IV. Unskilled and semiskilled	1	15	43	41
All groups	6	24	46	25

Source: Atkinson 1972, table 13.

Impact on the Distribution of Wealth

No studies of the type performed by Wedgwood and Harbury and Hitchens have been performed for Canada. However, Porter (1965) did investigate the family background of 611 Canadian-born members of the "economic elite"— a group of 760 Canadian residents "holding directorships in the 170 dominant corporations, the banks, insurance companies, and numerous other corporations not classified as dominant" (274). His results are shown here in the first column of table 7. They indicate that 50 percent of the elite came from "upper class" families, which included those where a parent was a member of one of the elites (economic, political, etc.) as well as those where the father was educated at a private school—a much more exclusive credential than it would be in most other countries.

A further feature of Porter's work that is especially interesting in the context of this essay is that he investigated the ethnicity (and religious affiliations) of his economic elite. This is of special interest since Canada is now ethnically diverse, and members of different ethnic groups have arrived at different points in time. At the turn of the century almost all Canadians were either of British or French origin, and wealthy Canadians were almost exclusively of British origin. A large proportion of twentieth century immigrants came from other European countries, and (with a few notable exceptions) arrived with little wealth. If inheritance is the most important way of getting into the top 1 percent or 5 percent of the wealth distribution, or if wealth mobility is very low, we would then expect that Canadians of British origin, and particularly those showing signs of middle and upper class British origins (e.g., in their religious affiliation) should be heavily overrepresented in the Canadian economic elite. This is, in fact, exactly what Porter found.

Porter (1965) found that almost all members of the Canadian economic elite were of British origin. The only significant exceptions were French

TABLE 7.   Class Origins of the Canadian Born Members of the "Economic Elite" in Percentages, Canada, 1951 and 1972

Origin	1951	1972
Upper Class	50	59.4
Middle Class	32	34.8
Working Class	18	5.8
Total	100	100
Sample Size	611	673

Source: The 1951 estimates are a condensed version of Porter 1965, table 28. The 1972 estimates are by Clement 1986, table 21.

Canadians (7 percent) or of United States origin (10 percent). Despite their numerical importance in professional occupations and commerce there were only six Jews in his group. Members of the Anglican and Presbyterian churches were overrepresented (making up 37 percent of the elite).

Porter's study of the class origins of the economic elite was repeated by his student, W. Clement (1986), using 1972 data. A startling result of this study was the finding that class origins had become *more* exclusive by 1972 than they had been in 1951. As shown in table 7, for 1972 Clement found that 59 percent of the elite had upper class origins, compared with Porter's 50 percent for 1951. (There was little change in ethnic origins, except that a few more Jews had penetrated the ranks of the elite.) The explanation for this upward trend is not apparent, but it certainly suggests that the impression many Canadians have that wealth mobility has increased in the period of rapid growth since World War II may be mistaken.

I referred to the flurry of studies in Britain in the 1970s that attempted to put an upper bound on the impact of inheritance on wealth distribution by constructing hypothetical life-cycle economies in which wealth differences would be due purely to age or earnings. Davies and Shorrocks (1978) called for the construction of complete models in order to get a better "fix" on the impact of inheritance. In Davies 1979a, I developed such a model using Canadian data—primarily the 1970 SCF wealth survey and the 1971 SCF income survey (the first such survey to be made available on a public use tape). Household utility was assumed to depend not only on parental consumption and family size over the lifetime, but also on the contemplated lifetime incomes of offspring. This results in a model with Beckerian "compensatory bequests." Inheritances were derived for an initial generation by applying mortality rates, estate division assumptions, etc., to an adjusted version of the 1970 SCF wealth distribution. Saving behavior was then simulated forward and parameters were selected, in part, to ensure that the simulated distribution of wealth among the living was similar to the observed Canadian distribution.

Results of the experiments performed with the microsimulation model as reported in Davies (1982) are presented here in table 8. These allow an attempt to *decompose* wealth inequality. That is, it is possible to see how wealth inequality would be reduced if we eliminated differences in earnings, inheritances, saving rates, rates of return, and age. The results indicate that the most important factor was inheritance, followed by differences in saving rates. Differences in earnings, rates of return, and age were of lesser importance (and similar to each other in impact).

Looking at table 8 in more detail, we see that it decomposes wealth inequality in two steps. First, the influence of inheritance is studied. Columns 3 and 4 of the table show what happens when (i) inheritances are equalized for

TABLE 8. Simulated Distributions of Wealth, 1970

	Estimated actual distribution[a]	Complete model			Model without inheritances or bequest				
		Base run	Equalizing		Base Run	Equalizing			
			Is	Is and bs		ρs	rs	Es	Ages
Share of									
top 1%	19.6%	20.6	19.6	18.8	9.4	5.8	8.2	7.1	8.4
top 5%	43.4%	47.8	46.0	43.9	30.3	19.6	27.4	26.2	27.8
top 10%	58.0%	61.7	59.0	56.6	46.4	32.4	43.3	42.5	43.5
top quintile	74.0%	76.9	73.7	71.8	66.6	52.4	63.9	63.7	64.2
2d quintile	17.8%	14.7	16.0	17.2	21.6	26.9	22.7	23.0	22.6
3d quintile	8.0%	6.5	8.0	8.7	9.2	14.6	10.2	10.5	10.2
4th quintile	1.7%	1.9	2.2	2.4	2.5	5.6	3.1	2.7	2.9
5th quintile	−1.5%	0.1	0.0	0.0	0.0	0.5	0.1	0.0	0.1
Atkinson's index, ϵ =									
0.5	n.a.	0.489	0.464	0.448	0.391	0.270	0.363	0.367	0.368
1.0	n.a.	0.782	0.769	0.759	0.732	0.593	0.706	0.718	0.712
2.0	n.a.	0.957	0.959	0.958	0.956	0.937	0.953	0.956	0.955
3.0	n.a.	0.977	0.978	0.978	0.978	0.973	0.977	0.978	0.977
Coefficient of variation	2.519	2.751	2.491	2.428	1.521	1.051	1.386	1.333	1.406
Gini coefficient	0.746	0.747	0.723	0.708	0.658	0.531	0.632	0.632	0.635
Mean	$27,600	29,017	27,371	25,186	16,793	10,360	15,892	13,339	16,793
Median	$11,000	9,191	10,939	10,735	7,592	7,508	8,010	6,918	8,456

Source: Davies 1982, table 1.

Note: I = inheritance, b = bequest, ρ = time preference, r = interest rate, E = labor earnings.

[a] Davies 1979b, 225, and more detailed unpublished figures.

parents, but they are free to pass on whatever bequests they desire (column 3), and (ii) both inheritances received and bequests made to the next generation are equalized (column 4). The effects on the simulated distribution of wealth are surprisingly small: the share of the top 1 percent falls from 20.6 percent in the base run to 19.6 percent in column 3 and 18.8 percent in column 4, for example.

In Davies 1982, I argued that a better way to assess the impact of inheritances and bequests on wealth inequality would be to eliminate them completely from the model. The result is a very sizeable decline in wealth inequality (column 5). The share of the top 1 percent, for example, falls to 9.4 percent, and the Gini coefficient declines to 0.658 from 0.747 in the base run.

A further interesting aspect of the Davies 1982 results is that earnings differences turn out to be less important than was perhaps supposed in the British literature of the mid-1970s. While equalizing earnings has a larger impact on the share of the top 1 percent than equalizing rates of return or age (also relatively weak influences), taking the distribution as a whole the impact is quite similar.

Differences in saving rates are generated in this model by allowing variation in the rate of time preference, ρ.[16] This turned out to have a surprisingly important impact on the wealth distribution. The proportional reduction in inequality indicators generated by making ρ uniform in the pure life-cycle model is of about the same order of magnitude as that produced by eliminating inheritances from the complete model.

Table 9 provides more detail on the various distributions. It shows that the distribution of inherited wealth used in the simulations is considerably more concentrated than the estimated actual wealth distribution for 1970. The top 1 percent of inheritors received 24.6 percent of total inheritances, whereas the top 1 percent of wealth holders in the population cross-section had just 19.6 percent of total wealth. But the table also makes the point that even with their high concentration, because inheritances are a small part of aggregate lifetime wealth (6 percent), their addition to lifetime earnings only increases inequality in lifetime wealth slightly according to any of the measures. This should temper some of the concern about unequal inheritance as a cause of economic inequality, although it must be emphasized that the table does not

---

16. The average value of ρ was set at 0. A normal distribution was assumed, and was parameterized so that if the after-tax rate of return was 0.04, 20 percent of the families would have negative desired growth rates of consumption. Time preference rates were assigned to families to give a mild negative correlation (-0.3) with lifetime wealth (see Davies 1982, 484). (Dispersion in the taste parameter governing the strength of the bequest motive, and in rates of return, were also allowed. Correlations with lifetime wealth equal to $+0.3$ were used in both cases.)

penetrate to the *extreme* upper tail, where the influence of inheritance is likely quite disproportionate.

A further spinoff from Davies 1982 is that it makes possible a calculation of the share of inherited wealth in aggregate wealth. I did not report this figure in Davies 1982 because I did not anticipate the importance that would be placed on such calculations in the wake of Kotlikoff and Summers 1981. However, the oversight was corrected in Davies and St. Hilaire 1987, 108, where I reported that the Kotlikoff and Summers inheritance share of current wealth was 53 percent in my model. If accumulated interest on inherited wealth is ascribed instead to life-cycle saving (in my view a dubious approach) the share drops to 35 percent.

At about the same time that I was developing my simulation model, Michael Wolfson (1977) built another model that he used to address similar questions. Wolfson worked with both incomplete and complete models. The incomplete model, however, included all factors other than inheritance so that it does a better job of estimating the impact of inheritance residually than did the Oulton 1976 or Flemming 1976 studies in Britain. Wolfson's modeling differs from mine in not attempting to endogenize behavior. It represents a kind of wealth accounting exercise.

Wolfson (1977) first uses the income and wealth data from the 1970 SCF to set up a simulation that applies the observed pattern of saving to the life

TABLE 9. Determinants of the Distribution of Lifetime Wealth

Share of	Lifetime Earnings	Inheritances	Lifetime Wealth
Top 1%	4.8%	24.6	5.1
Top 5%	14.6%	46.3	15.2
Top 10%	24.0%	60.0	24.7
Top quintile	39.3%	74.1	40.2
2d quintile	23.9%	15.8	23.8
3d quintile	18.2%	7.8	17.7
4th quintile	13.0%	2.3	12.7
Bottom quintile	5.6%	0.0	5.6
Atkinson's Index, $\epsilon =$			
0.5	0.105	0.474	0.106
1.0	0.230	0.766	0.225
2.0	0.644	0.957	0.568
3.0	0.899	0.978	0.853
Coefficient of variation	0.687	3.400	0.714
Gini coefficient	0.338	0.727	0.345
Mean	$272,000	$17,200	$289,200
Median	$248,800	$6,600	$256,100

Source: Davies 1982, table 3.

cycle of a cohort in order to see how much wealth inequality could be produced without inheritance. Steady growth and stationary wealth distribution both overall and within age groups are assumed. In addition to differences in age, earnings, and saving propensities, the model also introduces alternative assumptions concerning dispersion in rates of return, and a detailed demographic submodel that guides family formation, divorce, remarriage, and mortality over the life cycle of the cohort. The conclusion is that the factors listed can explain much of observed wealth inequality, but not the observed concentration in the extreme upper tail. In Wolfson's base run, for example, a Gini coefficient exceeding apparent actual is obtained, but the share of the top 1 percent is only 11.3 percent, versus an "actual" figure of 20.3 percent from the SCF.

In a second approach, like Davies 1979a, 1982, Wolfson simulated the process of bequest. Starting his simulation in 1970 he modeled the mortality of all cohorts and divided the wealth of decedents among heirs up until the year 2000, finding that under various assumptions a predicted distribution of wealth in the year 2000 very similar to that observed in 1970 was obtained. If inheritances were instead outlawed, by the year 2000 the shares of top 1 percent and 5 percent would have fallen from 20.3 percent and 41.2 percent to 13.6 percent and 36.0 percent respectively. Thus Wolfson's work shows a strong disequalizing impact of inheritance on the upper tail of the Canadian distribution of wealth. The similarity of this conclusion to those of Flemming 1976 and Davies and Shorrocks 1978 in Britain, and Davies 1979a, 1982 in Canada is striking.

Conclusion

This essay has reviewed what is known about inheritance and the distribution of wealth in Britain and Canada. We have seen that there was a trend toward considerably reduced wealth inequality in Britain over the period 1923–80, but that there has been no trend since 1980. In Canada the data are weak, but there is no evidence of trend. There appears to have been a considerable convergence between British and Canadian wealth concentration, but if comparable data were available for the two countries I have argued they would likely show that there is still greater wealth inequality in Britain.

I have suggested that an important influence on the distribution of wealth in Canada is the "missing millionaires" effect, generated by the 35 percent foreign ownership of Canadian business. This high level of foreign ownership, together with Canada's relatively small size, makes for a fairly small group of individuals and families with substantial corporate ownership and power. This, in turn, has led some Canadians to believe that wealth is more concentrated in Canada than in other countries. However, whatever the effect of the size of the Canadian corporate elite on concentration of economic and political *power* in Canada, the absence of a substantial number of wealthy persons who would be present if Canadian business was 100 percent Canadian-owned tends to reduce measured concentration in household wealth holding.

The composition of wealth in Britain and Canada shows points of similarity, but also some interesting differences. Despite the fact that 30 to 40 percent of Britons live in public housing, dwellings form a considerably larger fraction of assets than in Canada. Canadians appear to hold more in the form of liquid assets and corporate stock (despite the high level of foreign ownership of Canadian business), and have greater debt. To some extent these differences may reflect divergence in estimation methods between the two countries.

There has been considerable work on the age profile of wealth holding in both countries. The best work for Britain indicates that the "hump saving" of the life-cycle model is displayed by moderate wealth holders, but only in weak form in the upper tail. The best evidence in Canada obtains a slightly stronger contrast: hump saving for "blue collar" families, but no dissaving in retirement for "white collar" families. Thus the evidence from both countries allows room for a strong bequest motive for saving.

We have also seen that studies in both countries indicate that inheritance has an important effect on the upper tail of the distribution of wealth. Since wealth concentration has been declining fairly strongly in Britain over most of the present century, I have argued that it must surely be the case that the force of unequal inheritance in that country has been sapped. This appears to have been due to more equal division of assets between wealthy husbands and wives, the cumulative effect of redistributive estate and income taxes, and the spread of "popular" wealth holding (houses and consumer durables). Changes in fertility and selection of marital partners may also have had an effect. Despite these changes, it appears to remain true that at least half of the genuinely wealthy are "inheritors" rather than "self-made," and there is even evidence of an increasing correlation in the wealth of succeeding generations at death. Also, inequality in the division of estates among offspring does not appear to have fallen among the very wealthy. Thus care must be taken to avoid misleading statements about *how* inheritance has become a less important influence on the wealth distribution in Britain over time.

Unlike Britain, Canada has no evidence of a decline in wealth concentration over time. Also, there is evidence that the class origins of the economic "elite" became more exclusive in the postwar period. Thus, it is conceivable that, broadly speaking, while inheritance has become less important in explaining the British wealth distribution, at the same time it has been growing in importance in Canada. Much better evidence would be needed on the Canadian side, however, to make this a firm conclusion.

REFERENCES

Atkinson, A. B. 1971. "The Distribution of Wealth and the Individual Life Cycle." *Oxford Economic Papers* 23:239–54.

———. 1972. *Unequal Shares*. London: Penguin.

———. 1983. *The Economics of Inequality*. 2d ed. Oxford: Clarendon Press.

Atkinson, A. B., James P. F. Gordon, and Alan Harrison. 1989. "Trends in the Shares of Top Wealth-Holders in Britain, 1923–1981." *Oxford Bulletin of Economics and Statistics* 51:315–32.

Atkinson, A. B., and A. J. Harrison. 1978. *Distribution of Personal Wealth in Britain*. Cambridge: Cambridge University Press.

Avery, Robert B., Gregory E. Elliehausen, Glen B. Canner, and Thomas A. Gustafson. 1984. "Survey of Consumer Finances." *Federal Reserve Bulletin*, 679–92.

Avery, Robert B., Gregory E. Elliehausen, and Arthur B. Kennickell. 1988. "Measuring Wealth with Survey Data: An Evaluation of the 1983 Survey of Consumer Finances." *Review of Income and Wealth* 34 (December): 339–70.

Burbidge, J. B., and A. L. Robb. 1985. "Evidence on Wealth-Age Profiles in Canadian Cross-Section Data." *Canadian Journal of Economics* 18 (November): 854–75.

Clement, Walter. 1986. *The Canadian Corporate Elite*. Carleton Library, no. 89. Toronto: McClelland and Stewart.

Davies, James B. 1979a. "Life-Cycle Saving, Inheritance, and the Personal Distribution of Income and Wealth in Canada." Ph.D. diss., London School of Economics.

———. 1979b. "On the Size Distribution of Wealth in Canada." *Review of Income and Wealth* 25 (September): 237–59.

———. 1982. "The Relative Impact of Inheritance and Other Factors on Economic Inequality." *Quarterly Journal of Economics* 47:471–98.

———. Forthcoming. "The Distribution of Wealth in Canada." In *Research in Economic Inequality*, ed. E. Wolff. Greenwich, CT: JAI Press.

Davies, James B., and A. F. Shorrocks. 1978. "Assessing the Quantitative Importance of Inheritance in the Distribution of Wealth." *Oxford Economic Papers* 30:138–49.

Davies, James B., and France St. Hilaire. 1987. *Reforming Capital Income Taxation in Canada: Efficiency and Distributional Effects of Alternative Options*. Ottawa: Economic Council of Canada.

Dunn, A. T., and P. D. R. B. Hoffman. 1983. "Distribution of Wealth in the United Kingdom: Effect of Including Pension Rights and Analysis by Age Group." *Review of Income and Wealth* 29:243–82.

Fijalkowski-Bereday, G. Z. 1950. "The Equalizing Effects of the Death Duties." *Oxford Economic Papers* 2 (June): 176–96.

Flemming, J. S. 1976. "On the Assessment of the Inequality of Wealth." In *Selected Evidence Submitted to the Royal Commission: Report No. 1, Initial Report on the Standing Reference*, Royal Commission on the Distribution of Income and Wealth, paras. 34–70. London: HMSO.

Francis, Diane. 1986. *Controlling Interest: Who Owns Canada?* Toronto: Macmillan.

Good, F. J. 1990. "Estimates of the Distribution of Personal Wealth." In *Economic Trends,* Central Statistical Office, 133–57. London: HMSO.

Greenwood, Daphne T. 1987. "Age Income and Household Size: Their Relation to Wealth Distribution in the United Sates." *See* Wolff 1987a.

Harbury, C. D. 1962. "Inheritance and the Distribution of Personal Wealth in Britain." *Economic Journal* 72:845–68.

Harbury, C. D., and D. M. W. N. Hitchens. 1979. *Inheritance and Wealth Inequality in Britain.* London: George Allen and Unwin.

———. 1987. "The Influence of Relative Prices on the Distribution of Wealth and the Measurement of Inheritance." *See* Wolff 1987a.

Harrison, A. J. 1976. "Trends Over Time in the Distribution of Wealth." In *Economics and Equality,* ed. A. Jones. Oxford: Oxford University Press.

———. 1979. *The Distribution of Wealth in Ten Countries.* Royal Commission on the Distribution of Income and Wealth, Background Paper, no. 7. Her Majesty's Stationery Office.

Inland Revenue. 1991. *Inland Revenue Statistics.* London: Her Majesty's Stationery Office.

Kennickell, Arthur, and Janice Shack-Marquez. 1992. "Changes in Family Finances from 1983 to 1989: Evidence from the Survey of Consumer Finances." *Federal Reserve Bulletin* 78:1–18. U.S. Government Printing Office.

King, M. A., and L-D. L. Dicks-Mireaux. 1982. "Asset Holdings and the Life-Cycle." *Economic Journal* 92:247–67.

Kotlikoff, Laurence J., and Lawrence H. Summers. 1981. "The Role of Intergenerational Transfers in Aggregate Capital Accumulation." *Journal of Political Economy* 89:706–32.

Newman, Peter C. 1975. *The Canadian Establishment.* Vol. 1. Toronto: McClelland and Stewart.

Oja, Gail. 1986. "The Wealth of Canadians: A Comparison of Survey of Consumer Finances with National Balance Sheet Estimates." Labour and Household Surveys Analysis Division Staff Reports, Statistics Canada.

Oulton, Nicholas. 1976. "Inheritance and the Distribution of Wealth." *Oxford Economic Papers,* (March) 28:86–101.

Porter, John. 1965. *The Vertical Mosaic: An Analysis of Social Class and Power in Canada.* Toronto: University of Toronto Press.

Projector, Dorothy S., and Gertrude S. Weiss. 1966. *Survey of Financial Characteristics of Consumers.* Washington, D.C.: Board of Governors of the Federal Reserve System.

Royal Commission on the Distribution of Income and Wealth. 1977. *Report No. 5: Third Report on the Standing Reference.* London: Her Majesty's Stationery Office.

———. 1979. *Report No. 7: Fourth Report on the Standing Reference.* London: Her Majesty's Stationery Office.

Shorrocks, A. F. 1975. "The Age-Wealth Relationship: A Cross-Section and Cohort Analysis." *Review of Economics and Statistics* 57:155–63.

————. 1982. "The Portfolio Composition of Asset Holding in the United Kingdom." *Economic Journal* 92:268–84.

————. 1987. "U.K. Wealth Distribution: Current Evidence and Future Prospects." *See* Wolff 1987a.

Statistics Canada. 1986. *The Distribution of Wealth in Canada: 1984.* Publication no. 13-580. Ministry of Supply and Services, Canada.

————. 1990. *Income Distributions by Size in Canada: 1989.* Publication no. 13-207. Ministry of Supply and Services, Canada.

————. 1991. *National Balance Sheet Accounts, System of National Accounts.* Publication no. 13-214. Ministry of Supply and Services, Canada.

Wedgwood, Josiah. 1928. "The Influence of Inheritance on the Distribution of Wealth." *Economic Journal* 38:38–55.

————. 1929. *The Economics of Inheritance.* London: George Routledge & Sons.

Wolff, Edward N. 1989. "Long-Term Trends in U.S. Wealth Inequality: Methodological Issues and Results." In *The Measurement of Saving, Investment, and Wealth,* ed. Robert E. Lipsey and Helen Stone Tice. Chicago: University of Chicago Press.

Wolfson, Michael. 1977. *The Causes of Inequality in the Distribution of Wealth: A Simulation Analysis.* Ph.D. diss., Cambridge University.

————. 1979. "The Bequest Process and the Causes of Inequality in the Distribution of Wealth." In *Modelling the Intergenerational Transmission of Wealth,* ed. J. D. Smith. New York: NBER.

Contributors

Andrew B. Abel, University of Pennsylvania, United States

Luc Arrondel, CEREPI, France

Hiroyuki Chuma, Hitotsubashi University, Japan

James B. Davies, University of Western Ontario, Canada

Anil K. Gupta, Department of Finance, Canadian Government, Canada

Michael D. Hurd, State University of New York at Stony Brook, United States

Toshihiro Ihori, University of Tokyo, Japan

Laurence J. Kotlikoff, Boston University, United States

Hirohisa Maki, Ministry of Posts and Telecommunications, Japanese Government, Japan

Sergio Perelman, Université de Liège, Belgium

Pierre Pestieau, Université de Liège, Belgium

Toshiaki Tachibanaki, Kyoto University, Japan

Seiji Takata, Ministry of Posts and Telecommunications, Japanese Government, Japan

Steven F. Venti, Dartmouth College, United States

David A. Wise, Harvard University, United States

Tadashi Yagi, Nagoya University, Japan